Making Gay Okay

Robert R. Reilly

Making Gay Okay

How Rationalizing
Homosexual Behavior
Is Changing Everything

IGNATIUS PRESS   SAN FRANCISCO

Cover image by istockphoto.com

Cover design by John Herreid

© 2014 by Ignatius Press, San Francisco
All rights reserved
ISBN 978-1-58617-833-8
Library of Congress Control Number 2013916523
Printed in the United States of America ∞

*To Rev. James V. Schall, S.J., fearless seeker of truth,
who knows and has taught us the "Order of Things"*

People do not believe lies because they have
to but because they want to.

—*Malcolm Muggeridge*

A man may lie to himself very prettily, but he can never
really escape from the knowledge that it is a lie.

—*Melinda Selmys, former lesbian*

Do not accept anything as love which lacks truth.

—*Edith Stein*

Contents

Introduction

Many people are puzzled as to why anyone would or should get exercised over the issue of homosexual "marriage" because, when seen in isolation, it may appear to be a small matter that affects only a very tiny proportion of the population. If homosexuals constitute some 2 percent, an even smaller percentage of them will avail themselves of marriage, if it is allowed. That is certainly the evidence from countries, such as Canada and Sweden, where it has already been permitted for some years. So why all the fuss?

The concern can be understood only when the issue is seen within the broader perspective of the false reality of which it is a part and, in many ways, the completion. The foundation stone of this false reality, as we shall see particularly in terms of Supreme Court decisions, was contraception, and the capstone is same-sex marriage. The progression from the one to the other was logically inescapable.

In my last year in college many years ago, I was discussing with a classmate the status of objective morality. He was strongly inclined toward moral relativism, and soon we got down to the bedrock principle of noncontradiction (i.e., that a thing cannot both be and not be in the same way, at the same time, in the same place). To my amazement, my classmate was willing to dispute this, stating that we do not know if this is true and speculating that at some point it might be shown not to be so. The conversation had to end there because there was no longer any basis upon which it could proceed.

At the time, I did not know that he was a homosexual. Later, while still a young man, he died of AIDS. Put bluntly, he denied the principle of non-contradiction, and the principle of noncontradiction denied him. Ideas have consequences, and so do actions based upon them. This is what is going to happen to us as a society if we put the capstone of same-sex marriage into place. We will be living a lie.

My thesis is very simple. There are two fundamental views of reality. One is that things have a Nature that is teleologically ordered to ends that inhere in their essence and make them what they are. In other words, things have inbuilt purposes. The other is that things do not have a Nature with ends: things are nothing in themselves, but are only what we make them to be according to our wills and desires. Therefore, we can make everything, including ourselves, anything that we wish and that we have the power to do. The first view leads to the primacy of reason in human affairs; the second leads to the primacy of the will. The first does not allow for sodomitical marriage, while the second does. Indeed, the problem is that the second allows for anything. This is what the same-sex marriage debate is really about—the Nature of reality itself. Since the meaning of our lives is dependent upon the Nature of reality, it too hangs in the balance.

This book is also about how to live rightly in respect to our sexual Nature. This issue is addressed within the opposing perspectives of a teleological and nonteleological human Nature. In Plato's *Gorgias*, Callicles said to Socrates: "He who would live rightly should let his desires be as strong as possible and not chasten them, and should be able to minister to them when they are at their height by reason of his manliness and intelligence, and satisfy each appetite in turn with what it desires." As he so often did, Socrates responded with a question: "And the culmination of the case, as stated—the life of catamites—is not that awful, shameful, and wretched? Or will you dare to assert that these are happy if they can freely indulge their wants?" (491e–492a). Is right the rule of the stronger, as Callicles asserted, and can one therefore freely indulge one's desires? Or, as Socrates suggested, is there something in the constitution of human Nature that makes the sexual use of boys shameful because it is wrong? We will address these questions.

The plan of this book is first to present the nature of the culture war of which the struggle over same-sex "marriage" is a major part, to examine how rationalization operates as its animating force, and then to lay out the issues in a philosophical way, including the meaning of *Nature* as it was first used in Greek philosophy. Next, I will explicate the opposition to that understanding of Nature, utilizing the thought of Jean-Jacques Rousseau as its exemplar. The second part of the book will show how the homosexual rationalization and the thinking upon which it is based have marched through and devastated the institutions of American society and government—especially the judiciary, science and psychiatry, education, the Boy Scouts, the military, and US diplomacy. It is one thing to grasp the issues in the abstract and another to see how they work their way out in the practical details of daily life. Much of the natural-law argument against same-sex marriage will be given in responses to the arguments made in its favor in each of these settings, especially in the courtroom. I make no case from religion or revelation in this book, only from reason as it discloses to us the Nature of things.

It should be emphasized that this critique of the homosexual cause is not an attack upon homosexuals, nor is it generated by any animus against them. Over the course of several decades, my professional work in the arts has brought me into association with many homosexuals. I have been at pains to promote the work of those whose art I thought was stellar, without regard to this issue. In fact, in my many interviews and discussions with artists and composers whom I happened to know were homosexual, I have never had the subject of homosexuality arise in connection with their work or, in fact, in any other way. It was irrelevant. When someone once raised the subject when I was with a young homosexual artist who had already reached star status, the artist quickly dismissed the subject and simply responded, "It doesn't define me." This book is not about them and is not meant to offend them. It is about those who insist not only on defining themselves in this way, but on defining the rest of us as well.

My apologia would, of course, be hard to believe for anyone who has collapsed the distinction between the nature of an act and the person performing the act. It is this vital distinction that allows one to judge the act, not the person. It is also this distinction that removes any moral onus from a person whose homosexuality or, say, alcoholism is no fault of his own. But even a genetic predisposition, if such exists, to homosexuality or alcoholism does not deprive a person of his free will, so the person is still morally responsible for his homosexual acts or drunkenness. (Of course, if one has no free will—which is suggested by those who declare sexual restraint or abstinence to be impossible—then any notion of morality becomes absurd.) Only an omniscient God can finally judge the true condition of a man's soul, but this in no way means that we cannot come to an understanding of the moral nature of an act, that we cannot know that some acts are great evils. I am sure this statement will not allay the inevitable charges of homophobia, but it is meant sincerely.

Note on usage. The word *Nature* is capitalized when referring to the metaphysical concept and lowercased when it is used synonymously with "character". In different legal and cultural settings, the word *sodomy* has included different things at different times. But, in *every* variation, it has always encompassed anal intercourse and is meant to here as well. Among other things, *gender* means "the state of being male or female", according to the *Oxford Dictionary*. I do not surrender the word to those who use it to mean that the masculine and the feminine are artificial constructs socially or politically engineered for men and women. Therefore, someone of the feminine gender *is* a woman—not someone who *thinks* he is a woman. The word *good* is capitalized when it refers to the divine, as in its use by Plato.

Part 1

The Rationalization and How It Works

1

The Culture War

Writing about homosexuality has become a growth industry, one writer has quipped. Indeed, there has never been a time in our nation when we have been so publicly preoccupied with this subject. The love whose name dare not be spoken (once upon a time) is being shouted, if not from the rooftops, at least from the streets in demonstrations and parades, from the platforms in political rallies, and from the pages of various popular and intellectual journals. And from the White House. On June 29, 2009, President Barack Obama met in the East Room with more than 250 "gay" leaders to commemorate the fortieth anniversary of the birth of the modern "gay rights" movement, an event precipitated by a police raid on the Stonewall Inn, a Greenwich Village homosexual bar, owned at that time by the Mafia in New York City.

Mr. Obama singled out Franklin Kameny for special praise: "We are proud of you, Frank, and we are grateful to you for your leadership." Mr. Kameny had been close to the White House before. In 1957 he was arrested by the morals squad in Lafayette Park, a well-known trysting place for homosexuals, across from the White House. As a result, he was fired from his government job. At the time, "sexual perversion" was grounds for dismissal from the government. Kameny sued and fought all the way up to the Supreme Court, which refused to hear his case. "The government put its disqualification of gays under the rubric of immoral conduct, which I objected to," Kameny said, "because under our system, morality is a matter of personal opinion and individual belief on which any American citizen may hold any view he wishes and upon which the government has no power or authority to have any view at all. Besides which, in my view, homosexuality is not only *not* immoral, but is affirmatively moral."[1] In 1968 Kameny coined the phrase "gay is good".

Despite Mr. Kameny's eccentric vision of the American Founding, he felt in no way constrained from working to enforce his "personal opinion and individual belief" upon the government and American society. His recognition by President Obama in the White House was one measure of his success in doing so. In 2011, the year of his death, the National Park Service placed his Washington, DC, home on the National Register of Historic Places, because it "recognized the historic significance of gay rights activist Dr. Franklin E. Kameny."[2] His papers are archived at the Library of Congress. The National Museum of American History accepted his 1965 protest signs and "gay is good" button for display. Mr. Kameny achieved iconic status.

In 2008, before the White House meeting, Mr. Kameny expressed some of his views in a published letter to Americans for Truth. He wrote, "Let us have more and better enjoyment of more and better sexual perversions, by whatever definition, by more and more consenting adults. . . . If bestiality with consenting animals provides happiness to some people, let them pursue their happiness. That is Americanism in action."[3] It is hard to recall that in the not-too-distant past many states and cities had laws against sodomy (and still do against bestiality), and it would have been inconceivable that the White House would choose to honor publicly someone who openly espoused these views. Now homosexual intercourse is being proposed and accepted as equivalent to the marital act and as a basis for marriage—including by President Obama, who announced in his second inaugural, "Our journey is not complete until our gay brothers and sisters are treated like anyone else under the law, for if we are truly created equal, then surely the love we commit to one another must be equal, as well." One wonders how and why this change—from legal censure and suppression to public celebration and espousal in the East Room—happened.

---

[1] David W. Dunlap, "Franklin Kameny, Gay Rights Pioneer, Dies at 86", *New York Times*, October 12, 2001, http://www.nytimes.com/2011/10/13/us/franklin-kameny-gay-rights-pioneer-dies-at-86.html?_r=0.

[2] National Park Service Release, November 2, 2011, http://home.nps.gov/news/release.htm?id=1248.

[3] Peter LaBarbera, " 'Gay Rights' Icon Frank Kameny Says Bestiality OK 'as Long as the Animal Doesn't Mind' ", Americans for Truth about Homosexuality website, accessed August 2, 2013, http://americansfortruth.com/2008/05/31/gay-icon-kameny-says-bestiality-ok-as-long-as-the-animal-doesnt-mind/.

One reason is that the subject of homosexuality, much like that of abortion before it, has become inextricably enmeshed in the political rhetoric of rights. Rights, as the *Declaration of Independence* tells us, are founded firmly in and are fully dependent on the "Laws of Nature and of Nature's God". Anyone whose claim can be asserted on the level of a right, therefore, gathers tremendous moral and political impetus for his cause. For this reason, activist homosexuals and their supporters attempt to identify themselves as the new civil rights movement.

Others have joined them. Former first lady Laura Bush said, "When couples are committed to each other and love each other then they ought to have the same sort of rights that everyone has." Former secretary of state Colin Powell declared that "they should be able to get married.... It seems to me this is the way we should be moving in this country." Former vice president Dick Cheney's public endorsement of same-sex "marriage" in 2009 on behalf of his lesbian daughter is typical. He said: "I think that freedom means freedom for everyone.... I think people ought to be free to enter into any kind of union they wish. Any kind of arrangement they wish." This erstwhile conservative might well have been quoting Franklin Kameny. What does this mean for our society?

This attempt to legitimize *any* arrangement demands especially close scrutiny, because it questions the meaning of concepts critical to our moral and political understanding of ourselves, including the very meaning of the "Laws of Nature and Nature's God" upon which our Founders thought our existence as a free people depends.

Homosexual Acceptance

The case for the practice of homosexuality began with seeming modesty. Its proponents contended that sexual choices are private and therefore homosexuals should be left to their own predilections. "Stay out of my bedroom!" "Live and let live." At the same time, they insisted they were the objects of discrimination and wished to enact remedial legislation. This very complaint, however, revealed that there is a public aspect to their private choice.

First of all, they must be identifiable to others as homosexuals; otherwise it would be impossible to discriminate against them. In many cases this public aspect takes the form of the homosexual's telling others that he is a homosexual—"coming out of the closet", as it is called. Why should a homosexual feel impelled to do this, especially if he expects discrimination as a result? After all, the hidden homosexual who has not "come out of the closet" (or has not been "outed"—involuntarily identified as a homosexual) enjoys the privacy of concealment.

One reason homosexuals take this risk has been made fairly clear by militant homosexual organizations. By so doing, homosexuals wish not only to be tolerated in terms of their private sexual behavior, but to have that behavior publicly vindicated and recognized as normal. This is hardly a strange desire. Man is a social being. Though parts of his life take place in private, in the normal course of things even those private aspects have public manifestations. Indeed, public social life is organized in such a way as to ensure privacy for certain things. We learn what should be private from the public way in which certain privacies are protected. So by *private* we do not mean things that are nobody else's business. The private, in this sense, is everybody's business.

For example, certainly the sexual intimacy between a husband and wife is held to be private and inviolate. But what are the public manifestations of this privacy? Obviously, wedding rings, children, private property, homes, schools, communities—the whole structure and fabric of society, in fact, is built to protect and maintain the conditions for that intimacy and its results. The whole social and political order is supportive of this privacy. It is encouraged and protected by law because it is held to be of benefit to all.

This is the kind of support and acceptance that homosexuals are seeking. This is seen in their desire to have their relationships legally recognized as marriages or to have the ability to adopt children. This makes somewhat specious the claim that all that is at stake in the homosexual controversy is the right to privacy. The clandestine homosexual does not claim a right to do the things he wishes to conceal and so claims no public protection for his privacy. As a result, he implicitly acquiesces in society's implied judgment of his actions as wrong. For some time now, many homosexuals have no longer found this concession tolerable, and by advancing their cause at the level of moral principle—as a matter of human rights—they insist not only on repeal, but on a complete reversal of that public judgment.

In regard to marriage, for instance, no one today is interfering with any union that homosexuals or lesbians might wish to form. They may find clergy members who are willing to improvise liturgies with which to solemnize their arrangements. No one will stop them. There are no legal prohibitions to doing this. But that is not sufficient. What they want is legal recognition that obliges *everyone* to recognize the legitimacy of their act.

According to Jeffrey Levi, former executive director for the National Gay and Lesbian Task Force, "We [homosexuals] are no longer seeking just a right to privacy and a right to protection from wrong. We have a right— as heterosexuals have already—to see government and society affirm our lives." Homosexual author Urvashi Vaid declared, "We have an agenda to create a society in which homosexuality is regarded as healthy, natural, and normal. To me that is the most important agenda item."[4] Paula Ettelbrick, former legal director of the Lambda Legal Defense and Education Fund, stated: "Being queer means pushing the parameters of sex, sexuality, and family, and ... transforming the very fabric of society.... We must keep our eyes on the goals of providing true alternatives to marriage and of radically reordering society's view of reality."[5]

Since only the act of sodomy (along with other peculiarly homosexual practices) differentiates an active homosexual from a heterosexual, homosexuals want "government and society" to affirm that sodomy is morally equivalent to the marital act. "Coming out of the closet" can mean only an assent at the level of moral principle to what would otherwise be considered morally disordered.

The Power of Rationalization

Why is this happening? In his *Ethics* Aristotle wrote, "Men start revolutionary changes for reasons connected with their private lives." This is also true when revolutionary changes are cultural. What might these "private" reasons be, and why do they become public in the form of revolutionary changes? The answer to these questions lies in the intimate psychology of moral failure. For any individual, moral failure is hard to live with because of the rebuke of conscience. Habitual moral failure, what used to be called vice, can be tolerated only by creating a rationalization to justify it.

Rationalizations for moral misbehavior work like this. Anyone who chooses an evil act must present it to himself as good; otherwise, as Aristotle

---

[4] Quoted in Gabriel Rotello, *Sexual Ecology: AIDS and the Destiny of Gay Men* (New York: Penguin Books, 1997), 286.

[5] Quoted in "Since When Is Marriage a Path to Liberation?" in *Lesbians, Gay Men, and the Law*, ed. William B. Rubenstein (New York: New Press, 1993), 398, 400.

taught, he would be *incapable* of choosing it. When we rationalize, we convince ourselves that heretofore forbidden desires are permissible. As Hilaire Belloc wrote, in this case, "Every evil is its own good."[6] In our minds we replace the reality of the moral order to which the desires should be subordinated with something more compatible with the activity we are excusing. Or as Professor J. Budziszewski put it, "We seek not to become just, but to justify ourselves."[7] In short, we assert that bad is good. Conscience often wins out afterward, and the person repents—first of all by admitting to the evil nature of the act committed. The temporary rationalization crumbles, and moral reality is restored. Habitual moral failure, however, can be lived with only by obliterating conscience through a more *permanent* rationalization, an enduring inversion of morality.

It is often difficult to detect rationalizations when one is living directly under their influence, and so historical examples are useful. One of the clearest was offered at the Nuremberg trials by Dr. Karl Brandt, Adolf Hitler's personal physician, who had been in charge of the Nazi regime's Aktion T-4 euthanasia program to eliminate "life unworthy of life". He said in his defense: "When I said 'yes' to euthanasia I did so with the deepest conviction, just as it is my conviction today, that it was right. Death can mean deliverance. Death is life." He was hanged for war crimes in 1948.

Unlike Dr. Brandt, most people recover from their rationalizations when remorse and reality set in again. But when morally disordered acts become the defining centerpiece of one's life, vice can permanently pervert reason, and the inversion of reality becomes complete. The rationalization can turn into a prison from which one cannot escape.

The purpose of this analogy is not to suggest that homosexual acts are in any way comparable to the evil of euthanasia, but to illustrate the enormous power that rationalization can exercise over those whose consciences it corrupts. The Nazi example simply demonstrates the extraordinary extent to which the establishment of a false reality can distort human behavior. If it can justify and mandate the murder of millions, what can it not do?

Perhaps a more immediately apt analogy to this kind of rationalization is the practice and justification of abortion, itself a product of the sexual revolution, which is equally expansive in its claims upon society. The internal logic of abortion requires the spread of death from the unborn to the nearly

---

[6] H. Belloc, *This and That and the Other* (New York: Dodd, Mead and Company, 1912), 27.

[7] J. Budziszewski, *What We Can't Not Know: A Guide*, rev. ed. (San Francisco: Ignatius Press, 2011), 140.

born, and then to the infirm and to otherwise burdensome individuals. The very psychology of rationalization also pushes those involved with abortion to spread the application of its principles in order to multiply its sources of support. Witness the spread of euthanasia to Vermont, Oregon, Washington, and Montana, where doctors can now legally kill patients.

Like Dr. Brandt, if you are going to kill innocent persons, you had better convince yourself and others that it is right, that you do it out of compassion. Thus, Beverly Harrison, a professor of Christian ethics at Union Theological Seminary, contends that abortion is a "positive good" and even a "loving choice". But Jungian analyst Ginette Paris thinks it is even more. In her book *The Sacrament of Abortion*, she calls for "new rituals as well as laws to restore to abortion its sacred dimension". Defending the right to partial-birth abortions during a US Senate debate, Senator Barbara Boxer assured her colleagues that mothers who have aborted their children by this means "buried those babies with love". If abortion is love, then, indeed, as Dr. Brandt said, "death is life."

Abortion is the ultimate in the larger rationalization of the sexual revolution (of which the homosexual cause is part): if sex is only a form of amusement or self-realization (as it must be when divorced from the moral order), why should the generation of a child stand in the way of it or penalize its fulfillment? The life of the child is a physical and moral rebuke to this proposition. But the child is too weak to overcome the power of the rationalization. The virtual reality of the rationalization is stronger than the actual reality of the child. The child succumbs to the rationalization and is killed in a new "sacrament". With more than fifty-five million abortions performed since 1973, the investment in the denial of the evil of abortion and in the establishment of the alternative reality that allows it has become tremendous.

The homosexual movement shares in the larger rationalization of the sexual revolution and is invested in its spread. The acceptance of each variant of sexual misbehavior reinforces the others. The underlying dynamic is: If you'll rationalize my sexual misbehavior, I'll rationalize yours. Entrenched moral aberrations then impel people to rationalize vice not only to themselves but to others as well. Thus rationalizations become an engine for revolutionary change that will affect society as a whole. And so it must be. If you are going to center your public life on the private act of sodomy, you had better transform sodomy into a highly moral act. If sodomy is a moral disorder, it cannot be legitimately advanced on the legal or civil level. On the other hand, if it is a highly moral act, it should—in fact, *must*—serve as the basis for marriage, family (adoption), and community. As a moral act, sodomy should be normative. If it is normative, it should be taught in our schools as a standard. If it is a standard, it should be enforced. In fact, homosexuality should be hieratic: active homosexuals should be ordained as priests and bishops. Sodomy should be sacramentalized.

All of this is happening. It was predictable. The homosexual cause moved naturally from a plea for tolerance to cultural conquest because the rationalization upon which it is based *requires* the assent of the community to the normative nature of the act of sodomy. In other words, we all must say that the bad is good in order for the rationalization to be secure in itself.

The power of rationalization drives the culture war, gives it its particular revolutionary character, and makes its advocates indefatigable. It may draw its energy from desperation, but it is all the more powerful for that. Since failed rationalization means self-recrimination, it must be avoided at all costs. This is why the rationalization is animated by such a lively sense of self-righteousness and outrage. For these reasons, the differences over which the culture war is being fought are not subject to reasoned discourse. Persons protecting themselves by rationalizing are interested not in finding the truth, but in maintaining the illusion that allows them to continue their behavior. This necessarily becomes a group effort. For them to succeed in this, *everyone* must accede to the rationalization. This is why revolutionary change is required, using all the tools of compulsion.

The homosexual rationalization is so successful that even the campaign against AIDS is part of it, with its message that "everyone is at risk". If everyone is at risk, the disease cannot be related to specific behavior. Yet the homosexual act is the single greatest risk factor in contracting AIDS. According to a 2011 power point presentation by the Centers for Disease Control and Prevention, 94.9 percent of HIV diagnoses among teenage boys (13 to 19 years old) were linked to "male-to-male" sex; 94.1 percent of the cases among young men ages 20 to 24 were from "gay" sex.[8] These unpleasant facts invite unwelcome attention to the nature of homosexual acts, so they must be ignored.

Indeed, by this rationalization, homosexuals are victims, not perpetrators. This is a self-assumed role. According to Marshall Kirk and Hunter Madsen, "AIDS gives us a chance, however brief, to establish ourselves as

[8] *HIV Surveillance in Adolescents and Young Adults*, National Center for HIV/AIDS, Viral Hepatitis, STD and TB Prevention, http://www.cdc.gov/hiv/pdf/statistics_surveillance _Adolescents.pdf.

a victimized minority." The logic goes like this: the victim of a robbery is not responsible for the crime; the thief is. Likewise, homosexuals are not responsible for the contraction or the spread of AIDS; they are its victims. In fact, they are martyrs to the greater cause of sexual liberation. As the famous refrain from the play *Marat/Sade* proclaims, "What's the point of a revolution without general copulation?"

If those who have AIDS are martyrs, who martyred them? Lesbian lobbyist Hilary Rosen explained in her *Washington Post* column that "hundreds of thousands of gay people died because [Sen. Jesse] Helms and his allies were more successful than not in those early days [in opposing expanded support for the Centers for Disease Control]."[9] (What about the hundreds of thousands of people who died because *they* were victimized by AIDS carriers?) In their 1989 book, *After the Ball: How America Will Conquer Its Fear and Hatred of Gays in the '90s*, Kirk and Madsen wrote: "In any campaign to win over the public, gays must be portrayed as victims in need of protection so that straights will be inclined by reflex to adopt the role of protector.... The public should be persuaded that gays are victims of circumstance, that they no more chose their sexual orientation than they did, say, their height, skin color, talents, or limitations.... Gays should be portrayed as victims of prejudice."[10] It worked. By a huge margin, AIDS gets more research money per patient than any other disease. Should those dying of other diseases blame their illnesses on this displacement of research funds? Should cigarette smokers who contract lung cancer blame their disease on those who failed to increase funds for cancer research?

Since the necessity for self-justification requires the complicity of the whole culture, holdouts cannot be tolerated, because they are potential rebukes. The self-hatred, anger, and guilt that a person possessed of a functioning conscience would normally feel from doing wrong are redirected by the rationalization and projected upon society as a whole (if the society is healthy) or upon those in society who do not accept the rationalization. These latter are labeled homophobes, though it is they who become the objects of hatred. They are blamed for the misfortunes in homosexual life, which are no longer ascribable to the behavior that produces them, but to those who do not accept the behavior as moral, thus discomfiting its practitioners.

[9] Hilary Rosen, "My Family's Fight for Equality", *Washington Post*, March 29, 2013, A15.
[10] Marshall Kirk and Hunter Madsen, *After the Ball: How America Will Conquer Its Fear and Hatred of Gays in the 90's* (New York: Plume Books, 1989), 184.

Coercion is the solution to this dilemma. Those who do not accept homosexual behavior as normative must be legally forced to embrace the rationalization or be silent in the face of it. In the same way we once learned of the inherent goodness of married life, we must now be taught—and compelled to accept—the "new morality" of homosexuality. The instruments of coercion are first cultural and then political. The homosexual campaign marches through the institutions of society—the press, the entertainment media, medical associations (particularly psychiatric and psychological ones), religious bodies and the clergy, civic societies, businesses and corporate executives, leaders in the arts, educational institutions, and finally the military—transforming them one by one to its cause. After the long march, it is ready for the political assault—to gain the levers of government through either the courts or legislatures to enforce compliance.

E. Michael Jones, one of the pioneers in revealing the extent to which the power of rationalization operates in the corruption of culture, wrote that "the paradise of sexual liberation was only plausible in so far as it aspired to universality. It could only calm the troubled conscience in an effective manner when it was legitimized by the regime in power. In this regard, what better conscience machine could there be than one which confidently banned God and his law from public life and then went on in the name of high moral purpose to make this vision normative for the entire world?"[11] Jones wrote this in regard to Max Eastman and the Soviet Union, but the same point pertains particularly to the US government's embrace of sexual license and its acceptance of homosexual marriage. The American regime is now consecrating the principles of the sexual revolution by reading them into the US Constitution and by exporting them in its foreign policy, as will be seen later.

The Divorce of Law and Morality: Demoting Marriage

Ironically, the logic behind this process of legitimization of homosexual behavior undercuts any objective standards by which we could judge the moral legitimacy of anything. This is the ultimate danger it poses—including to America's political foundations.

---

[11] E. Michael Jones, *Libido Dominandi: Sexual Liberation and Political Control* (South Bend: St. Augustine Press, 2000), 221.

Why this should be so requires some understanding of the moral foundation of law and its prescriptive nature. The legal protection of heterosexual relations between a husband and wife involves a public judgment on the nature and purpose of sex. That judgment teaches that the proper exercise of sex is within the marital bond because both the procreative and unitive purposes of sex are best fulfilled within it. The family alone is capable of providing the necessary stability for the profound relationship that sexual union both symbolizes and cements and for the welfare of the children who issue from it.

The legitimization of homosexual relations changes that judgment and the teaching that emanates from it. What is disguised under the rubric of legal neutrality toward an individual's choice of sexual behavior—"equality and freedom for everyone"—is, in fact, a demotion of marriage from something seen as good in itself and for society to just one of the available sexual alternatives. In other words, this neutrality is not at all neutral; it teaches and promotes indifference, where once there was an endorsement. Since the endorsement purported to be based upon knowledge of the objective good of marriage, it taught not only that marriage is good, but that we can *know* what is good. The latter is, in a way, a far more critical lesson.

The implied indifference in a law that is neutral to one's choice of sexual alternatives teaches that we are incapable of knowing in an objective way the goodness or evil of those sexual alternatives and that therefore their worth can be determined only subjectively by the private individual. An example of a similar teaching was provided by the preceding legalization of pornography, which prepared the ground for the homosexual cause. Go to almost any newsstand, and you will see side by side on the shelf *Playboy* and *Good Housekeeping*. What does any sensible person learn from seeing this odd juxtaposition? Certainly the way of life espoused by *Playboy* is inimical to good housekeeping. Yet there they are together; take your pick.

In other words, the person learns, if only by osmosis, that it is a matter of public indifference as to whether one properly uses or abuses sex. More accurately, legal commerce in pornography teaches that no such distinction exists. Once this teaching has been learned, where does one draw the line? If heterosexual sex is only a form of play or recreation, what could be wrong with a little sodomy? Or even incest?

So far from not embodying any moral view, legal neutrality gives public status to and fosters a highly subjective view of life, which, of course, extends to things other than sexual behavior. As Germain Grisez wrote,

"One cannot long adopt certain specific moral precepts without adopting the entire view from which such precepts rise." In his satiric way, Evelyn Waugh said much the same thing when asked why there were no good professional proofreaders left in England. "Because", he responded, "clergymen are no longer unfrocked for sodomy."[12] One cannot abandon one standard without affecting all others.

[12] Quoted in Paul Fussell, "A Hero of Verbal Culture", review of *The Letters of Evelyn Waugh*, ed. Mark Amory, *New York Times*, November 2, 1980, http://www.nytimes.com /books/99/10/10/specials/waugh-letters80.html.

2

Order in the Universe: Aristotle's Laws of Nature

At the heart of the debate over same-sex marriage are the most fundamental questions about who man is and how he decides what makes for his flourishing. Ineluctably the issue of "gay marriage" is about far more than sexual practices. The case for it becomes plausible only if one accepts certain assumptions about how to distinguish what is natural from what is unnatural and what is right from what is wrong. The intellectual origins of the debate stretch all the way back to the Greeks, but radical changes in philosophy over the past two hundred years have altered its character. It is now not so much about understanding reality as it is, but about, as lesbian advocate Paula Ettelbrick proclaimed, "transforming the very fabric of society ... [and] radically reordering society's views of reality".[1]

Since how we perceive reality is at stake in this struggle, the question inevitably rises: What *is* the nature of reality? Is any given practice necessarily good for us as human beings? Is it according to our Nature? Each side in the debate claims that what they are defending or advancing is natural. Opponents of same-sex marriage say that it is against Nature; proponents say that it *is* according to Nature and that therefore they have a right to it. Yet the purported realities to which each side points are not just different but mutually exclusive: each negates the other. What does the word *Nature* really mean in these contexts? The word may be the same, but its meanings are directly contradictory. Therefore, it is vitally important to understand the broader contexts in which it is used, how they developed, and the larger views of reality of which they are a part—since the status and meaning of *Nature* will be decisive in the outcome of this matter.

[1] Quoted in Ed Vitagliano, "Gay Activists War against Christianity", *American Family Association Journal* (February 2006): 16, http://afajournal.org/2006/february/206GayWar.asp.

Let us then review briefly what the natural law understanding of *Nature* is and the kinds of distinctions an objective view of reality enables us to make in regard to our existence in general and to sexuality in particular. The point of departure must be that Nature is *what is*, regardless of what anyone desires or abhors. We are part of it and subject to it. We do not make Nature. It is not subject to us. It is the given. We shall see how, once the objective status of Nature is lost or denied, we are incapacitated from possessing any true knowledge about ourselves and about how we are to relate to the world. This discussion may seem at times somewhat unrelated to the issues directly at hand, but it is not. It is at the heart and soul of these issues. Without it, the rest of our discussion would be a mere prattle of opinions.

At the core of the dispute over same-sex marriage are two basic, profoundly different anthropologies, or notions of man's origin. For an understanding of the original notion of Nature, we will turn to those who began the use of the term in classical Greece, especially Plato and Aristotle. To present the antithesis of this understanding, we will then go to Jean-Jacques Rousseau, who eviscerated the word of its traditional meaning in the eighteenth century and gave it its modern connotation. The older Aristotelian anthropology claims that man is by Nature a rational, political animal for whom the basic societal unit is the family. Human beings are born into and live in families, which in turn exist as part of larger social units that are necessary to man's fulfillment. This understanding will be delineated in the discussion of homosexuality and the Greeks, which follows in the next section. The Rousseauian anthropology claims that man is not a rational, political animal and that society in any form is fundamentally alien, and alienating, to individuals. In his origins, man was isolated and essentially complete on his own and in himself.

These anthropologies presuppose, in turn, two radically different metaphysics: one is teleological (things have an inner orientation or aim); the other is nonteleological (things have no inner aim), or antiteleological. The first claims with Aristotle that "Nature is a cause that operates for a purpose."[2] The purpose is a given in the thing itself; it is not man-made. The laws of Nature are preexisting, immutable, and universal. The second denies ends in Nature—it is man, not Nature, who gives things their purpose. Insofar as they pertain to man, these so-called laws are mutable, conditioned

---

[2] Aristotle, *Physics* 2.8.199b32.

by historical accidents, and therefore malleable. According to this view, reason itself is grounded in the irrational or accidental. These two schools, which will be more fully explicated as we proceed, provide the philosophical perspectives within which to understand the uses of the words *natural* and *unnatural* as they are employed, respectively, by the proponents and opponents of homosexual acts and same-sex marriage today.

The momentous discovery of Nature was the first product of Greek philosophy. Thoughtful persons first deduced the existence of Nature when they became aware of order in the universe. The regularity with which things happen could not be accounted for by random repetition and required explanation. All activity seems governed by a purpose, by ends to which things are designed to move. Before this discovery, ancient man was immersed in mythological portrayals of the world, the gods, and himself. These mythopoeic accounts made no distinction between custom and Nature, or between convention (the *way* things happen) and Nature (the reason *why* they happen). A dog wagged its tail because that was the way of a dog. Egyptians painted their funeral caskets in bright colors because that was the way of the Egyptians. There was no way to differentiate between the two—the one being according to Nature and the other according to custom—because the word *Nature* was not available in the vocabulary of the prephilosophical world. Once discovered, this distinction enabled man to discern the difference between custom, which can be changed, and Nature, which cannot. Nature was internal to and inseparable from what a thing is; custom was external and separable.

How is it that we can understand Nature or anything of the world around us? Why do our minds correspond with external reality? How is it that our idea of something like a tree can tally with what a tree actually is? It was perhaps Heraclitus (though some claim Anaximander) who first grasped that the universe is *intelligible* and that therefore man is able to comprehend its order. If this is true—and *only* if it is true—man's inquiry into the Nature of reality becomes possible. (Obviously, if the world is unintelligible, such inquiry is futile.) The very idea of Nature then becomes possible. How could this be? Heraclitus said that the universe is intelligible because it is ruled by and is the product of "thought" or wisdom. If it is the product of thought, then it can be apprehended by thinking. One can understand the workings of a clock because they are the result of a rational design and of an intelligent designer. We can know reality, or *what is*, because it was made by *logos* or reason. We can have thoughts about things that are themselves the product of thought. If things were merely the product of accident, they would not be accessible to reason because their source would be in the irrational.

As far as we know, Heraclitus and Parmenides were the first to use the word *logos* to name this "thought" or wisdom behind all things. *Logos* means "reason" or "word" in Greek. For them, *logos* is the intelligence behind the intelligible whole. It is *logos* that makes the world accessible to the endeavor of philosophy (i.e., reason). In the *Timaeus,* Plato writes, "Now the sight of day and night, and the months and the revolutions of the years, have created number, and have given us a conception of time; and the power of inquiring about the nature of the universe; and from this source, we have derived philosophy, than which no greater good ever was or will be given by the gods to mortal man." Through reason, said Socrates, man can come to know *ta onta* ("what is", i.e., the Nature of things).

In turn, Aristotle taught that the essence, or Nature, of a thing is what makes it what it is and not something else. This is not a tautology. As an acorn develops into an oak tree, there is no point along its trajectory of growth when it will turn into a giraffe or something other than an oak. That is because it has the Nature of an oak tree and not of anything else. Hence, by Nature or natural law, we mean the principle of development that makes any living thing what it is and, given the proper conditions, what it will become when it fulfills itself or reaches its end. For Aristotle, "Nature ever seeks an end",[3] and "always the tendency in each is towards the same end, if there is no impediment."[4] This end state is its *telos*, the reason for which it is—what it is *meant* to be. In nonhuman creation this design is manifested through either instinct or physical law. Every living thing has a *telos*, an inner aim, toward which it purposefully moves. In plants or animals, this involves no self-conscious volition. In man, it does.

Anything that operates contrary to this principle in any given thing is unnatural to that thing. By *unnatural,* we mean something that works against what a thing would become were it to operate according to the principle of its development. For instance, an acorn will grow into an oak unless its roots are poisoned by highly acidic water. One would say that the acidic water is unnatural to the oak or against its "goodness"—its "goodness" being the fulfillment of its Nature.

[3] Aristotle, *Generation of Animals* 1.715b15.
[4] Aristotle, *Physics* 2.8.199b15–18.

The term *teleological*, when applied to the universe, implies that everything has an end, and the ends inhere in the structure of things themselves. There is what Aristotle called entelechy, "having one's end within". The purpose of an eye, for instance, is built-in; it is for seeing. Were this not so, one would have to believe that the eye—and indeed every organ of the body—came about by chance and that the eye can see by sheer accident. *Teleological* means the goal of the thing is intrinsic, not extrinsic, to it. These laws of Nature, then, are not an imposition of order from without by a commander in chief, but an expression of it from within the very essence of things, which have their own integrity. In inanimate objects, the physical laws of the universe make this obvious. Likewise, all living creatures, except for man, are determined by what they are to act in the ways they do. They are preordained to their end, or to their "good". Man is also ordained to an end, but he alone can choose to conform himself to his "good" or not.

This also means that the world is comprehensible precisely and only because it operates on a *rational* basis. It is by their Natures that we are able to know what things are. Otherwise, we would know only specificities and be unable to recognize things in their genus and species. In other words, we would experience this piece of wood (a tree) only as opposed to that piece of wood (another tree), but we would not know the word *tree* or even the word *wood*, because we would not know the essence of either. In fact, although we might experience many things, we would know nothing.

Nature is also what enables one person to recognize another person as a human being. All human beings have a human Nature, which means that all human beings are fundamentally the same—and different from all other things—in their very essence, which is immutable. Hence every human soul is ordered to the same transcendent good, or end. This is what it means to be human. Both Socrates and Aristotle said that men's souls are ordered to the same good and that therefore there is a single standard of justice that transcends the political order of any city. There should not be one standard of justice for Athenians and another for Spartans. There is only one justice, and it is the same at all times, everywhere, for everyone. As Aristotle wrote in the *Rhetoric*, "Universal law is the law of Nature. For there really is, as everyone to some extent divines, a natural justice and injustice that is binding on all men, even on those who have no association or covenant with each other."[5]

---

[5] Aristotle, *Rhetoric* 1.13.

This is the foundation for the declaration that "all men are created equal". This is what allows us also to say, with Marcus Tullius Cicero in *De Legibus*, that "wicked and unjust statutes" are "anything but 'laws'", because "in the very definition of the term 'law' there inheres the idea and principle of choosing what is just and true." In other words, positive law, that made by legislatures or rulers, is legitimate only to the extent to which it incorporates natural law, which is the objective source of the distinction between what is just and what is unjust. A positive law made contrary to natural law would be, by definition, unjust.

Cicero added that

> true law is reason, right and natural, commanding people to fulfill their obligation and prohibiting and deterring them from doing wrong. Its validity is universal; it is immediate and eternal. Its commands and prohibitions apply effectively to good men, and those uninfluenced by them are bad. Any attempt to supercede this law, to repeal any part of it, is sinful; to cancel it entirely is impossible. Neither the Senate nor the Assembly can exempt us from its demands; we need no interpreter or expounder of it but ourselves. There will not be one law in Rome, one in Athens, or one now and one later, but all nations will be subject all the time to this one changeless and everlasting law.[6]

Assimilating this notion into Christianity, Thomas Aquinas, wrote that the natural law is "nothing else than the rational creature's participation in the eternal law".[7]

Because of Greco-Roman philosophy, reason replaced force as the arbiter of human affairs. Reason becomes *normative*. It is through reason—not from the gods of the city or from custom—that man discerns what is just from what is unjust, what is good from what is evil, what is myth from what is reality. Behaving reasonably or doing what accords with reason becomes the standard of moral behavior. We see one of the highest expressions of this understanding in Aristotle's *Nicomachean Ethics*. As classics scholar Bruce S. Thornton expressed it: "If one believes, as did many Greek philosophers from Heraclitus on, that the cosmos reflects some sort of rational order, then 'natural' would denote behavior consistent with that order. One could then act 'unnaturally' by indulging in behavior that subverted that order

---

[6] Cicero, *On the Commonwealth* 3.33.
[7] Thomas Aquinas, *Summa Theologica* I-II, 94.

and its purpose."[8] Behaving according to human Nature therefore means acting *rationally*. Concomitantly, behaving unnaturally means acting irrationally. This notion of reality necessitates the *rule* of reason for human beings because of their rational Nature.

This is relevant to man alone because only he possesses reason and free will. He can choose the means to his end or choose to frustrate his end altogether. This, of course, is why moral laws are applicable only to man. These moral laws are what natural law means in regard to man. That man can defy moral law in no way lessens the certainty of its operation. In fact, man not so much breaks the moral law as the moral law breaks man, if he transgresses it. In short, when we speak of man's Nature, we mean the ordering of man's being toward certain ends. It is the fulfillment of those ends that makes him fully human.

What is man's end? In the *Apology*, Socrates said, "A man who is good for anything ... ought only to consider whether in doing anything he is doing right or wrong—acting the part of a good man or bad." *The Republic* states that "the idea of the Good ... is seen only with an effort; and when seen, is also inferred to be the universal author of all things beautiful and right, parent of light and the lord of the light of this visible world, and the source of truth and reason in the intellect." Since Socrates, we have called man's end "the good". This end carries within it an intimation of immortality for, as Diotima said in the *Symposium* (207a): "Love loves the good to be one's own forever. And hence it necessarily follows that love is of immortality."

The good for man, Aristotle tells us, is happiness. Happiness is not whatever we say it is, however, but only that which is consistent with our Nature truly makes us happy. "Happiness", Aristotle says in his *Ethics*, is "an activity of soul in accord with virtue." Aristotle explains that happiness is achieved only through virtuous actions—the repetition of good deeds. Deeds are considered good or bad, natural or unnatural, in relation to the effect they have on man's progress toward his end in achieving the good. Since man's Nature is fundamentally rational, happiness consists in the knowledge and contemplation of the ultimate Good. (That Good, theologians tell us, is God.) Aristotle says that "the activity of God, which surpasses all others in

[8] Bruce S. Thornton, *Eros: The Myth of Ancient Greek Sexuality* (Boulder: Westview Press, 1997), 100.

blessedness, must be contemplative; and of human activities, therefore, that which is most akin to this must be most of the nature of happiness."

Homosexuality and the Greeks

We shall see the relevance of this idea of man's good to his sexual behavior as we examine the subject of sexuality in ancient Greece. It is ironic that the proponents of homosexuality so often point to ancient Greece as their paradigm because of its high state of culture and its partial acceptance of homosexuality, or more accurately, pederasty. Some ancient Greeks did write paeans to, and depict in art, homosexual/pederastic love, and male erotic attraction obviously had enough currency in Greek society to be a serious topic of discussion in the Platonic dialogues. However, it did not occur to the celebrants of this kind of love to propose homosexual relationships as the basis for marriage in their societies.

The homosexual association that was mostly publically accepted—and then only in the upper reaches of society—was between an adult male and a male adolescent. This largely pedagogical relationship, whose purpose was to form good and noble citizens, was to be temporary, as the youth was expected to marry and start a family as soon as he reached maturity. The idea that someone was a homosexual for life or had this feature as a permanent identity would have struck the ancient Greeks as more than odd. In other words, homosexuality, for which a word in Greek did not exist at the time (or in any other language until the late nineteenth century), was mostly transitory. It also appears that many of these mentoring relationships in ancient Greece were chaste and that the ones that were not rarely involved sodomy, which was widely considered a shameful outrage.

Homosexual relationships between mature male adults were not accepted by Greek society at large. In fact, they were often the object of derision. According to classics professor Bruce S. Thornton, the passive homosexual, the adult *kinaidos*, became the symbol in Greek culture of "unrestrained compulsive sexual appetite, of surrender to the chaos of natural passion that threatens civilized order, traitor to his sex".[9] As Thornton points out, Aristophanes often skewered the *kinaidos* in his plays as the emblem of sexual incontinence and political corruption. In a fifth-century B.C. allegory

[9] Ibid., 101.

composed by Prodicus, Virtue accuses Vice of "using men like women".[10] In the fourth century B.C., in Aeschines' prosecution against Timarchos, the latter is charged with "outraging his own body contrary to nature [*para phusin*]" in playing the passive homosexual.[11] The older "Just lover" does not seek physical gratification, said Aeschines, but is a "witness to chastity". This hardly matches the idealized homosexual paradise that our contemporaries hark back to in an attempt to legitimize behavior the ancient Greeks would have considered shameful, despite their relatively liberal sexual attitudes.

What is especially ironic is that, as mentioned, ancient Greece's greatest contribution to Western civilization was philosophy, which discovered that the mind can know things, as distinct from just having opinions about them, that objective reality exists, and that there is some purpose implied in its construction. The very idea of Nature and natural law arose as a product of this philosophy, whose first and perhaps greatest exponents, Socrates and Plato, were unambiguous in their condemnation of homosexual acts as unnatural. In the *Laws*, Plato's last book, the Athenian speaker says, "I think that the pleasure is to be deemed natural which arises out of the intercourse between men and women; but that the intercourse of men with men, or of women with women, is contrary to nature, and that the bold attempt was originally due to unbridled lust."[12] By its nature, lust is unbridled, irrational, and therefore destructive of what it is to be human. Giving in to it is therefore dehumanizing.

For Socrates, the sight of beauty, as in a beautiful male youth, is not to be taken as something in itself, but as a reflection of divine Beauty and the ultimate Good toward which Eros directs the soul. In this sense, as Diotima said in the *Symposium* (207a), "Eros is of immortality." Beauty awakens the soul to the desire for transcendent beauty. It is an error, therefore, to be diverted by the reflection in one's search for the ultimate Good. Beauty stirs the soul, but it is philosophy, not physical gratification, that provides the means of perceiving and coming to know the Good. One cannot come to this knowledge if one is mired in the sensual, which blocks the vision of the ultimate reality. (In this latter sense Eros can be, as Apollonius of Rhodes called it, that "unspeakable evil thing".)[13]

[10] Ibid., 107.
[11] Ibid., 114.
[12] Plato, *Laws* 636c; see also *Symposium of Xenophon* 8:34, Plato, *Symposium* 219b–d.
[13] Thornton, *Eros*, 217.

As a consequence of this metaphysical view, Socrates sees the erotic attraction of a grown man (*erastes*) for a beautiful male youth (*eromenos* or *paidika*) within the perspective of the erotic drive for wisdom. This drive will be thwarted by a life of self-indulgence and can proceed only with a life of self-discipline. As Fr. James Schall has pointed out, "The sober lesson of Plato's *Symposium* is that beauty and virtue are to go hand in hand."[14] Therefore, the relationship between the *erastes* and the *eromenos* should be of the older man enlightening the younger one in philosophical education. This means that any physical touching by the older man of the younger must be in regards to the latter "as a son", as Socrates puts it, and not further than that.

What went further than that, Socrates condemned. He loathed sodomy. According to Xenophon in *Memorabilia* (1.2.29f.), Socrates saw that Kritias was sexually importuning the youth of whom Kritias was enamored, "wanting to deal with him in the manner of those who enjoy the body for sexual intercourse". Socrates objected that "what he asks is not a good thing". Socrates said that "Kritias was no better off than a pig if he wanted to scratch himself against Euthydemos as piglets do against stones."

In *Phaedrus* (256a–b), Socrates makes clear the moral superiority of the loving male relationship that avoids being sexualized: "If now the better elements of the mind, which lead to a well ordered life and to philosophy, prevail, they live a life of happiness and harmony here on earth, self-controlled and orderly, holding in subjection that which causes evil in the soul and giving freedom to that which makes for virtue." By their chastity, these platonic lovers have, according to another translation of the text, "enslaved" the source of moral evil in themselves and "liberated" the force for good. This was the kind of mentoring relationship of which Socrates and Plato approved. On the other hand, "he who is forced to follow pleasure and not good" (239c) because he is enslaved to his passions will perforce bring harm to the one whom he loves because he is trying to please himself, rather than seeking the good of the other.

In the *Laws* Plato makes clear that moral virtue in respect to sexual desire is not only necessary to the right order of the soul, but is at the heart of a well-ordered polis. The Athenian speaker says,

> I had an idea for reinforcing the law about the natural use of the intercourse which procreates children, abstaining from the male, not

---

[14] James Schall, *The Order of Things* (San Francisco: Ignatius Press, 2007), 215.

deliberately killing human progeny or "sowing in rocks and stones", where it will never take root and be endowed with growth, abstaining too from all female soil in which you would not want what you have sown to grow. This law when it has become permanent and prevails—if it has rightly become dominant in other cases, just as it prevails now regarding intercourse with parents—confers innumerable benefits. In the first place, it has been made according to nature; also, it effects a debarment from erotic fury and insanity, all kinds of adultery and all excesses in drink and food, and it makes men truly affectionate to their own wives: other blessings also would ensue, in infinite number, if one could make sure of this law. (838–839)

The central insight of classical Greek political philosophy is that the order of the city is the order of the soul writ large. If there is disorder in the city, it is because of disorder in the souls of its citizens. This is why virtue in the lives of the citizens is necessary for a well-ordered polis. This notion is reflected in the Athenian's statement concerning the political benefits of the virtue of chastity. The relationship between virtue and political order is, of course, par excellence, the subject of Aristotle's works. It was a preoccupation of not only philosophy, but of drama as well, as can be seen in Euripides' *Bacchae*. Euripides and the classical Greeks knew that Eros is not a plaything. In *The Bacchae*, Euripides showed exactly how unsafe sex is when disconnected from the moral order. When Dionysus visits Thebes, he entices King Pentheus to view secretly the women dancing naked on the mountainside in Dionysian revelries. Because Pentheus succumbs to his desire to see "their wild obscenities", he agrees to undergo the humiliation of dressing as a woman. Dionysus ironically asks him, "Why have you fallen upon this great eros?" Pentheus, the embodiment of the political order, capitulates to the irrational and, as a result, the order of the city is toppled. Pentheus' enslavement to his passions leads to the literal enslavement of his city. The queen mother, Agave, one of the bacchants, ends up with the severed head of her son Pentheus in her lap—an eerie premonition of abortion. Pentheus' decapitation is a literal dramatization of his losing his mind.

The lesson is clear: once Eros is released from the bonds of family, Dionysian passions can possess the soul. Giving in to them is a form of madness, because erotic desire is not directed toward any end that can satisfy it. It is insatiable—what Plato calls in the *Laws* "endless and insatiate of evils". Once loosed, it will destroy the rational order of things. "That which causes evil in the soul"—in which Plato includes homosexual intercourse—will ultimately result in political disorder. The liberation of Eros is not freedom but annihilation.

For Aristotle, the irreducible core of a polity is the family. Thus, Aristotle begins his *Politics* not with a single individual, but with a description of a man and a woman together in the family, without which the rest of society cannot exist. He says: "First of all, there must necessarily be a union or pairing of those who cannot exist without one another." Later, he states that "husband and wife are alike essential parts of the family." The family is the nursery of virtue, which reaches its perfection in the polis. "Every state is [primarily] composed of households", Aristotle asserts. Without the family, there are no villages, which are associations of families, and without villages, there is no polis. In other words, without households—meaning husbands and wives together in families—there is no state. In this sense, the family is the *prepolitical* institution. The state does not make marriage possible; marriage makes the state possible. Homosexual marriage would have struck Aristotle as an absurdity since a polity cannot be founded on its necessarily sterile relations. This is why the state has a legitimate interest in marriage—because, without it, it has no future.

If Aristotle is correct—that the family is the primary and irreducible element of society—then chastity becomes the indispensable political principle because it is the virtue that regulates and makes possible the family. Without the practice of this virtue, the family becomes inconceivable. Without it, the family disintegrates. A healthy family is posited upon the proper and exclusive sexual relationship between a husband and wife. Violations of chastity undermine not only the family, but society as a whole.

This accounts for Aristotle's pronounced condemnation of adultery, which he finds all the more odious if committed while the wife is pregnant: "For husband or wife to be detected in the commission of adultery—at whatever time it may happen, in whatever shape or form, during all the period of their being married and being called husband and wife—must be made a matter of disgrace. But to be detected in adultery during the very period of bringing children into the world is a thing to be punished by a stigma of infamy proportionate to such an offense."[15] Aristotle understood that the laws were, or should be, ordered toward the formation of a certain kind of person—toward the realization of a virtuous citizenry. This is why Aristotle forbids adultery and wants to make it disgraceful in all

[15] Aristotle, *Politics* 16.18.

circumstances not only because it subverts virtue, but because it attacks the political foundations of society.

Adultery becomes a political problem because it violates chastity, which is indispensable to a rightly ordered polis. There is no comparable condemnation of adultery in homosexual marriage in Aristotle because such an institution would have been inconceivable to him, as it has been throughout history until recent times. That is because it is a self-contradiction. Marriage cannot be based on an act which is in itself a violation of chastity, because something cannot be its opposite. (In *Nicomachean Ethics*, Aristotle places "sex between males" among the "diseased things", like the habit of plucking out the hair or of gnawing the nails, or even coals or earth, which may "arise in some by nature and in others, as in those who have been the victims of lust from childhood, from habit" [7.1148].) A homosexual household would not make sense to Aristotle since it could not contain parents and all the generational relations that spring from them, which makes the polis possible. What did not make sense then does not make sense now, and for the same reasons.

So, it is through Nature that we come to understand the proper use of things. The enormous importance of this for our topic is that, since the ends of things are intrinsic to them, man does not get to make them up, but only to discover them through the use of his reason. He can then choose to conform his behavior to these ends in a life of virtue or to frustrate them in a life of vice. He can choose to become fully human or to dehumanize himself.

If his choice is the latter, he will not present it to himself in those terms. As Aristotle said, he must see what he selects as a good in order to be able to select it. If he chooses to rebel against the order of things, he will present this choice to himself not as one in favor of disorder, but as one *for* order—but of another sort. He will, as we have said, rationalize: vice becomes virtue. It is to the construction of this other sort of "order", to this alternate reality, that we now turn. One of its modern architects was Jean-Jacques Rousseau.

3

Rousseau's Inversion of Aristotle

Rousseau turned Aristotle's notion of Nature on its head. Aristotle said that Nature defined not only what man is but what he should be. Rousseau countered that Nature is not an end—a telos—but a beginning: man's end is his beginning, or, as Allan Bloom expressed it, "There are no ends, only possibilities."[1] Since man has no immutable Nature, "we do not know what our nature permits us to be", as Rousseau wrote in his *Emile*. A twentieth-century version of this view was offered by John Dewey, who said: "Human nature is not to have a nature." Hence, there is nothing man "ought" to become, no moral imperative, no ends in man or Nature. Existence is therefore bereft of any rational principle. There is no entelechy, no such thing as "having one's end within", as Aristotle put it. Rousseau could not have been more profoundly antiteleological. Let us see what this means.

Contra Aristotle, Rousseau asserted that man by Nature is not a social, political animal endowed with reason. In fact, according to Rousseau, reason itself is not natural to man—whereas Aristotle said it is man's very essence. Rather, reason developed accidentally, and its roots are therefore in the irrational. For Rousseau, man's prepolitical life begins not with the family, but with himself, as an isolated individual in the "state of nature", where the pure "sentiment of his own existence" was such that "one suffices to oneself, like God".[2] The state of nature becomes a secular substitute for the Garden of Eden. Yet this self-sufficient god was asocial, amoral, and prerational. His couplings with women were random and formed no lasting attachment. The family was not natural to him. As Rousseau wrote

[1] Allan Bloom, "Jean-Jacques Rousseau", in *History of Political Philosophy*, ed. Leo Strauss and Joseph Cropsey, 2nd ed. (Chicago: University of Chicago Press, 1972), 537.

[2] Jean-Jacques Rousseau, *The Reveries of a Solitary Walker* (New York: Burt Franklin, 1971), 114.

in his *Discourse on the Origin of Inequality*, "There was one appetite which urged him to perpetuate his own species; and this blind impulse, devoid of any sentiment of the heart, produced only a purely animal act. The need satisfied, the two sexes recognized each other no longer, and even the child meant nothing to the mother, as soon as he could do without her." The Marquis de Sade expressed a thoroughly Rousseauian sentiment in his novel *Juliette*, when he wrote that "all creatures are born isolated and with no need of one another"[3] That is why there is no family in the state of nature.

It was only when, through some unexplainable "accident", one man was forced into association with another that his godlike autonomy ended. "Man is by nature good", said Rousseau, but has somehow fallen from nature. What man has become is the result of this unexplained and unexplainable "accident", which also in some way ignited his use of reason. Rousseau stresses the *accidental* character of man's association in society in order to emphasize its unnaturalness and artificiality. It was not necessary and should not have happened because man was perfect in the state of nature. Aristotle taught that man cannot reach perfection by himself; he needs society and the political order to reach his full potential. The polis is necessary to him. Rousseau asserted the opposite: man begins in perfection, which the formation of society then takes from him.

Here is how Rousseau stated his thesis in his *Discourse on the Origin of Inequality*: "This state [of nature] was the least subject to upheavals and the best for man, and that he must have left it only by virtue of some fatal chance happening that, for the common good, ought never to have happened. The example of savages, almost all of whom have been found in this state, seems to confirm that the human race had been made to remain in it always; that this state is the veritable youth of the world; and that all the subsequent progress has been in appearance so many steps toward the perfection of the individual, and in fact toward the decay of the species."[4]

In his *Discourse on the Sciences and Arts*, Rousseau purported to show the destructive influences of civilization and "progress" on men, whose "minds have been corrupted in proportion as the arts and sciences have improved". In his work *Rousseau, Judge of Jean-Jacques*, he describes himself as having advanced the "great principle that nature made man happy and good, but that society depraves him and makes him miserable.... Vice and

---

[3] Cited in Jones, *Libido Dominandi*, 22.

[4] Jean-Jacques Rousseau, "Discourse on the Origin of Inequality", in *The Basic Political Writings*, trans. and ed. Donald A. Cress (Indianapolis: Hackett Publishing Company, 1987), 65.

error, foreign to his constitution, enter it from outside and insensibly change him." Speaking of himself in the third person, Rousseau wrote that "he makes us see the human race as better, wiser, and happier in its primitive constitution; blind, miserable, and wicked to the degree that it moves away from it."

The society resulting from that "fatal chance happening" has corrupted man. This is Rousseau's substitution for original sin. Through his association with others, man lost his self-sufficient "sentiment of his own existence". His love of himself relies on the esteem of others, instead of on his own self-love independent of others. In this way man becomes "alienated" from himself and enslaved to others. This is what Rousseau meant when he said, "Man is born free and everywhere he is in chains." Here we see in Rousseau the origin of Marx's idea of exploitation, carried through, in more recent times, to Jean-Paul Sartre's existential assertion: "Hell is other people." But if hell is other people, then heaven must be just oneself. Some eighteenth-century French aristocrats were so taken by Rousseau's vision that they released their children in the woods to raise themselves, free from society's contamination.

While there is nothing natural about civil society, Rousseau nonetheless knew that the prerational, asocial state of blissful isolation was lost forever, much as was the Garden of Eden. But he thought that an all-powerful state could ameliorate the situation of alienated man. How could this be done? The closest man can come to secular salvation is to abolish those dependent forms of association that have enslaved him to other men and kept him always outside of himself. He must therefore sever, as much as possible, his relations with his fellow members of society so that he can return the sentiment of his own existence to himself. Rousseau described the accomplishment of this condition: "Each person would then be completely independent of all his fellowmen, and absolutely dependent upon the state." The state could restore a simulacrum of that original well-being by removing all of man's subsidiary social relationships. By destroying man's familial, social, and political ties, the state could make each individual totally dependent on the state and independent of each other. Since all relationships are artificial, the state alone will construct man's relations. The state is the vehicle for bringing people together so they can be apart: a sort of radical individualism by and through state sponsorship.

Rousseau's program was to politicize society totally, and his first target was society's foundation—the family—the primary means by which men

are curbed of that total self-absorption to which Rousseau wished them to
return. To destroy the family Rousseau proposed that its primary function
of educating its children be taken from it and given to the state. "The public authority, in assuming the place of father and charging itself with this
important function [should] acquire his [the father's] rights in the discharge
of his duties." The father is supposed to console himself with the thought
that he still has some authority over his children as a "citizen" of the state.
His relationship with his children has now metamorphosed into a purely
political one.

Rousseau's attack upon the family and his exclusive reliance upon the
state as the vehicle of man's redemption is the prototype for all future rev-
olutionaries. The program is always the same: society, responsible for all
evils, must be destroyed. To promote universal "brotherhood", the only
source from which the word *brother* can draw meaning—the family—must
be eliminated. Once society is atomized, once the family ceases to interpose
itself between the individual and the state, the state is free to transform the
isolated individual by force into whatever version of "new man" the revolutionary visionaries espouse.

Here is the point of huge significance for our subject. If the family is
artificial in its origins, as Rousseau claimed, then it can be changed and rear-
ranged in any way the state or others may desire. Any such change is simply
a shift in *convention* (as there is no teleological Nature), a change in a cultural
artifact. We can revise human relations in any way we choose. Whoever
has sufficient power may make these alterations to suit himself. There is no
standard in Nature to which we must adhere or by which we can be judged.
This, of course, includes marriage. If we do not have a Nature with a telos,
then there could not possibly be a problem with homosexual acts or same-
sex marriage—or with many other things, as well.

Pointing out that there has never been such a thing as homosexual marriage in history is superfluous if man's Nature is malleable, the product of
history. History moves on, and man and all his social arrangements change,
or "evolve", with it; or rather, man can change himself according to his
desires, as long as he has the means to do so. Since things do not have ends
in themselves, they can be given purposes by whoever is powerful enough
to assign them.

This is the philosophy of the Sophist Callicles in Plato's *Gorgias*, the same
dialogue quoted in the introduction: "The fact is this: luxury and licentious-
ness and liberty, if they have the support of force, are virtue and happiness,

and the rest of these embellishments—the unnatural covenants of mankind—are all mere stuff and nonsense" (492c). With the support of force, virtue becomes *whatever* you choose. Virtue is not conforming your behavior to the rational ends of Nature, but conforming things to your desires. Reason becomes the instrument for doing this; it rationalizes for you.

For Rousseau, man is a creature of desire and appetites, to which his reason is subordinated. Rousseau's host in England, David Hume, wrote in *A Treatise on Human Nature*, "Reason is, and ought only to be, the slave of the passions and may never pretend to any office other than to serve and obey them." Reason is not, then, the means by which man reaches his end in the knowledge and contemplation of the Good. It is a tool for satisfying the passions. Reason is based upon unreason. The inversion of Aristotle is complete.

A modern-day version of Callicles would not speak as frankly as he did to Socrates. He would cloak his inversion of natural law in the language of "rights", so that it might seem to be the same, while actually being its opposite. If you are an active homosexual, you appropriate natural law rhetoric and claim a "right" to sodomitical acts and same-sex marriage. Fr. James Schall has uncovered this deception. He writes:

> Modern natural right theory is a theory of will, a will presupposed to nothing but itself. In its politicized formulation, it has been the most enduring and dangerous alternative to a natural law that is based in the ontological reality of what man is. Once natural right becomes the understood foundation of political life, the state is free to place any content into it that it wants, including the rewriting or elimination of natural law. The older constitutional tradition thought that the state was itself both a natural result of man's nature and, in that capacity, a check on the state. But if man has no nature, he is freed from this restriction. Modern natural right means that nothing limits man or the state except what he wills. He can will whatever he can bring about whether or not it was held to be contrary to natural law.[5]

Nothing less than this, is playing itself out in the same-sex marriage struggle.

Though not directly speaking of Callicles or Rousseau when he was interviewed for *Salt of the Earth*, the then Cardinal Joseph Ratzinger said

[5] James V. Schall and Ken Masugi, "An Easter Conversation with James V. Schall, S.J.", Claremont Institute, April 10, 2013, http://www.claremont.org/publications/pubid.826/pub_detail.asp.

something that characterizes this school of thought: "The idea that 'nature' has something to say is no longer admissible; man is to have the liberty to remodel himself at will. He is to be free from all of the prior givens of his essence. He makes of himself what he wants, and only in this way is he really 'free' and liberated. Behind this approach is a rebellion on man's part against the limits that he has as a biological being. In the end, it is a revolt against our creatureliness. Man is to be his own creator—a modern, new edition of the immemorial attempts to be God, to be like God."[6]

Today, Rousseau's influence is all around us. For instance, the condition of the forested county park across from my home stands in testimony to him. At the beginning of Rousseau's *Emile*, we read that "everything is good as it leaves the hands of the Author of things; everything degenerates in the hands of man." Thus, the forest is unkempt, deliberately kept in a state of disrepair, infested with poison ivy and decaying trees, as a tribute to Rousseau's advancement of the state of nature as superior to man's molestation of it (meaning forestry). Good for organic matter and bugs; bad for man (and my children). In short, it is unusable by human beings but for the narrow macadam path that snakes through it. The Garden of Eden was not Rousseau's state of nature because Nature, within the garden, was subject to man, meaning to his reasoned order. He gardened in it. Nature needs to be put in order; otherwise it is a jungle. That is what man does—in fact, it is what he is told to do in Genesis.

Rousseau's influence was also clearly present in the 2012 Obama presidential campaign. Consider "The Life of Julia", a Flash animation illustrating how the state, guided by President Obama's policies, would support a woman over her lifetime. In fact, Julia's life is portrayed *only* insofar as it exists in relation to the state. This is the Rousseauian ideal. The family is practically nowhere present. At age three, Julia is enrolled in a Head Start program. She receives government loans and tax credits for her college education. When she is twenty-two, her surgery is covered because of government health care. By age twenty-five, Julia can pay off her student loans, thanks to the government. Also, thanks to government health care, her birth control is covered, and she can concentrate on her work, for which she gets equal pay, thanks to the state. When she turns thirty-one, Julia decides to have a child. How? No husband (or man, for that matter) is mentioned, yet clearly (as we know from the generous birth control she

[6]Joseph Cardinal Ratzinger, *Salt of the Earth* (San Francisco: Ignatius Press, 1997), 133.

has received prior to this) hers is not a virgin birth. Perhaps this child was the result of one of the random couplings that Rousseau described in the state of nature. Then several years later the government helps get her son into a public kindergarten. This is the second and last mention of the child. (Perhaps, like Rousseau's children, he was left in a foundling home.) At age forty-two, Julia gets a Small Business Administration loan to start her own company. At sixty-five, Medicare is there for her and, at sixty-seven, so is Social Security. This supposedly appealing narrative of government dependence and family absence is presented as a success, rather than as a warning.

Another recent revelation of Rousseau's influence upon contemporary thinking on the family came from Melissa Harris-Perry, an MSNBC TV hostess. In April 2013 she proclaimed that "we haven't had a very collective notion that these are our children. We have to break through our kind of private idea that kids belong to their parents or kids belong to their families, and recognize that kids belong to their communities." When criticized for this remark, she defended herself by giving a version of Rousseau's theory of the "general will": "This is about whether we as a society, expressing our collective will through our public institutions, including our government, have a right to impinge on individual freedoms in order to advance a common good."[7] The general will is self-justifying. *Whatever* it decides defines the common good, including the welfare of one's children.

Rousseau's ideology also seeped into the art world. A prime example was the famous American composer John Cage. Typical of Cage were compositions whose notes were based on the irregularities in the composition paper he used, selected by tossing dice, or written with the help of charts derived from the Chinese *I Ching*. Perhaps Cage's most notorious work is his *4' 33"*, during which the performer silently sits with his instrument for that exact period of time, then rises and leaves the stage. The "music" is, whatever extraneous noises the audience hears in the silence the performer has created. In his book *Silence*, Cage announced: "Here we are. Let us say Yes to our presence together in Chaos."

What was the purpose of all this? Precisely to make the point that there is no purpose, no telos, or to express what Cage called a "purposeful purposelessness", whose aim was to emancipate people from the tyranny of meaning. With his aleatoric compositions, Cage worked out musically the

---

[7] Jack Mirkinson, "Melissa Harris-Perry Stands by Promo: 'Our Children Are Not Our Private Property' ", *Huffington Post*, updated April 14, 2013, http://www.huffingtonpost.com /2013/04/13/melissa-harris-perry-promo-children-msnbc_n_3076195.html.

full implications of Rousseau's nonteleological view of nature. Cage did for music what Rousseau did for philosophy. If man's reason is rooted in the irrational, shouldn't his music also be? Cage shared Rousseau's denigration of reason, the same notion of alienation, and a similar solution to it. In both men, the primacy of the accidental eliminates Nature as a normative guide and becomes the foundation for man's total freedom. Like Rousseau's man in the state of nature, Cage said, "I strive toward the nonmental." The quest is to "provide a music free from one's memory and imagination". Life itself is very fine "once one gets one's mind and one's desires out of the way and lets it act of its own accord".

But what is its own accord? Of music, Cage said, "The requiring that many parts be played in a particular togetherness is not an accurate representation of how things are" in Nature, because in Nature there is no order. In other words, life's accord is that there is no accord. As a result, Cage desired "a society where you can do anything at all".

In the Stony Point experimental arts community, where he spent his summers, Cage observed that each summer's sabbatical produced numerous divorces. So he concluded, "All the couples who come to the community and stay there end up separating. In reality, our community is a community for separation." Rousseau could not have stated his ideal better. Nor could Cage have made the same point in his art more clearly. For instance, in his long collaboration with choreographer Merce Cunningham, Cage wrote ballet scores completely unconnected to and independent of Cunningham's choreography. The orchestra and dancers rehearsed separately and appeared together for the first time at the premiere performance. The dancers' movements have nothing to do with the music. The audience is left to make of these random juxtapositions what it will. There is no shared experience— except of disconnectedness. The dancers, musicians, and audience have all come together in order to be apart.

According to Cage, the realization of the disconnectedness of things creates opportunities for wholeness. "I said that since the sounds were sounds this gave people hearing them the chance to be people, centered within themselves where they actually are, not off artificially in the distance as they are accustomed to be, trying to figure out what is being said by some artist by means of sounds." Here, in his own way, Cage captures Rousseau's notion of alienation. People are alienated from themselves because they are living in the estimation of others. Cage's noise, like Rousseau's philosophy, can help them let go of false notions of order, to "let sounds be themselves, rather than vehicles for man-made theories", and to return within themselves to the sentiment of their own existence.

This is the anthropological and metaphysical perspective within which the same-sex-marriage movement makes its case. To accept same-sex marriage means to accept the entire perspective from which it comes, including the assertion that "human nature is not to have a nature". But natural law is nothing other than what it is to be a human being. Without it, there is no natural standard of what is noble or what is right. Its rejection is a denial of humanity, of *what is*.

The Telos of Sex

Because we do have a Nature, there is a problem with the Rousseauian fantasy. If the rule of reason is incumbent upon us by our Nature—because acting rationally *is* acting in accord with Nature—then we must ask the question: Is sodomy *reasonable*? We can answer this only by addressing the Nature of sexual acts. We can begin with the overwhelmingly obvious fact that human bodies are better designed for heterosexual intercourse than for homosexual. As George Gilder put it, "Procreative genital intercourse stands at the crux of sexual differentiation, and is for the normative pinnacle of sexual relationships to which all other sexual energies aspire, and from which they flow." And William May expressed the combined unitive and reproductive Nature of the sexual act: "There is something of paramount human significance in the fact that one especial kind of touch, the touch of coital sex, not only requires for its exercise a difference between male and female, but also is an act that of its own inherent dynamism is capable of expressing an intimate, exclusive sharing of life and love between a man and a woman and at the same time is capable of communicating that life and that love to a new human being." In other words, only a unitive act can be generative, and only a generative act can be unitive—in that only it makes two "one flesh". That is why the unitive and procreative aspects of sex are inseparable. Separating them, as we shall see, does irreparable harm.

As procreative, this pinnacle of sexual relationships is naturally ordered to the family, whose structure places a couple in a context larger than just themselves. Compared with the act of marital union, homosexual acts are, as Michael Novak has pointed out, "self-centered in a way that is structural, independent of the goodwill of the individual". They have in them an inescapable element of solipsism. "The other side of the bed is occupied, as it were, by more of the same—the same half of humanity, instead of the other half for whom each person is constitutionally seeking." The renunciation of the other half leaves homosexuals bereft not only of a role in continuing the human race, but of the personal growth entailed in adjusting oneself, as Samuel McCracken expressed it, "to someone so different from oneself as to be in a different sex entirely". A woman is the Other through whom the man can come to know himself fully in his manhood, just as, for a woman, the man is the Other through whom she can come to know fully her womanhood. In *On the Meaning of Sex*, Budziszewski wrote, "The essential difference between men and women, the underlying reality that gives rise to all the other differences, is that men are in potentiality to be fathers, and women in potentiality to be mothers."[8] Same-sex relationships exchange this potency for impotency.

So what *is* sex for? The end of sex, as said earlier, is to make "one flesh". Two becoming "one flesh" encompasses both the generative and unitive Nature of sex. By Nature, only men and women are physically capable of becoming "one flesh". (Otherwise the pieces don't fit.) The end of sex is not simply pleasure; if it were, any kind of sex that produces pleasure would be natural. That something occurs, or can occur, does not make it natural. Cancer occurs, but one would not say, by that fact, that cancer is therefore natural to, say, the lungs. Why not? Because we know that lungs are for breathing and that cancer impedes and eventually prevents breathing.

A great deal of human ingenuity has gone into finding other uses for sex that go directly against its unitive and generative Nature. Those who misuse its powers are saying, in effect: We will take the pleasure, but not the thing toward which the pleasure is directed. It is like divorcing nutrition from the pleasure of eating—to the point of getting sick from it. As Fr. James Schall has written, "Whenever we seek pleasure without it being grounded in what is right in the action in which it exists, we isolate the pleasure, the act, from reality." In this sense, it becomes unreal, just as pornography is unreal. Pleasure becomes a form of alienation, instead of integration. Sex is a language of the body. Every act of coition presupposes the commitment within which it must take place in order to be real. That is what it naturally expresses. And when the commitment is not there, it is ineluctably felt as a betrayal, as a lie with the body. It is followed by

[8] J. Budziszewski, *On the Meaning of Sex* (Wilmington, DE: ISI Books, 2012), 97.

emptiness, by alienation. There is something inherently false, one might even say unjust, about sexual acts outside of marriage because, as Aristotle would say, the pleasure in them is not consistent with the Nature of the act or with man's final end.

Sex is a very strong passion, however, and it is difficult, as the Greeks knew, for anyone to contain. The only thing that can tame Eros and direct it to an end that can satisfy the sexual passion is love, which leads Eros away from death and, quite literally, toward new life. When a specific person is the object of love, no substitute will do. Love demands exclusivity and receives it in marriage. The desire for oneness in marital union is also a thirst for fecundity. The wild and complete abandon of the marital act is a joyful affirmation of the possibility of more—in children.

In their souls, what people truly love is goodness. And when they love goodness, it is what they seek to serve. This is true with sex also. Sex is directed to goodness by love. Love sublimates lust and restores the original innocence of sex. It is no longer self-seeking, self-consuming, but self-giving and life-generating. Sex receives its inherent completion only in *spousal* love. It seeks the unity that is available only in "one flesh." Spousal love requires becoming "one flesh". This is not a matter of "who says", but of how we are constituted by Nature. Anything else is counterfeit. To make the counterfeit official, as in legal same-sex marriage, is to substitute the unreal for the real. If you cannot become "one flesh" with the person you love, that is Nature's way of telling you that the character of your love is not spousal, but something else.

Love has its proper expression according to its subject and object—sisterly love, parental love, conjugal love, and the love of friendship are each distinct and are expressed accordingly. A child does not love his father with parental love, because the child is not the parent of his father. It may seem silly to state something so obvious, but this is what must be done when reality is being contested.

It is just as necessary and obvious to say that two men, or two women, cannot become husband and wife because that relationship requires a person of the other gender. No matter how many times homosexual advocates say it, two flesh of the same kind is not, and cannot become, "one flesh". We are now being told that this is not so—that if one man loves another man, sexualizing that love in the form of an act of sodomy is not only not harmful, but provides a sound moral basis for marriage. The sanctification of sodomy in marriage is the ultimate rationalization of sexual misbehavior.

So what is sodomy for? If sodomy is an expression of "love", how does it bring about the perfection of the person performing it or of the person on whom it is performed? Is there an objective good toward which it is intrinsically ordered? Sodomy is purposeless in that it serves neither unitive nor procreative ends. Its only good is pleasure, but it is pleasure contrary to what is right in the action—as the action itself is ordered to the unitive and procreative. As such, it is a perversion. Not being ordered to a good is what makes it, by Nature, disordered and irrational. Sodomy is onanism with another person. In this way, it fits in with Rousseau's description of sex in the state of nature—random and momentary. There is in sodomy an inbuilt futility, rather than the fruitfulness to which sex is essentially directed. A family with children provides a sense of fulfillment and completion that a same-sex couple cannot achieve.

As seen through Rousseau's influence, the case for homosexuality is a vulgarization of a philosophical anarchism that denies the existence of teleological Nature and therefore the ability to discriminate between the use and the abuse of things. This is popularly manifested in the most frequent defense of homosexuality, which takes the form of an anthropological survey of societies that invariably produces a tribe or two in which homosexual behavior is accepted as normal. This is offered as proof that either homosexuality is an expression of natural law or that such a variety of human behavior proves there is no such thing as natural law. The first conclusion is simply a way of robbing the word *Nature* of its meaning by including within its definition anything man is capable of doing. But this approach becomes less attractive when we recall that besides sodomy, it includes incest, human sacrifice, and mass suicide, for all of which there are numerous historical— and some recent—examples. The second conclusion errs by supposing that there can be a natural law only if it is universally acknowledged and obeyed. This overlooks the fact that man is unique in that he can affirm or deny his Nature. His denial of his Nature, however, in no way refutes its existence, any more than the denial of the law of gravity will keep one from falling.

Opposition to Natural Law

To see more specifically the way in which Nature is removed as an objective standard in order to argue for the morality of homosexuality, we may turn to a more contemporary example provided by Professor Burton Leiser, who offers a fairly typical argument against natural law in his chapter on homosexuality in *Liberty, Justice, and Morals*, a college textbook. He quotes Pope Pius XI as a representative of the natural law position: "Private individuals have no other power over the members of their bodies than that which pertains to their natural ends." Leiser goes on to question: "Is it true that every organ has one and only one proper function?" He gives the example of a woman's eyes as well adapted to seeing, but also well adapted to flirting. He then asks, "Is a woman's use of her eyes for the latter purpose sinful merely because she is not using them, at the moment, for their primary purpose?" Similarly, he questions whether any use of sex can be condemned because it is not being used for its principal procreative purpose: "Why should any other use of these organs, including their use to bring pleasure to their owner, or to someone else, or to manifest love to another person, or even, perhaps, to earn money, be regarded perverse, sinful or unnatural?"

The natural law theory that Leiser pretends to debunk is a straw man. The natural law argument has never been (nor is it in any way suggested by Pius XI's statement) that there is one and only one purpose or function of an organ, but that within the other ends an organ may be intended to serve by Nature, there is a hierarchy that subordinates some ends to others. While flirting with one's eyes is not unnatural, it is certainly subordinate to seeing. In fact, one can hardly flirt with one's eyes while not seeing. Strange indeed would be the woman who flirted with her eyes so as to impair her sight. Moreover, this hierarchy is arranged according to the one final end that is expressive of the whole Nature of man: the Good of which Socrates spoke or the God of revealed religion.

But the real crux of the natural law position is that however many ends an organ (or any other natural object) has, those ends originate in Nature and not in man's desires. Leiser, on the other hand, contends that "the purpose or function of a given organ may vary according to the needs or desires of its owners." With this argument, he justifies the use of sex not only "for pleasure, or for the expression of love" but "for some other purpose"—whatever that may be. Homosexuality, under this dispensation, is not wrong, because there is no "objectively identifiable quality in such behavior that is unnatural".

This removal of the objective quality of human acts leaves the true reality of things residing in man's desires or in his will. This is the world of Callicles. Morality is reduced to human intentions. In other words, an act such as sodomy has no meaning in and of itself, apart from the meaning it happens to be given by the person acting (i.e., what he intends or desires the act to be). As a consequence of this, we are unable to say that the act of sodomy is inherently wrong (or right) but are required to look to the person performing the act. It is according to his interior disposition or desires that the act becomes evil or good.

As mentioned in the introduction, while the natural law position emphasizes the moral Nature of an act, it does not disregard the intent of the actor. Indeed, the very idea of a moral act presupposes that the necessary conditions for it are present (i.e., a thorough understanding by the actor of what he is doing, full and free consent in the performance of the act, and so on). But at the same time, when we say that an act is objectively good or evil in itself, we mean that intention cannot change the goodness or evil of the act, which is intrinsic to it. A good intention—love—cannot change an evil act into a good one. It will harm the Nature of the person acting and the person acted upon, regardless of intent. Intention may affect the guilt or innocence of the actor, however, if, for example, the person is not fully aware of the evil of the act or does not perform it with full consent.

But by what standard are these desires to be judged? If human acts are not objectively good or evil and only individual desires are real, how can distinctions between desires be made? This is the existential dilemma created by the abandonment of the objectivity of Nature. Since the moral quality of an act cannot be discerned, one is left with a quantitative standard of intensity. How intensely (genuinely) is the desire felt? Adultery, incest, pederasty, masturbation—according to the school of desire, no moral distinction can be made between any of these acts and, say, the act of marital union. This is sexual equality with a vengeance.

How the White House Evolved

President Barack Obama has called for this equality—all loves are equal—but both he and Vice President Joseph Biden used to oppose homosexual marriage. Now they openly espouse it. How did this come about ? It came to be because they first embraced the larger view of reality of which the rationalization is only a part. Both Obama and Biden have said that their positions regarding same-sex marriage evolved. When you are "evolving", you should watch your grammar. Otherwise people might suspect you are devolving instead. Take, for instance, the hapless Joe Biden's pronouncement of why he now supports same-sex marriage. It's all a matter of "Who do you love?" His statement is both substantively and grammatically incorrect. It should, of course, be "Whom do you love?". *You* is the subject and *whom* is the object of the verb *love*. Biden's grammatical error reveals the problem with same-sex marriage. It has two subjects without an object.

What is the object of marriage? As we have said, it is for two to become "one flesh". Anatomically and morally, only a man and a woman can do this. Only spousal love is properly sexual, for only it provides for the protection of that at which the marital act aims both in its unitive and procreative senses.

But what about "love"? Isn't it a bit mean-spirited not to allow people who love each other to get married, even if they are of the same gender? Real love always seeks the well-being of the loved one. This is true in all sorts of love, including that between parents and children or between brothers and sisters or between friends of the same gender. To sexualize the love in these relationships would be profoundly mistaken because none of these loving relationships is or could be spousal in character. Sex between parents and children, between siblings, or between friends of the same gender is objectively disordered and will inflict harm on the parties involved, no matter how they *feel*, because nonconjugal sex, by its Nature, is opposed to the loved one's well-being and therefore antithetical to real love and to the human perfection at which it aims. For this reason, sex between unmarried friends of opposite genders is also harmful. This means that Mr. Obama's statement at his second inaugural that "surely the love we commit to one another must be equal" cannot be true unless we deny that there are different kinds of love, some of which ought not be sexual.

How does one evolve into this curious position? One undertakes what Nietzsche called the transvaluation of values. The president did this by twisting the immutable truths in the Constitution and in Christianity into their opposites. On September 25, 2004, Obama said: "I'm a Christian. And so, although I try not to have my religious beliefs dominate or determine my political views on this issue, I do believe that tradition, and my religious beliefs say that marriage is something sanctified between a man and a woman."[9] Indeed, that is what Christianity teaches. One wonders what in

---

[9] Tom Curry, "The 'Evolution' of Obama's Stance on Gay Marriage", NBCNews .com, May 9, 2012, http://nbcpolitics.nbcnews.com/_news/2012/05/09/11623172-the -evolution-of-obamas-stance-on-gay-marriage?lite.

Christianity Obama considers inconsistent with his political views. How are his political views formed? Are they consistent with moral philosophy? Is the judgment of moral philosophy, as in a work like Aristotle's *Ethics* or in Socrates' condemnation of sodomy, inconsistent with Christian teaching on same-sex marriage? If not, why doesn't Obama's moral reasoning lead him in the same direction as his Christian faith?

In his book *The Audacity of Hope*, Obama gives us a clue. He writes: "Implicit in [the Constitution's] structure, in the very idea of ordered liberty, was a rejection of absolute truth, the infallibility of any idea or ideology or theology or 'ism', and any tyrannical consistency that might lock future generations into a single, unalterable course." In other words, truth leads to tyranny. Truth does not set you free; it imprisons. Moral relativism sets you free. Then you can do what you want. But it is absurd for Obama to say that the Founders of the United States did not believe in absolute truths. Had this been so, there would have been no Declaration of Independence ("We hold these truths . . .") and no Constitution. Obama is reading his own moral relativism back into the document and then trying to use it to legitimize the very opposite of what it proclaims.

Here is another example of the transvaluation of values. On January 28, 2010, during a town hall meeting at the University of Tampa, Obama said: "My belief is that a basic principle in our Constitution is that if you're obeying the law, if you're following the rules, that you should be treated the same, regardless of who you are. I think that principle applies to gay and lesbian couples." Only a moral relativist would or could read same-sex marriage back into the Constitution. What Obama is really proposing to do is change the rules so that those who are not following them can have their own special set of rules. So, in the name of equality before the law—a sound constitutional principle—he subverts equality before the law.

This all leads to Obama's striking statement on Wednesday, May 9, 2012. Here it is with the personal pronouns and adjectives italicized:

> *I* have to tell you that over the course of several years as *I* have talked to friends and family and neighbors when *I* think about members of *my* own staff who are in incredibly committed monogamous relationships, same-sex relationships, who are raising kids together, when *I* think about those soldiers or airmen or marines or sailors who are out there fighting on *my* behalf and yet feel constrained, even now that Don't Ask Don't Tell is gone, because they are not able to commit themselves in a marriage, at a certain point *I've* just concluded that for *me* personally it is important for

me to go ahead and affirm that *I* think same-sex couples should be able to get married.[10]

Ten personal pronouns or adjectives in one sentence. That is an impressive feat of solipsism that undergirds the moral relativism that authorizes what "is important for me" as the standard by which to judge what is right and wrong.

The transvaluation of values necessitates more than the denial of objective morality. It requires that the negation—the transvaluation—becomes the new religion. It is the sanctification of nihilism, the Church of Nada. It needs to be sacramentalized, as in same-sex marriage. That is why Obama insists upon it. Listen to this final, breathtaking part of Obama's rationalization. Just as he used the Constitution to justify its opposite, he now employs Christianity in the same way. Christianity, which has unambiguously condemned sodomy for more than two thousand years, is enlisted to endorse it: "The thing at root that we think about is, not only Christ sacrificing himself on our behalf, but it's also the golden rule—you know, treat others the way you would want to be treated. And I think that's what we try to impart to our kids, and that's what motivates me as president." After all, he might as well have said, Christ died to make the world safe for sodomy.

In other words, if you would like your moral misbehavior to be rationalized, you should be willing to rationalize the moral misbehavior of others. That is only fair play. That way, we are all equal. That is equal opportunity. This is Obama's new golden rule. The transvaluation of values is complete.

---

[10] Rick Klein, "Obama Flip Flops on Gay Marriage", FoxNews.com, accessed July 31, 2013, http://nation.foxnews.com/president-obama/2012/05/09/obama-reverses-position-same-sex-marriage.

4

The Argument from Justice

The transvaluation also requires an inverted notion of justice. The ultimate level of absurdity has been reached by the claim that *justice* requires the legalization of same-sex marriage. Consider the following two protestations.

Celebrating the passage of such a law in New York in 2011, *Washington Post* columnist Richard Cohen wrote: "I am the brother of a woman in a longtime same-sex relationship.... This is a cause whose justness has long been apparent to me. The opponents have no case other than ignorance and misconception and prejudice."[1]

And when Edwin O'Brien, the Catholic archbishop of Baltimore, attempted to remonstrate with Maryland Governor Martin O'Malley, a Catholic, over his sponsorship of a same-sex marriage bill, the governor responded: "When shortcomings in our laws bring about a result that is unjust, I have a public obligation to try to change that injustice."[2]

But before justice can be enlisted on behalf of this cause, we should ask ourselves: What *is* justice? The classical answer to this question is that justice is giving to things what is their due according to what they *are*. In other words, to act justly, one must first know what things are. Without this knowledge, one cannot act justly. This may seem self-evident, but its application is far more difficult than one might at first think. In order to know what things are, one needs metaphysics and epistemology. The question of justice necessarily leads to the question of the Nature of things. One also

---

[1] Richard Cohen, "Mario Cuomo Beats the Odds—Spectacularly", Washington Post, June 27, 2011, http://articles.washingtonpost.com/2011-06-27/opinions/35235299_1_andrew -mark-cuomo-mario-cuomo-kerry-kennedy.

[2] Brian Witte, "Maryland Same-Sex Couples Prepare for Marriages Today", *Daily Chronicle*, January 1, 2013, http://www.daily-chronicle.com/mobile/article.xml/articles/2012/12/31 /61004ae6f2144e20b1bb339aa6e56041/index.xml.

needs accurate language, so that words can be deployed that capture the essence of what things are. When one knows what something is according to its Nature, one then understands what it is for. The end of the thing then determines whether an action toward it is a use or an abuse. This is where the matter of justice comes in.

It is necessary to apprehend things as they are before one can act justly. A simple example suffices. If one does not know the difference between a man and a dog, one may end up treating a man as if he were a dog. This would be acting unjustly. Justice in no way pertains to how we *feel* about things but rather to what they *are*. In our anthropomorphic enthusiasm, we may feel that our pet dog is human. It would be absurd, however, to pass legislation requiring the dog's consent to its owner's rule, because the dog is not human and is incapable of giving its consent. Confusion over the distinction between the human and the nonhuman leads to such absurdities as the lawsuit filed in New York on December 2, 2013, to establish the "legal personhood" of chimpanzees. Steven Wise, the president of the Nonhuman Rights Project, asked the court to declare Tommy, a 26-year-old chimpanzee, "a cognitively complex autonomous legal person with the fundamental legal right not to be imprisoned". He said chimpanzees "possess complex cognitive abilities that are so strictly protected when they're found in human beings". Therefore, he asserted, "There's no reason why they should not be protected when they're found in chimpanzees."[3]

However, chimpanzees and dogs do not have free will. It is therefore just for men to rule over chimpanzees and dogs, and it is unjust to "free" them from their owners on the basis that the animals have not consented to their ownership.

Likewise, no feeling can justify the enslavement of another human being, because a human being has the inalienable right to consent in his rule. This, of course, is the problem with slavery. Only the understanding of what a human being is allows one to make this vital distinction between the human and the nonhuman. It is something one knows or does not know (or refuses to acknowledge), with huge consequences. This act of recognition is the basis of Western civilization. We have forever since called barbarian those who are either incapable of seeing another person as a human being or who

[3] Bernard Vaughan and Daniel Wiessner, "New York Lawsuit Seeks 'Legal' Personhood for Chimpanzees", *Reuters*, http://www.reuters.com/article/2013/12/02/us-usa-chimpanzees-lawsuit-idUSBRE9B10UE20131202.

refuse to do so. It is precisely the loss of this distinction upon which the practice of slavery was grounded and upon which the practice of abortion is based today.

Epistemological Amnesia and Tyranny

Has the ability to make distinctions grounded in Nature been lost with respect to the marriage debate? If so, how does the loss affect it and us? The modern premise, so evident in the campaign for same-sex marriage, is that any preexisting rational end constitutes a limitation on human freedom. Therefore, freedom requires the denial that rational ends inhere in things. Everything is a tabula rasa, a blank slate upon which we can write anything we desire. Things, being without ends in themselves, have only the purposes we choose for them. Therefore, we give them whatever names we desire. The purpose of language is no longer to apprehend things as they are, but to transform them into what we want them to be.

Misnaming things necessarily leads to moral and political disorder. In the *Analects*, Confucius taught: "If names be not correct, language is not in accordance with the truth of things. If language be not in accordance with the truth of things, affairs cannot be carried on to success. When affairs cannot be carried on to success, proprieties and music do not flourish." Without the right word, one will not only get the relationship of things wrong, but what something actually *is* will be wrong, as well. The corruption of language spells the termination of justice, for it prevents us from knowing what things are, or how properly to speak of them, or to use rather than abuse them—just as when a black man was called a piece of property and used as an "article of merchandise", rather than a human being.

An injustice of similar magnitude is perpetrated by naming same-sex couplings "marriage". Socrates and Plato said that a chaste loving relationship between a man (*erastes*) and a male youth (*eromenos*) is morally superior to one in which sexual touching takes place. Marriage for those who engage in sodomy reverses this moral judgment, and places sodomitical behavior on a higher moral plane than chastity. This inversion of the classical moral order cannot take place without a corresponding inversion of the classical definition of justice. One will give to things what is their due no longer according to what they are. In other words, justice will reside in one's desires or will, rather than in the reality of *what is*. For same-sex marriage to be just, justice has to be *whatever* we say it is.

This is a very dangerous teaching—that we get to make up what things are. If Nature is denied, then justice will necessarily be reduced to what is willed, which, in turn, becomes *right as the rule of the stronger*. This is what Callicles espoused, as did Thrasymachus in Plato's *Republic*. This is what tyrants do. What is arbitrary is by definition tyrannical. It is based upon pure will, unguided by reason. Those who wish to base their freedom upon the supposed purposelessness of things, which obtains in the absence of Nature, should face the consequences of this view. What seems unmitigated freedom is, in fact, the foundation of tyranny.

Unfortunately, this solipsistic view of reality has reached high places, as we shall see when we discuss Supreme Court rulings in detail in the next chapter. For now, we excerpt this sentence from the 1992 *Planned Parenthood v. Casey* ruling, in which the court opined that "at the heart of liberty is the right to define one's own concept of existence, of meaning, of the universe, and of the mystery of human life." Well, actually not. The universe is already here. It has already been defined for us; otherwise it would not be in existence. Our choice is not to make up the meaning of the universe but to discern its meaning and then either conform ourselves to it or revolt against it.

The choice today is revolt. Igor Stravinsky wrote, "The old original sin was one of knowledge, the new original sin is one of non-acknowledgment." It is the refusal to acknowledge anything outside the operation of the human will—most especially the good toward which the soul is ordered. The good is what must ultimately inform human justice. Therefore, moral relativism is inimical to justice, as it removes the epistemological ground for knowing the good. As Max Planck, the founder of quantum theory, wrote, "Everything that is relative presupposes the existence of something that is absolute, and is meaningful only when juxtaposed to something absolute."[4] What happens if the absolute is absent? If what is good is relative to something other than itself, then it is not the good but the expression of some other interest that only claims to be the good. Claims of "good" then become transparent masks for self-interest. This is the surest path back to barbarism and the brutal doctrine of "right is the rule of the stronger". The regression

[4] Max Planck, *Scientific Autobiography, and Other Papers* (New York: Philosophical Library, 1949), 46–48.

is not accidental. Relativism inevitably concludes in nihilism, and the ultimate expression of nihilism is the supremacy of the will.

The Restoration of Ends

The defense against this descent into tyranny is the restoration of Nature. As mentioned earlier, once we know what something *is*, we can know what it is for. Its purpose is within it. How does this pertain to the issue of the justice of same-sex marriage? Fr. James Schall has written that "cities were established to render each his due, to render justice."[5] Since the family is the irreducible core unit of cities or any other political order, one may say the same thing of marriage: it was established to render justice, to give each his due—in this case, what is due between husband and wife in the inimitably unique relationship that they form. Owing to the exceptional complementarity and procreative potential of a husband and a wife, the legal form for their relationship is likewise distinctive, and not replicable for other relationships that are neither complementary nor potentially reproductive. To use the legal form of marriage for these latter associations is to transfer the goods proper to marriage to those to whom they are not proper. This is an act of injustice—treating something as other than what it *is*.

Consider this analogy. Marriage is a legally acknowledged station in life. So, too, is being an officer of the law. If we were to treat as officers of the law those who are not—and who are not even qualified to serve in that capacity—it would be an act of injustice, both to *real* law officers and to the community they are supposed to serve. Confusion and dysfunction would abound, as people would be unable to tell the real from the unreal. All the greater would be the dysfunction and confusion from faux marriages. Some who were not married would think they were, and some who were married would wonder whether they were. And the children—whose are they? Are they from the real marriages or from the unreal ones?

The magnitude of the injustice involved in the redefinition of marriage comes most clearly into view in regard to children, to whom justice is also owed. As Seana Sugrue writes, "The ability of same-sex couples to be parents depends crucially upon the state declaring that they possess such rights, and by extinguishing or redefining the rights of biological parents. With the

---

[5] Schall, *The Order of Things*, 174

rise of same-sex marriage, the obligations parents owed to their biological children are reduced to mere convention. This is true for everyone. Parents come to owe obligations to their children not because they are parents, but because they choose to be parents."[6] What is owed to children by right or Nature becomes optional by convention. This is a staggering loss for them.

Same-sex "families" with children are broken by definition because in no instance will both parents be present. Such "families" are made to be broken, or rather broken to be made, *by design*. This is especially so in the cases in which a child is bred—with the outside assistance of a person of the other gender—to be placed with the same-sex couple, only one of whom is, or could be, the parent of the child. This is a grotesque act of injustice to the children who are misused in this way and for this purpose. They are deliberately denied the possibility of being with both parents. They are made rootless, or rather made to be rootless in the essential aspect of the missing parent—an intentionally truncated genealogy. Indeed, they are willfully wrenched out of the chain of being. In an appearance at a hearing of the Minnesota House Civil Law Committee, on March 14, 2013, Grace Evans (age eleven) asked its members, who were considering a redefinition of marriage: "Which parent do I not need, my mom or my dad?"[7] No one answered. The committee went on to approve the legislation to repeal the state law defining marriage as between a man and a woman. It passed the Minnesota Legislature and was signed into law on May 14, 2013.

The adoption of children by same-sex couples is an extension of the rationalization of their misbehavior, no matter how motivated it may be by accompanying eleemosynary motives. Children are the fruit of a mother and a father, ideally in matrimony as a husband and a wife. If same-sex couples, too, can have children, this will mean that they also have "real" marriages. The possession of a child by the same-sex couple completes the rationalization for them. Just as most active homosexuals practice faux intercourse, they can have faux progeny from it. They can pretend that this is so, and they can insist that society pretend along with them. What is worse, the same-sex couples will make the children pretend too. The children will

---

[6] Robert P. George and Jean Bethe Elshtain, eds., *The Meaning of Marriage* (Dallas: Spence Publishing Company, 2006), 189.

[7] "Which Parent Don't I Need, My Mom or My Dad?", YouTube video, 2:05, of Grace Evans' statement before the Minnesota House Civil Law Committee, posted by "mnformarriage", March 14, 2013, http://www.youtube.com/watch?v=kUfYaFys4Aw& feature=youtu.be.

be indoctrinated to participate in the lie. And therein lies a good deal of the harm that homosexual couples will bring to the children, despite the love and affection they may provide. As one mother explained to me, "Most kids understand intuitively the idea that everything has a purpose. How does one explain to them that the purpose is ignored by adults? The children are caught in that web of deceit."

Robert Oscar Lopez, raised by a lesbian couple, stated that "children deeply feel the loss of a father or mother, no matter how much we love our gay parents or how much they love us. Children feel the loss keenly because they are powerless to stop the decision to deprive them of a father or mother, and the absence of a male or female parent will likely be irreversible for them."[8] Elsewhere, Lopez added, "Conferring marriage on same-sex couples means some children will never be able to invoke the words 'father' and 'mother' in order to describe the household that their parents are now allowed to describe as a 'marriage.' In order to grant validation and prestige to mom and mom or dad and dad, the kids lose access to the value of celebrating a maternal and paternal line of ancestry. Come Mother's Day and Father's Day, they will not be equal to their peers, due directly to the fact that their same-sex guardians fought so hard to be equal to their peers' parents".[9]

In regard to justice, one might also ask: What of same-sex, heterosexual couples who live with and cherish each other, but who do not engage in homosexual acts? Are they less worthy of marriage? If the only thing that distinguishes them from homosexual couples is sodomitical behavior, and if only homosexual couples are to be extended the privilege of marriage, then something of special merit must obtain precisely to the act of sodomy itself. Why should sodomy be privileged in this way? Otherwise, why would marriage not be appropriate for chaste or heterosexual same-sex friendship? The tax advantages obtaining to an estate left by one spouse to another are great. Should they be only for lesbian and homosexual couples and not, say, for brothers, sisters, or others who may love each other and live together?

All of this makes richly ironic Richard Cohen's and Governor O'Malley's invocation of justice to advance a cause based upon the denial of the Nature of marriage. They are, in fact, complicit in perpetrating fraud—an unjust act.

---

[8] Robert Oscar Lopez, "What Do the Children Say?", Mercator.net, May 12, 2013, http://www.mercatornet.com/articles/view/what_do_the_children_say.

[9] Robert Oscar Lopez, "Truth, Metaphor, and Race in the Marriage Debate", Witherspoon Institute, February 11, 2013, http://www.thepublicdiscourse.com/2013/02/7871/.

5

The Lessons from Biology

How are we to discriminate between the real and the unreal in this matter of marriage? Primarily, it has to do with the procreative and unitive powers of our sexual organs. Today we seem to know the purpose of every part of our bodies except our genitals. Is there any other part of our bodies about which we claim to know so little? Is there any doubt as to what our hands are for, or our eyes, nose, and ears? Each of these appendages or organs has a functional structure that dictates its proper use. How is it that we know this about all the other parts of our bodies except the genitals? This is a case of selective amnesia.

Therefore, we must return to the point that sex has a natural purpose. In using or treating any part of our body, the critical question is: What are the ends to which the Nature of the thing directs it, and is the action outside of, or within, those ends? For instance, our lungs are for breathing. Breathing oxygenates our blood through the alveoli. If anyone suggested that our lungs are for imbibing water, they would be set straight in short order and informed that water in the lungs would lead to death. If they nonetheless insisted that water is good for the lungs and applied this teaching to themselves, they would soon be asphyxiated.

No one has really been tempted to do this. People have, however, found a great deal of pleasure in smoking cigarettes. This has been shown to be a misuse of the lungs, because the tars and nicotine from the tobacco smoke cause lung cancer. Therefore, we can say with some confidence that the end or purpose of the lungs is not pleasure from smoking. The purpose of a thing cannot be fulfilled in an action that leads to its destruction. On the basis of this, the government has taken vigorous steps to dissuade people from smoking. Laws have been passed prohibiting young people from buying cigarettes and requiring the labeling of cigarettes as injurious to health.

No one today, however, can publicly suggest that our genitals are not made for sodomy or even, without becoming the objects of obloquy, point out the deleterious health consequences of this unclean practice. Well before HIV/AIDS arrived on the scene, the life expectancy of practicing homosexuals was substantially below that of the heterosexual male population because of the harmful health effects of this behavior. What things *are* have a way of fighting back against those who deny what they are and who act in such a way as if they weren't.

As unpleasant as the subject matter may be, it is necessary to report on the physical effects of sodomitical behavior and of other homosexual acts. Their consequences are significantly more injurious to health than smoking, so much so that ignorance or denial of these effects is one of the most remarkable barometers of the strength of the rationalization that insists this behavior is normal and normative.

A person stuffing objects into his ears is endangering his hearing, because he could puncture his eardrums or precipitate an infection. Ears are made for hearing, not for the storage of objects. Using them for the latter endangers the former. Any responsible person would advise someone stuffing objects into his ears not to do this because of the harm it could bring.

This is likewise true of the male genitals and the anus. Human generative organs are perfectly matched, the male for penetration, the female for reception. The matching takes place *only* in heterosexual intercourse and is a perfect biological fit, which causes no physical harm to either party. There is no anatomical fit in same-sex couplings. There is and can be no union of sexual organs in any same-sex act.

Unlike the vagina, the anus is solely an excretory organ; it is an exit, not an entrance. It is designed to eliminate fecal matter. When it is used in homosexual intercourse as a stand-in for the female vagina, it is being subjected to an activity for which it was clearly not designed. One of the indications of this is the physical harm that it brings. If one insisted on using a highway exit as an entrance, one would be told that this is extremely hazardous to one's health and safety and to that of others. Why is this so difficult to state when it comes to human anatomy?

Before proceeding on the subject, one might ask how typical anal intercourse is in homosexual behavior. Is it fundamentally characteristic or anomalous? Some claim that homosexual behavior does not necessarily mean that male couples engage in anal intercourse. The answer, however, is that it predominates. In *Homosexuality and the Politics of Truth*, psychiatrist Dr. Jeffrey Satinover writes:

The typical homosexual (needless to say there are exceptions) is a man who has frequent episodes of anal intercourse with other men, often with many different men. These episodes are 13 times more frequent than heterosexuals' acts of anal intercourse, with 12 times as many different partners as heterosexuals. These statistics, it should be added, are quite conservative. The most rigorous single study—the Multicenter AIDS Cohort Study [1987]—recruited nearly 5000 homosexual men and found that: "a significant majority of these men ... (69 to 83 percent) reported having 50 or more lifetime sexual partners, and over 80 percent had engaged in receptive anal intercourse with at least some of their partners in the previous two years."[1]

That is not all. A national survey of "gay" men, reported by the *Advocate* (August 23, 1994: 20), showed that 41 percent performed anilingus (tongue on or in the anus), 46 percent received it in the prior year, and 46 percent of the men sometimes had sex that they themselves considered risky.

Health Consequences: Mortality and Disease

When it is misused, the body understandably becomes confused. For instance, reports journalist Susan Brinkmann, "there are substances in seminal fluid called 'immuno-regulatory macromolecules' that send out 'signals' that are only understood by the female body, which will then permit the 'two in one flesh' intimacy required for human reproduction. When deposited elsewhere, these signals are not only misunderstood, but cause sperm to fuse with whatever somatic body cell they encounter. This fusing is what often results in the development of cancerous malignancies."[2]

According to "Correlates of Homosexual Behavior and the Incidence of Anal Cancer" in the *Journal of the American Medical Association*, the risk of anal cancer soars by 4,000 percent among those who engage in anal intercourse.[3] At the Fourth International AIDS Malignancy Conference at the

---

[1] Jeffrey Satinover, *Homosexuality and the Politics of Truth* (Grand Rapids: Baker Books, 1996), 55.

[2] R.J. Ablin and R. Stein-Werblowsky, "Sexual Behavior and Increased Anal Cancer", *Immunology and Cell Biology* 75 (1977): 181–83.

[3] J.R. Daling et al., "Correlates of Homosexual Behavior and the Incidence of Anal Cancer", *Journal of the American Medical Association* 247, no.14 (April 9, 1982): 1988–90; cited in Susan Brinkmann, "Health Risks of the Homosexual Lifestyle", Catholic Education Resource Center, accessed July 31, 2013, http://catholiceducation.org/articles/homosexuality/h00088.html.

National Institutes of Health in May 2000, Dr. Andrew Grulich said that the incidence of anal cancer among homosexuals with HIV "was raised 37-fold compared with the general population".[4]

Cancer is not the only or even the greatest peril to active homosexuals. Anal sex increases the risk of rectal prolapse, perforation that can go septic, chlamydia, cryptosporidiosis, giardiasis, genital herpes, genital warts, isosporiasis, microsporidiosis, gonorrhea, viral hepatitis B and C, and syphilis.[5]

In 2006 homosexual journalist Simon Fanshawe wrote in the *Guardian*: "Hooked on drugs and sex and looks, we call it gay culture. The figures are staggering: 20 percent of gay men in London use the incredibly damaging crystal meth. Studies show that men who do are twice as likely to become HIV positive. Since 1999, the figures for HIV infections have continued to rise in the UK. Syphilis infection rates among gay men have increased by 616 percent in the past five years."[6]

All of this has resulted in a substantially reduced life expectancy for active homosexuals. In *The Health Risks of Gay Sex*, Dr. John R. Diggs Jr. reports:

> An epidemiological study from Vancouver, Canada, of data tabulated between 1987 and 1992 for AIDS-related deaths reveals that male homosexual or bisexual practitioners lost up to 20 years of life expectancy. The study concluded that if 3 percent of the population studied were gay or bisexual, the probability of a 20-year-old gay or bisexual man living to 65 years was only 32 percent, compared to 78 percent for men in general. The damaging effects of cigarette smoking pale in comparison—cigarette smokers lose on average about 13.5 years of life expectancy.... There are additional major causes of death related to gay sex. For example, suicide rates among a San Francisco cohort were 3.4 times higher than the general US male population in 1987. Other potentially fatal ailments such as syphilis, anal cancer, and Hepatitis B and C also affect gay and bisexual men disproportionately."[7]

[4] "Studies Point to Increased Risks of Anal Cancer", *Washington Blade*, June 2, 2000, cited in Timothy J. Dailey, PhD, "The Negative Health Effects of Homosexuality", Family Research Council, accessed July 31, 2013, http://www.frc.org/get.cfm?i=Iso1B1.

[5] Ibid.

[6] Simon Fanshawe, "Society Now Accepts Gay Men as Equals. So Why on Earth Do So Many Continue to Behave Like Teenagers?", *Guardian*, April 20, 2006, http://www.guardian.co.uk/commentisfree/2006/apr/21/gayrights.comment.

[7] John R. Diggs Jr., MD, "The Health Risks of Gay Sex", Catholic Education Resource Center, accessed July 31, 2013, http://www.catholiceducation.org/articles/homosexuality/h00075.html#05.

Dr. Satinover reports that a presentation on the homosexual life span to the Eastern Psychological Association, April 1993, "found that the gay male lifespan, *even apart from AIDS* and *with* a long term partner, is significantly shorter than that of married men in general *by more than three decades*. AIDS further shortens the lifespan of homosexual men by more than 7 percent" (emphasis in original).[8] Elsewhere, Dr. Satinover states that "the incidence of AIDS among twenty- to thirty-year-old homosexual men is roughly 430 times greater than among the heterosexual population at large."[9]

The severity of these mortality rates has been reduced with more recent advances in the treatment of AIDS. In late 2001, in the *International Journal of Epidemiology*, a group of Canadian researchers gave an update to the study referenced earlier by Dr. Diggs that they had done in the late 1980s and early 1990s:

> We demonstrated that in a major Canadian centre, life expectancy at age 20 years for gay and bisexual men is 8 to 21 years less than for all men. If the same pattern of mortality continued, we estimated that nearly half of gay and bisexual men currently aged 20 years would not reach their 65th birthday. Under even the most liberal assumptions, gay and bisexual men in this urban centre were experiencing a life expectancy similar to that experienced by men in Canada in the year 1871. In contrast, if we were to repeat this analysis today the life expectancy of gay and bisexual men would be greatly improved. Deaths from HIV infection have declined dramatically in this population since 1996. As we have previously reported there has been a threefold decrease in mortality in Vancouver as well as in other parts of British Columbia.[10]

Further improvements in the treatment of AIDS mean that the death rate from HIV was some nine times greater in 1990 than in 2010. This, of course, is good news, but it remains the case that, as British Dr. David Delvin asserts, "anal intercourse carries a higher transmission risk than almost any other sexual activity."[11] What's more, the improved treatment

---

[8] Satinover, *Homosexuality and the Politics of Truth*, 69.

[9] Ibid., 57.

[10] Robert S. Hogg, Steffanie A. Strathdee, Kevin J. P. Craib, Michael V. O'Shaunessy, Julio Montaner, and Martin T. Schechter, "Gay Life Expectancy Revisited", *International Journal of Epidemiology* 30, no. 6 (December 2001), http://ije.oxfordjournals.org/content/30/6/1499 .full.

[11] David Delvin, "Anal Sex", NetDoctor, accessed July 31, 2013, http://www.netdoctor .co.uk/sexandrelationships/analsex.htm.

of AIDS also carries risks. Unfortunately, according to *New York Blade News*, "Scientists believe that the increased number of sexually transmitted diseases (STD) cases is the result of an increase in risky sexual practices by a growing number of gay men who believe HIV is no longer a life-threatening illness."[12]

Also, "new data from the US Centers for Disease Control and Prevention (CDC) show that gay, bisexual, and other men who have sex with men (MSM) are over 44 times more likely than other men to contract HIV, and over 40 times more likely than women to contract HIV. Further, MSM are over 46 times more likely to contract syphilis than other men, and over 71 times more likely than women to contract syphilis. According to the CDC, MSM comprised 57 percent of people newly infected with HIV in the United States in 2006, even though MSM are only 2 percent of the adult population."[13] According to Dale O'Leary, "While MSM make up for only a tiny percentage of the population, they account for 72 percent of primary and secondary syphilis cases, plus 79 percent of HIV diagnoses among men, and a significant percentage of other STDs."[14]

There is more evidence supporting the disease and mortality figures but, rather than larding more of it into the text of the book, I have placed it in the appendix.

Warning Labels?

Why, then, are there no warning labels? Where are the skulls and cross-bones? How is it that there can be warning labels on cigarettes and alcohol, on almost every package of food, health alerts for the level of air pollution, mandatory use of seat belts in cars, and yet no cautionary admonitions regarding homosexual practices? Why are we counseled to change our dietary habits if we tend toward obesity because of the health hazards it presents, but not asked to modify our behavior if we engage in sodomy, which can be far more lethal?

[12] Bill Roundy, "STD Rates on the Rise" *New York Blade News*, December 15, 2000, 1.

[13] "Gay Men Still More Likely to Contract HIV", *BCMJ* 52, no. 4 (May 2010), http://www.bcmj.org/pulsimeter/gay-men-still-more-likely-contract-hiv.

[14] Dale O'Leary, "The Syndemic of AIDS and STDs among MSM," *Linacre Quarterly* 81, no. 1 (February 2014).

There are no warning labels because they would disturb the rationalization for homosexual behavior by inviting the observation that there is something in Nature itself that rebels against it. Rather than face the clear implication that what they are doing is unnatural to their own bodies, active homosexuals evade or even deny the overwhelming evidence of the health dangers to which they subject themselves. Therefore, focus is transferred from the homosexual behavior that spreads AIDS to the virus itself. And so it is with a host of other sexually transmitted diseases and illnesses spread throughout the homosexual community.

This is like fighting lung cancer while remaining silent about the dangers of smoking. Some homosexuals behave toward AIDS exactly as the tobacco lobby behaved toward lung cancer. Condemn the cancer and justify the smoking. The motivation to cure lung cancer is not so that people can continue smoking. Likewise, would one say to an alcoholic suffering from liver damage that we are going to spend billions of dollars more on research so that his liver can withstand his drinking habits, with which there is nothing wrong?

The purpose of medicine is to restore an organ to health, not to allow its continued abuse. Yet some homosexuals appear to feel that the purpose of a cure for AIDS is to emancipate them from any restraint in the pursuit of their sexual pleasures. Fr. James Schall remarked, "The purpose of government, as a consequence, is to make whatever we want to do possible for us with little or no cost to ourselves. If our activities cause diseases or derangements of human lives, the solution is not, through self-discipline, to stop the activities that cause the damage but to find a 'cure' that will enable us to continue what we want without any consequences to ourselves. We look to technology to substitute for our own lack of self-rule."[15]

This attitude is so manifest that the clearest path to AIDS prevention is ignored or neglected because it does not fit into the liberal sexual ethos. Harvard researcher Edward Green reports that Uganda's ABC program, which focuses on abstinence for the unmarried and "zero grazing" for the rest, is the most effective means of dealing with the AIDS epidemic. In his book, *Broken Promises: How the AIDS Establishment Has Betrayed the Developing World* (2011), he recounts how at an AIDS conference in Washington in

---

[15] Rev. James V. Schall, S.J., "The Goodness and Humanity of God", *Crisis Magazine*, January 3, 2013, http://www.crisismagazine.com/2013/the-goodness-and-humanity-of-god.

2004 his presentation received muted applause. "But, when a female college student came to the microphone and exclaimed, 'I think people should be able to have as much sex as they want, with as many people as they want', she received a thunderous, standing ovation."[16]

Promiscuity and Homosexual "Marriage"

What else is typical of homosexual behavior that might belie its naturalness and suitability for marriage? If the love between homosexuals is *spousal* in nature, as the advocates of homosexual marriage claim, we would then expect it to be as exclusive as it is in heterosexual marriage. In other words, since the loved one is irreplaceable, the characteristic sexual expression of spousal love would be fidelity and monogamy. But if the primary interest is sexual, then the other person is replaceable, in fact, disposable. So, which is it?

Let us compare the two—the spousal and the promiscuous. Dr. Diggs writes that "the most extensive survey of sex in America found that 'a vast majority [of heterosexual married couples] are faithful while the marriage is intact.' The survey further found that 94 percent of married people and 75 percent of cohabiting people had only one partner in the prior year." Overall, the authors of *Sex in America* reported that 90 percent of heterosexual women and more than 75 percent of heterosexual men have *never* engaged in extramarital sex. This comports more or less, given human frailty, with what one would expect from the natural exclusivity of spousal love. In short, heterosexual couples were 41 times more likely to be monogamous than homosexual couples.[17]

As already intimated by the prior quote from Dr. Satinover, fidelity is not typically the case with homosexual couples. He cites *The Male Couple*, researched and written by two homosexual authors, as "one of the most carefully researched studies of the most stable homosexual pairs". He states that "its investigators found that of 156 couples studied, only seven had maintained sexual fidelity; of the hundred couples that had been together for more than five years, none had been able to maintain sexual fidelity. The authors noted that 'the expectation for outside sexual activity was the rule

---

[16] Quoted by Carolyn Moynihan in "Heads in the Sand over AIDS", *MercatorNet*, December 2, 2011, http://www.mercatornet.com/articles/view/heads_in_the_sand_over_aids.

[17] Michael Brown, *A Queer Thing Happened to America* (Concord, NC: EqualTime Books, 2011), 383.

for male couples and the exception for heterosexuals.'" This should hardly be a surprise. Fidelity requires chastity. How could an act (sodomy) that is in its essence—meaning in *every* instance—a violation of chastity serve as a source of fidelity or as the foundation for monogamy? To say that it could leads one perilously close to a violation of the principle of noncontradiction.

How does this infidelity express itself? Dr. Satinover reports that "a 1978 study found that 43 percent of male homosexuals estimated having sex with 500 or more different partners and 28 percent with 1000 or more different partners. Seventy-nine percent said that more than half of these partners were strangers and 70 percent said more than half were men with whom they had sex only once."[18]

A 1997 survey of 2,583 sexually active homosexual men in Australia reported that "only 15 percent of the men reported having fewer than 11 sex partners to date, while on the other end of the spectrum 15 percent had over 1000 sex partners. A whopping 82 percent had over 50 partners and nearly 50 percent had over 100."[19] Another Australian survey, this one in 2000, according to Dr. Diggs, "tracked whether men who had sex with men were associated with the gay community. Men who were associated with the gay community [though not necessarily in couples] were nearly four times as likely to have had more than 50 sex partners in the six months preceding the survey as men who were not associated with the gay community." It appears the more "gay" a person is, the more promiscuous he is.

A 2004 article reporting on a study by Professor Edward O. Laumann and his colleagues regarding homosexuality and promiscuity states the following:

> A new study by a group of University of Chicago researchers reveals a high level of promiscuity and unhealthy behavior among that city's homosexual male population. According to the researchers, 42.9 percent of homosexual men in Chicago's Shoreland area have had more than 60 sexual partners, while an additional 18.4 percent have had between 31 and 60 partners. All total, 61.3 percent of the area's homosexual men have had more than 30 partners, and 87.8 percent have had more than 15, the research found. As a result, 55.1 percent of homosexual males in Shoreland—known as Chicago's "gay center"—have at least one sexually transmitted disease, researchers said.

[18] Satinover, *Homosexuality and the Politics of Truth*, 55.
[19] Brown, *A Queer Thing Happened to America*, 382.

The three-year study on the sexual habits of Chicago's citizens was done for the book *The Sexual Organization of the City* (University of Chicago Press).[20] The *Journal of Human Sexuality* (volume 1, 2009) related that

> John Rechy, a well-known homosexual author, reports that he has had sex with more than 7,000 men and that "thousands of sex encounters [with as many different male partners] are not rare in the gay world" (Goode & Troiden, 1980, p. 58). The results from Goode and Troiden's study reveal that "the number of partners with whom our respondents admitted having engaged in sex was, by heterosexual standards, prodigious" (p. 52). One respondent reported that he had engaged in sex with more than 10,000 men. Only 35 percent reported that they had engaged in sexual intercourse with fewer than 100 men; 42 percent reported that they had engaged in sexual intercourse with between 100 and 499 men; and 23 percent admitted to having had 500 or more partners.

Homosexual activist Michelangelo Signorile, author of *Queer in America*, stresses that for "'gay' men the term 'monogamy' simply doesn't necessarily mean sexual exclusivity.... The term 'open relationship' has for a great many gay men come to have one specific definition: a relationship in which the partners have sex on the outside often, put away their resentment and jealousy, and discuss their outside sex with each other, or share sex partners."[21] Therefore, Signorile suggests that "rather than being transformed by the institution of marriage, gay men—some of whom have raised the concept of the 'open relationship' to an art form—could simply transform the institution itself, making it more sexually open, even influencing their heterosexual counterparts."[22]

In 1995 Thomas Schmidt, PhD, wrote in *Straight and Narrow?* that "promiscuity among homosexual men is not a mere stereotype, and it is not merely the majority experience—it is virtually the only experience. And even if we set aside infidelity and allow a generous definition of 'long-term relationships' as those that last at least four years, under 8 percent of either male or female homosexual relationships fit the definition. In short, there is practically no comparison possible to heterosexual marriage in terms of either fidelity or longevity. Tragically, lifelong faithfulness is almost

[20] Michael Foust, "Marriage Digest: New Study: Homosexual Men Prone to Promiscuity", Baptist Press News, January 16, 2004, http://www.bpnews.net/bpnews.asp?ID=17458.

[21] Michelangelo Signorile, *Life Outside* (New York: Harper Collins, 1997), 213.

[22] Michelangelo Signorile, "I Do, I Do, I Do, I Do, I Do", *OUT* (May 1996): 30.

nonexistent in the homosexual experience."[23] In other words, the popular depiction in the media of the faithful homosexual couple of decades' duration is largely a fiction.

If the nature of the love between homosexuals were *spousal*, what could account for such behavior? In a spousal relationship, the spouse is not replaceable because it is the *person* who is loved. Another person simply will not do. According to Dr. Anne-Marie Ambert of York University, in *Same Sex Couples and Same-Sex-Parent Families* (2003), "There is general agreement across the various sources of statistics on this topic. First, within homosexual unions, men are overwhelmingly non-monogamous."

What then does the near-universal level of promiscuity mean? Former homosexual William Aaron answered that question: "In the gay life, fidelity is almost impossible. Since part of the compulsion of homosexuality seems to be a need on the part of the homophile to 'absorb' masculinity from his sexual partners, he must be constantly on the lookout for [new partners]. Consequently the most successful homophile 'marriages' are those where there is an arrangement between the two to have affairs on the side while maintaining the semblance of permanence in their living arrangement."[24] *The Male Couple* study reports that "the single most important factor that keeps couples together past the 10-year mark is the lack of possessiveness.... Many couples learn very early in their relationship that ownership of each other sexually can be the greatest internal threat to their staying together."[25]

What all this means precisely is that the nature of the love between homosexuals is *not* spousal, as sexual substitutes seem to be the norm. Where is the commitment to fidelity on which marriage is based? Without such commitment, a marriage cannot be said to exist. Some homosexuals are startling frank about his. Gareth Kirby, editor of the homosexual newspaper *Xtra West*, on September 6, 2001, stated that "legal marriages" are contrary to homosexual culture:

> In our [gay] culture, we haven't created the same hierarchy as has heterosexual culture. We know that love has many faces, and names,

---

[23] Thomas E. Schmidt, *Straight and Narrow?* (Downers Grove, IL: InterVarsity Press, 1995), 108.

[24] William Aaron, *Straight* (New York: Bantam Books, 1972), 208, cited by Joseph Nicolosi in *Reparative Therapy of Male Homosexuality* (Lanham, MD: Rowman and Littlefield Publishers, 1997), 125; quoted by Robert H. Knight in "How Domestic Partnerships and 'Gay Marriage' Threaten the Family", *Insight*, (June 1994): 9.

[25] David P. McWhirter and Andrew Mattison, *The Male Couple: How Relationships Develop* (Englewood Cliffs, NJ: Prentice Hall, 1984), 256.

ages, places.... We know that a 30-year relationship is no better than a nine-week, or nine-minute, fling—it's different, but not better. Both have value. We know that the instant intimacy involved in that perfect 20-minute ... in Stanley Park can be a profoundly beautiful thing. We know a two-year relationship where people live apart is as beautiful, absolutely as beautiful, as a 30-year relationship where people live together. We know that the people involved in an open relationship can love each other as deeply as the people in a closed relationship.[26]

Also, the anonymity of much of the substitute sex indicates exactly the absence of love altogether, as one does not relate to the other as a person, but as an object. Anonymous sex is dehumanized and dehumanizing. It treats another human being as a mere appurtenance to one's desires. American composer Ned Rorem remarked that "anonymity can be so uninhibited, the sex so incredibly fulfilling, that it could never be repeated with the same person, precisely because the next time he would *be* a person."[27] What German theologian Josef Pieper said about pornography is equally applicable to this compulsive behavior: it removes the fig leaf from the genitals and places it over the human face.

Though not specifically speaking of anonymous promiscuity, former lesbian Melinda Selmys provides acute insight into the psychology of same-sex encounters: "We did not make love to one another, but each consented to serve as a cipher for the other's archetypal ideals. Through sex, I was able to become a different, stylized, idealized self and to become one, as it were, with a certain projection of my own psyche, a perfected 'other' who had the capacity to fulfill my deepest longings."[28] Of course, this insight applies to any sex in which the other person becomes an object. In his *Ethics,* Aristotle wrote: "Those who love for the sake of pleasure do so for the sake of what is pleasant to *themselves,* and not in so far as the other is the person loved" (emphasis in original).

This level of promiscuity is pornography in action. It has all the symptoms; it is not directed toward any end that can satisfy it. It is insatiable. The sheer number of partners easily illustrates this point. Why so many? Yet, no matter how many, it never seems to be enough. "Never enough"

[26] Cited in C. Gwendolyn Landolt, "Same-Sex Unions Are Not Marriages", REAL Women of Canada, May 18, 2004, http://www.realwomenofcanada.ca/publications/analysis-reports/same-sex-unions-are-not-marriages/.

[27] Cited in Melinda Selmys, *Sexual Authenticity* (Huntington, IN: Our Sunday Visitor, 2009), 108.

[28] Melinda Selmys, *Sexual Authenticity,* 187.

is an appetitive disorder and a recipe for social and political disaster. Because it promises something it cannot deliver, promiscuous behavior eventually produces a sense of betrayal. The futility inherent in it generates fury that often leads to violence and despair that often leads to self-destruction.

If the love between homosexuals is *not* spousal in its character, why should it be blessed in a supposed marriage? What is the point of insisting on homosexual marriage when promiscuity prevails? Why should some homosexuals push for and insist upon it? The answer, as indicated previously, is simple: to complete the rationalization of their misbehavior, they must sacramentalize it. Anything short of this would not be acceptable. The purpose is to reach the ultimate rationalization—the sanctification of sodomy.

Ronald G. Lee, who describes himself as "a refugee from the homosexual insane asylum", wrote that homosexual journalist

> Andrew Sullivan wants us to believe that legalizing same-sex "marriage" will domesticate gay men, that all that energy now devoted to building bars and bathhouses will be dedicated to erecting picket fences and two-car garages. What Sullivan refuses to face is that male homosexuals are not promiscuous because of "internalized homophobia", or laws banning same-sex "marriage". Homosexuals are promiscuous because when given the choice, homosexuals overwhelmingly choose to be promiscuous. And wrecking the fundamental social building block of our civilization, the family, is not going to change that.[29]

Legalizing homosexual marriage is not, then, as some have suggested, being "inclusive" or making room for another kind of marriage. It requires the denial of the true nature of marriage. Some homosexual activists will admit this. Journalist and activist Masha Gessen stated on a public panel in Sydney, Australia, "It's a no-brainer that the institution of marriage should not exist.... Fighting for gay marriage generally involves lying about what we are going to do with marriage when we get there—because we lie that the institution of marriage is not going to change, and that is a lie."[30]

What can one conclude from all this evidence? One might say with Professor Harry Jaffa that "nature itself seems to reward chastity with health,

---

[29] Ronald G. Lee, "The Truth about the Homosexual Rights Movement", *New Oxford Review* (February 2006), http://www.newoxfordreview.org/article.jsp?did=0206-lee.

[30] Robert P. George, "What Few Deny Gay Marriage Will Do", *First Things*, April 16, 2013, http://www.firstthings.com/blogs/firstthoughts/2013/04/16/what-few-deny-gay-marriage-will-do/.

and punish promiscuity with disease.... It would certainly seem that nature has an interest in the morality that is conducive to the family, and punishes behavior inimical to it."[31] As we have seen, this is especially true of homosexual behavior. Substituting it for marital relations as a foundation for marriage would be, in moral terms, analogous to substituting a cancerous lung for a healthy one on the basis that we cannot tell the difference between them. Such a claim would obviously subvert medical care and would represent a huge injustice to cancer patients. Sodomy is the cancer version of coition. Exchanging it for spousal intercourse on the basis that there is no difference between them is an act of injustice that will subvert marriage and the body and soul of the society that accepts it.

[31] "Clarifying Homosexuality and Natural Law: A Review of *Gays / Justice: A Study of Ethics, Society, and Law* by Richard D. Mohr", Claremont Institute, February 1, 1991, http://www.claremont.org/publications/pubid.694/pub_detail.asp.

6

Inventing Morality

The wider social and political implications of this moral egalitarianism are not hard to deduce. If there are not preexisting, intelligible ends toward which man is ordered by Nature, every individual must invent, in an arbitrary and subjective manner, some ends by which to guide his actions and order his life. The way one lives then becomes a matter of lifestyle. The elevation of the word *lifestyle* to its present prominence is an indication of the total loss of any serious meaning in one's choice of how to live. What used to be man's most profound ethical concern has been reduced to an element of fashion. The choice of homosexuality or family life becomes equally valid in this denatured context. If the concept of an intelligible common good is denied, so are the moral grounds for social approval or disapproval of personal behavior. With each person a law unto himself, political community becomes impossible.

And here we finally arrive upon the supreme irony that makes the homosexual's appeal to "gay rights" so grotesque. Our rights reside in and derive from the "Laws of Nature and of Nature's God" to which the Declaration of Independence refers for our justification as a nation. Yet the proponents of homosexuality are supporting a cause that can succeed only by obliterating that very understanding of Nature upon which our existence as a free people depends. The moral view from which their vindication of homosexuality emanates is one that ultimately makes impossible the very conception of rights. Their appeal to rights subverts the rights to which they appeal.

Yet it would be wrong to assign the major share of blame for this to the homosexual apologists. Homosexuality is simply the latest in a series of *causes célèbres* that are the logical consequences of the loss of objective reality—a loss that is transforming the right to life into death (abortion), liberty into license, and the pursuit of happiness into hedonism.

Nor is this argument against the promotion of homosexual behavior meant to suggest that homosexuals should have anything but the full exercise of their civil rights, as should any other citizen. Rights, since their source is Nature, are, after all, universal by definition. It is the espousal of fictitious and self-contradictory gay rights that must be opposed because it elevates homosexual behavior to, and advances it on, the level of moral principle. This claim threatens the health of the whole community, not because it would mean a wholesale defection to the ranks of the homosexuals, but because the teaching itself is pernicious and will affect and form the attitudes of the body politic in other matters as well.

Legislating Immorality from the Bench of the Supreme Court

It has certainly affected the attitudes of the judiciary, which has done so much to prepare the groundwork for the legalization of homosexual marriage through a series of extraordinarily misconceived rulings that have legitimized the separation of sex from procreation. As George Will said, "The Supreme Court is where America does much of its political philosophy."[1] Seldom, however, are the justices themselves political philosophers. Rather, they are under the influence of political philosophers. To borrow generously from John Maynard Keynes' famous lines, with alterations, one might say that "the ideas of political philosophers, both when they are right and when they are wrong, are more powerful than is commonly understood. Indeed the world is ruled by little else. Justices, who believe themselves to be quite exempt from any intellectual influence, are usually the slaves of some defunct political philosopher. Madmen in authority, who hear voices in the air, are distilling their frenzy from some academic scribbler of a few years back."

Therefore, we will examine from the perspective of political philosophy what the high court has been saying about the issues of family and the fundamental character of sexual relations. Unfortunately, it is not Aristotle they have been channeling, but someone closer to Rousseau. We will find that they have fallen victim to a profoundly antiteleological view of reality that would be unfamiliar to the profoundly teleological views held by America's Founders, who believed deeply in the "Laws of Nature"—not the slightest

[1] Said in the author's presence at the Bradley Prize Awards, Terrace Theater, Kennedy Center, June 13, 2013.

echo of which can be detected in these decisions. As such, they have been—almost unawares, it seems, perhaps from hearing voices in the air—undermining the primacy of reason upon which the existence of the United States (and their own authority as judges) is premised and nourishing the notion of the primacy of will, which is antithetical to it.

We shall see this strange notion work its way through the following cases: *Griswold v. Connecticut, Eisenstadt v. Baird, Carey v. Population Services International, Roe v. Wade, Lawrence v. Texas, Stenberg v. Carhart, Planned Parenthood of Southeastern Pennsylvania. v. Casey*, with special emphasis on the *Lawrence* decision for reasons that will become apparent. We will then see the repercussions in several state and federal district court cases, most especially *Perry v. Schwarzenegger*, until they boomerang back in the *Hollingsworth v. Perry* and *United States v. Windsor* cases, which the Supreme Court decided in June 2013.

Blackstone on Sodomy

To see the court's rulings in their proper light, a little history regarding the moral and legal status of sodomy in America is in order. First of all, the word *homosexuality* is of rather recent coinage, originating in the late nineteenth century. German-Hungarian writer Károly Mária Kertbeny (1824–1882) created the word *Homosexualität* in order to promote the notion that homosexuality is normal. In English the word *homosexual* appeared around 1891 and was used in 1892 in the English translation of Richard von Krafft-Ebing's 1886 German reference work on sexual perversions, *Psychopathia Sexualis*.

Long before the invention of the word *homosexual*, however, sodomy was morally regarded as a gravely disordered act, no matter who performed it. It was a crime in common law. William Blackstone's *Commentaries on the Laws of England* had a great influence in the American colonies and on the formation of the American legal system. Blackstone wrote that sodomy is "an offense of so dark a nature, the very mention of which is a disgrace to human nature, a crime not fit to be named" (vol. 4, 1769). United States Supreme Court Justice John Marshall cited Blackstone several times and, according to the Blackstone Institute, "the *Commentaries*, in fact, were cited nearly 10,000 times in the reports of American courts between 1789 and 1915."[2]

[2] Blackstone Institute, "Bashing Blackstone: The Reconstructionists' Attack in America's Culture War", Blackstone Institute website, accessed July 31, 2013, http://www.blackstoneinstitute.org/sirwilliamblackstone.html.

Blackstone's detestation of sodomy must be seen against his understanding of marriage, which he defined as a relationship "of husband and wife ... founded in nature, but modified by civil society: the one directing man to continue and multiply his species, the other prescribing the manner in which that natural impulse must be confined and regulated". Sodomy was obviously an unconfined and unregulated use of "that natural impulse".[3] Marriage was also a step to the next great relationship, "that of parent and child, which is consequential to that of marriage, being its principal end and design: and it is by virtue of this relation that infants are protected, maintained, and educated".[4] Justice Joseph Story, whose *Commentaries on the Constitution of the United States* was a cornerstone of nineteenth-century American jurisprudence, agreed with Blackstone on the natural law foundation of marriage. He wrote, "Marriage is treated by all civilized societies as a peculiar and favored contract. It is in its origin a contract of natural law."[5]

In complete agreement with Aristotle's understanding of marriage as *the* prepolitical institution, James Wilson, signer of both the Declaration of Independence and the Constitution, said of the family: "It is the principle of the community; it is that seminary, on which the commonwealth, for its manners as well as for its numbers, must ultimately depend. As its establishment is the source, so its happiness is the end, of every institution of government, which is wise and good."[6] In order to be the *source* of every institution of government, the family must *precede* every institution of government. In short, marriage does not need the government in order to exist. Rather, the government needs marriage in order to exist. (The obverse is true for same-sex marriage.) That is why attacks against the family endanger the very principle of government—most especially of those forms of government that rely on the virtue of their citizenry for their very existence. If the happiness of the family is the end or goal of every institution of government, as Wilson proclaimed, then the government would naturally promote chastity and discourage violations of it, including sodomy.

---

[3] William Blackstone, *Commentaries on the Laws of England* (Oxford: Clarendon Press, 1765), bk. 1, ch. 15.

[4] Ibid.

[5] Joseph Story, *Commentaries on the Conflict of Laws*, cited in Matthew Spalding, *We Still Hold These Truths: Rediscovering Our Principles, Reclaiming Our Future* (Wilmington, DE: ISI Books, 2009), 157.

[6] James Wilson, "Of the Natural Rights of Individuals", in *Collected Works of James Wilson*, ed. Kermit L. Hall and Mark David Hall (Indianapolis: Liberty Fund, 2007), 1081.

These views on marriage were echoed in later Supreme Court decisions, such as *Murphy v. Ramsey* (1885) and *Maynard v. Hill* (1888). *Murphy* stated that "no legislation can be supposed more wholesome and necessary ... than that which seeks to establish it on the basis of the idea of the family, as consisting in and springing from the union for life of one man and one woman in the holy estate of matrimony."[7] And *Maynard* declared that marriage "is an institution, in the maintenance of which in its purity the public is deeply interested, for it is the foundation of the family and of society, without which there would be neither civilization nor progress".[8]

One of the more recent Blackstone citations came in Supreme Court Justice Warren Burger's concurring opinion in *Bowers v. Hardwick* (1986), which upheld the constitutionality of an Alabama law against sodomy. Justice Byron White, delivering the court's decision, said the Constitution does not confer "a fundamental right to engage in homosexual sodomy".[9] Agreeing, Burger wrote:

> The proscriptions against sodomy have very "ancient roots". Decisions of individuals relating to homosexual conduct have been subject to state intervention throughout the history of Western civilization. Condemnation of those practices is firmly rooted in Judeo-Christian moral and ethical standards. Homosexual sodomy was a capital crime under Roman law.... During the English Reformation when powers of the ecclesiastical courts were transferred to the King's Courts, the first English statute criminalizing sodomy was passed. Blackstone described "the infamous *crime against nature*" as an offense of "deeper malignity" than rape, a heinous act.... To hold that the act of homosexual sodomy is somehow protected as a fundamental right would be to cast aside millennia of moral teaching.[10]

It would be, precisely, to cast aside Socrates, Plato, Aristotle, the Old Testament and the New, Augustine, and Aquinas, to say nothing of the teachings of other civilizations. It would be to ignore not only the moral teachings regarding sodomy, but the vision of a virtuous citizenry that the

---

[7] Murphy v. Ramsey, 114 U.S. 15, 45 (1885), http://supreme.justia.com/cases/federal/us/114/15/.

[8] Maynard v. Hill, 125 U.S. 190, 211 (1888), http://supreme.justia.com/cases/federal/us/125/190/case.html.

[9] Bowers v. Hardwick, 478 U.S. 186 (1986), http://supreme.justia.com/cases/federal/us/478/186/case.html.

[10] Ibid.

laws aimed at helping to form. Sodomitical man is different from a man living chastely—different enough to require a different sort of rule, as we shall see. Sodomy reflects a disorder in the soul that can strike at the public order for the reasons that Plato and Aristotle gave.

Blackstone said that rape is a "heinous act" because it is coerced intercourse. But there is nothing wrong with intercourse itself in the right circumstances. This cannot be said of sodomy, which is at all times and in every circumstance wrong. This is why Blackstone found in it a "deeper malignity". This is no doubt why, as the *Bowers* ruling pointed out, "*Sodomy* was a criminal offense at common law and was forbidden by the laws of the original 13 States when they ratified the Bill of Rights. In 1868, when the Fourteenth Amendment was ratified, all but 5 of the 37 States in the Union had *criminal sodomy laws*. In fact, until 1961, all 50 states outlawed sodomy, and today, 24 states and the District of Columbia continue to provide criminal penalties for sodomy performed in private and between consenting adults."[11] During the colonial period, there were some twenty sodomy prosecutions and four executions. In 1778 Thomas Jefferson's Bill for Proportioning Crimes and Punishment proposed: "Whosoever shall be guilty of Rape, Polygamy, or Sodomy with man or woman shall be punished, if a man, by castration, if a woman, by cutting thro' the cartilage of her nose a hole of one half inch diameter at the least."[12] The Virginia legislature rejected the proposed legislation, preferring to maintain the death penalty as the maximum punishment. From 1880 to 1995, there were 203 prosecutions "for consensual, adult homosexual sodomy reported in the West reporting system", according to Justice Antonin Scalia's dissenting opinion in *Lawrence*.[13]

Lawrence v. Texas

"Cast aside millennia of moral teaching" is exactly what the *Lawrence v. Texas* ruling did in 2003, seventeen years after *Bowers*. This decision declared a Texas statute "forbidding two persons of the same sex to engage

[11] Bowers, 478 U.S. 186.

[12] Gaye Wilson, "Bill 64", *Thomas Jefferson Encyclopedia*, Monticello.org, accessed July 31, 2013, http://www.monticello.org/site/research-and-collections/bill-64.

[13] Lawrence v. Texas, 539 U.S. 558 (2003), http://supreme.justia.com/cases/federal/us/539/558/case.html.

in certain intimate sexual conduct" unconstitutional and, in order to do so, overturned the *Bowers* ruling. The reasoning in *Lawrence v. Texas* needs to be examined closely because it clearly followed the logic and pattern of preceding decisions, except for *Bowers*, regarding reproductive and sexual matters and provided the basis for the challenge against the legal definition of marriage as being between a man and a woman. It also revealed the distressing level of intellectual poverty that has infected the legal profession at its highest level, as few of its members seem capable of grasping the relationship between morality and law.

The critiques of court cases that follow are given not to address the constitutional legal issues of whether "due process" or "equal protection" was jeopardized in some way, but to expose the underlying philosophical assumptions in the justices' reasoning. In their thinking we shall see reflected the progressive abandonment of the idea of virtue traditionally held to be necessary to a free people and the substitution of a specious form of liberty based upon a manufactured "right to privacy" that is untethered from any notion of morality. While the court may at first seem indifferent to the question of virtue, it gradually becomes overtly hostile to it and to the concomitant notion of morality as the basis of law.

In delivering the *Lawrence* opinion, Justice Anthony Kennedy claimed that "liberty presumes an autonomy of self that includes freedom of thought, belief, expression, and certain intimate conduct" upon which the state should not intrude.[14] The list of freedoms is very familiar and the statement seems unexceptionable, but the formulation is unusual. Why did Justice Kennedy not simply say that liberty includes these freedoms, or, if it was necessary for him to give an account of liberty, that liberty itself is rooted in unalienable God-given rights? Why the presumption of "an autonomy of self" as the supposed foundation for it? What does this mean?

Autonomy, of course, means self-rule and is usually applied to states or institutions in the sense of giving themselves their own laws. One assumes, then, that Justice Kennedy's "autonomy of self" means giving oneself one's own laws. But upon what are these laws of self based? Does he mean self-rule in the classical sense of a person's mastering his passions through a life of virtue? Such a person lives by moral laws that he does not get to make up. They preexist him. His freedom does not consist in creating his *own* moral order, but in constraining his passions so that he is not enslaved by them.

---

[14] Ibid.

That, as Aristotle said, is what self-rule means. He is then free to choose the good and, by habitually doing so, becomes a virtuous man. That is what true freedom means and, in this sense, only the good man is free.

As we shall see, this is not what Justice Kennedy had in mind. He meant a more modern, existential, profoundly anti-Aristotelian notion of freedom, more in line with Rousseau's, in which one gets to make up one's *own* moral universe. It has nothing to do with virtue or, really, with the US Constitution.

A careful examination of *Lawrence* will demonstrate these points. The case involved two men who were prosecuted by the state of Texas for engaging in anal intercourse. They pled no contest and were fined $125. They appealed their convictions on Fourteenth Amendment equal protection grounds, claiming the Texas statute was unconstitutional. The law's constitutionality was upheld in Texas; so they appealed to the Supreme Court, which overthrew it. Justice Kennedy said the case "involves liberty of the person both in its spatial and in its more transcendent dimensions".[15] Therefore, the Court asked: Is it constitutional for a state to make "it a crime for two persons of the same sex to engage in certain intimate sexual conduct"? One would think that the answer would in large part depend on the moral character of the act in question, in this case, anal intercourse; but the court stated, "The fact that the governing majority in a state has traditionally viewed a particular practice as immoral is not a sufficient reason for upholding a law prohibiting the practice."[16]

That may be well and good, but at least such a tradition should invite, one would think, an examination of whether the "practice" in question *is*, in fact, immoral, and whether the governing majority in Texas was correct in its assessment of it. And if not, why not? What else could provide a sufficient reason for upholding the law against sodomy other than the immorality of the act? Remarkably, the court *never* addressed this issue except tangentially. In invalidating the law, however, the court implicitly overturned the moral judgment on which it was based. Sodomy, in other words, must not be so bad, after all.

At least the court showed some awareness that American sodomy laws historically had "sought to prohibit noncreative sexual activity more generally", but seemed clueless as to why anyone should wish to have done so or

[15] Ibid.
[16] Ibid.

whether they should have. Rather, the court put on display the inexorable logic behind a succession of cases that it cited which, step-by-step, went about separating sex from procreation or, more accurately, showing what the separation of sex from procreation means. We will now review these cases and follow their logic as it leads to the altar of same-sex marriage.

First came *Griswold v. Connecticut* (1965), in which the court invalidated an 1879 state law that prohibited the sale of any "drug, medicinal article, or instrument for the purpose of preventing conception" to anyone. Why was there such a law in the first place? Professor Robert George stated that "Connecticut sought to promote marital fidelity and stable families by discouraging attempts to avoid the possible consequences of nonmarital sexual relations through the use of contraceptives. Prominent judges in Connecticut recognized the legitimacy of these purposes, and the state's supreme court upheld the laws against several constitutional challenges from 1940 to 1964."[17]

In 1961, Estelle Griswold, executive director of Planned Parenthood League of Connecticut, opened a birth control clinic deliberately to challenge the law. She was arrested for providing contraceptive information, instruction, and medical advice to a married couple and fined $100. She appealed. The Supreme Court of Connecticut upheld her conviction. It was then appealed to the US Supreme Court. In the *Griswold* ruling, Justice William Douglas, writing for the majority, famously found an "implied constitutional right of privacy" in the "penumbras formed by emanations from those guarantees" found in the Bill of Rights.[18] Therefore, according to the court's reading, married couples could legally obtain contraceptives. The significance of this decision can be seen in hindsight from the more recent advocacy for same-sex marriage expressed by E. J. Graff, who avowed that redefining marriage would change the "institution's message" so that it would "ever after stand for sexual choice, for cutting the link between sex and diapers".[19] *Griswold* broke the first link in the chain connecting sex and

---

[17] Robert P. George and David T. Tubbs, "The Bad Decision That Started It All", Catholic Education Resource Center, accessed July 31, 2013, http://catholiceducation.org/articles/abortion/ab0099.html.

[18] Griswold v. Connecticut, 381 U.S. 479 (1965), http://supreme.justia.com/cases/federal/us/381/479/case.html.

[19] Cited in Ryan T. Anderson, "Marriage: What It Is, Why It Matters, and the Consequences of Redefining It", Heritage Foundation, Backgrounder no. 2775, March 11, 2013, http://www.insideronline.org/summary.cfm?id=19525.

diapers. Subsequent decisions simply worked out the implications of the break until the link was completely severed.

Step two, after *Griswold*, was *Eisenstadt v. Baird* (1972), in which the court found unconstitutional a law prohibiting the distribution of contraceptives to *unmarried* persons. The court declared that "if the right of privacy means anything, it is the right of the *individual*, married or single, to be free from unwarranted governmental intrusion into matters so fundamentally affecting a person as the decision whether to bear or beget a child."[20] The "right to privacy", therefore, inheres not in the marital bond—as marriage, it turns out, is nothing more than an "association between two individuals"—but in any individual adult. Traditionally, one would have thought that a decision to get married or not would have *preceded* "the decision whether to bear or beget a child", or at least that those who decided to bear or beget a child would have understood that it was necessary to get married first.

But what of those who decide *not* "to bear or beget a child" and *not* to get married? Can the government possibly intrude upon something they decide *not* to do? Well, only if they actually do decide to do something—which is to copulate with the expressed intention of not begetting a child. Do they possess a *right* to do this, along with a concomitant right to obtain the necessary tools to effect this purpose? *Eisenstadt* answered yes. After all, in order to copulate, you need an "association between two individuals", apparently much like that of marriage, even if it lasts only half an hour. While it lasts, each *individual* preserves his "right to privacy". In other words, contracepting an act of fornication is a right under the Constitution, just as marital contraception is.

But if married couples and adult singles who temporarily form a couple have a right to contracept, what about minors under the age of sixteen? What about *their* privacy rights? With impeccable logic, the court took step three in *Carey v. Population Services International* (1977), in which it found it unconstitutional to prohibit the sale of contraceptives to minors because minors are entitled to the same constitutional protections as adults. *Everyone* has the right to contracept. In fact, in April 2013, US District Judge Edward R. Korman ruled that the Food and Drug Administration must make the morning-after pill, Plan B One-Step, heretofore available without a prescription only to those seventeen or older, available over the counter

---

[20] Eisenstadt v. Baird, 405 U.S. 438 (1972), http://supreme.justia.com/cases/federal/us /405/438/case.html.

to females of all ages.[21] The Obama administration appealed to delay the ruling and restrict the pill to those fifteen and older. Nancy Northrup, president of the Center for Reproductive Rights, complained that Obama's "administration has decided once again to deprive women of their right to obtain emergency contraception without unjustified and burdensome restrictions".[22] After all, what's a fourteen-year-old girl to do when she needs this "emergency contraceptive" after having experienced an "association between two individuals"? Without irony, Judge Korman called the age restrictions "politically motivated" and "scientifically unjustified". In June the Obama administration abandoned its position and gave in to the inherent logic of *Griswold* and *Eisenstadt*. On cue, Cecile Richards, president of the Planned Parenthood Federation of America, crowed, "This is a huge breakthrough for access to birth control and a historic moment for women's health and equity."[23] Indeed, now girls will be able to get an abortifacient right next to the bubblegum at their local drugstore.

Step four chronologically preceded step three, but comes last in the inexorable chain of logic. Step four is, of course, *Roe v. Wade* (1973), in which the court found that an unborn child is not a "person" and therefore not sheltered by either due process or equal protection. The court declared that the "right of privacy ... is broad enough to encompass a woman's decision whether or not to terminate her pregnancy". This ruling perfected the fissure created by the preceding separation of sex from procreation, "cutting the link between sex and diapers", by physically eliminating the tiny human beings who would wear those diapers. As the *Lawrence* decision pointed out, "The opinions in *Griswold* and *Eisenstadt* were part of the background for the decision in *Roe v. Wade*."[24] Indeed they were. If couples have a right to contracept a generative sexual act, why should they be held accountable if the contraception fails and a child is generated? Hasn't the child violated

---

[21] Pam Belluck, "Drug Agency Lowers Age for Next-Day Birth Control", *New York Times*, April 30, 2013, http://www.nytimes.com/2013/05/01/health/fda-lowers-age-for-morning -after-pill.html?partner=rss&emc=rss&_r=0.

[22] Terry Baynes, "FDA Appeals Make 'Morning-After' Pill Available to All Ages", *Reuters*, May 1, 2013, http://www.reuters.com/article/2013/05/02/us-usa-planb-appeal-idUSBRE 94100H20130502?feedType=RSS&feedName=domesticNews&rpc=76.

[23] Brady Dennis and Sarah Kliff, "Obama Administration Drops Fight to Keep Age Restrictions on Plan B Sales", *Washington Post*, June 10, 2013, http://www.washingtonpost .com/national/health-science/obama-administration-drops-fight-to-keep-age-restrictions -on-plan-b-sales/2013/06/10/a296406e-d22a-11e2-a73e-826d299ff459_story.html.

[24] Lawrence, 539 U.S. 558.

their right to privacy? What right had the child to intrude? Recall that the *Eisenstadt* case had said that there should be no "unwarranted governmental intrusion into matters so fundamentally affecting a person as the decision whether to *bear* or *beget* a child" (emphasis added). Obviously, in a contracepted act of intercourse, a decision has been made *not* to *beget* a child. In apparent disregard for this decision, however, a child arrives anyway. What is one to do? If the child has already been begotten, can one's "right to privacy" still cover the *bearing* of the child? Yes, said *Roe v. Wade*. One can decide *not* to *bear* a begotten child. One can kill him, with state approbation.

The legalization of abortion through this decision was an act of barbarity, as barbarism is defined as the inability or unwillingness to recognize another person as a human being. Abortion brings to completion the denial of procreative sex by nullifying its effects, which are seen as accidental. If you have an accident and conceive a baby, you can just clean up the mess by aborting him. The disavowal of the relationship between sex and procreation eliminates the child. The child is, or rather should have been, the incarnation of the love between the man and the woman. The denial of the child is the denial of this love. It also raises a troubling question: If the fruit of the tree must be destroyed, what of the tree itself?[25]

The ancients understood that sex outside the moral order leads to death. In abortion, this result could not be more explicit. This can be stated another way, as it has been by Fr. James Schall, though not directly in relation to abortion: "The state can take, and the democratic state seems more and more inclined to take, the direction of ... killing anything that stands in the way of its imposing its order on the souls of men, men too often willing to let it happen."[26] This sounds like a Rousseauian dream come true. The child stands in the way of this imposition, as his presence is a refutation of the manufactured "right to privacy", and he suffers death as a result.

Planned Parenthood of Southeastern Pennsylvania v. Casey

The next few cases simply amplified the magnitude of the great divide between sex and procreation, and its consequences. *Planned Parenthood of*

---

[25] See Jean Vanier, *Man and Woman He Made Them* (Mahwah, NJ: Paulist Press, 1989).

[26] In interview by Kathryn Jean Lopez, "Helping Us 'Turn Around'", *National Review Online*, March 2, 2013, http://www.nationalreview.com/articles/342029/helping-us-turn-around-interview/page/0/4.

Southeastern Pennsylvania v. Casey (1992) reiterated *Eisenstadt's* understanding of the "right to privacy" and reaffirmed abortion rights, which "could not be repudiated without serious inequity to people who, for two decades of economic and social developments, have organized intimate relationships and made choices that define their views of themselves and their places in society, in reliance on the availability of abortion in the event that contraception should fail".[27] This is a marvelously candid admission that abortion has been *shaping* the lives and character of a substantial number of the American people in a fundamental way. Because of contraception and abortion, these people have changed into something other than they would have been without them. If your actions are contingent on your ability to abort an unborn child, what kind of person have you become? What does it mean to engage in sexual relations only on the condition that you are able to eliminate any results from them?

To what kind of "intimate relationships" might the *Casey* court have been referring? In an imaginary conversation, Professor Anthony Esolen gave this characterization: "You and I will now engage in the act that brings new human life into being, a human life that extends far beyond the present moment, in memory and in hope; but we will treat what we are doing as the act of a moment, and no more, and that will be all right."[28] This sounds exactly like what a man would have said to a woman before one of the random couplings described in Rousseau's state of nature. The court concurs that it "will be all right". So, go ahead.

In other words, the "right to privacy" means that you do not have to accept responsibility for your sexual behavior or suffer any consequences from it. The available statistics easily demonstrate that those who "have organized intimate relationships" with the highest number of sexual partners have the greatest number of abortions. The psychology works something like this: if the intimacy was a lie, the product of it must be destroyed. There should be no evidence left of this false "intimacy".

What kind of view of oneself must one have to behave in this way? And how might one's "place in society" be defined by this behavior? Abortion makes available a process of dehumanization—one in which abortion

---

[27] Planned Parenthood of Southeastern Pa. v. Casey, 505 U.S. 833 (1992), http://supreme .justia.com/cases/federal/us/505/833/case.html.

[28] Anthony Esolen, "Felix and Oscar: A Post-Modern Marriage", *Crisis Magazine*, April 2, 2013, http://www.crisismagazine.com/2013/felix-and-oscar-a-post-modern-marriage.

becomes all the more important, the more dehumanized one becomes. What is lost here is any notion that man ought to have moral control over himself and his life—certainly over his procreative powers. As usual, the court does not address this subject, as apparently it believes it is not a subject it *should* address, leaving the impression of indifference as to whether citizens serve their passions or control them.

Instead, it found that the part of the Pennsylvania law that required a woman to notify—not obtain consent from, but notify—her husband that she was having an abortion created an "undue burden", was an infringement on her liberty, and was therefore unconstitutional. The court said that, if required to notify their spouses, "a significant number of women will likely be prevented from obtaining an abortion just as surely as if Pennsylvania had outlawed the procedure entirely.... Furthermore, it cannot be claimed that the father's interest in the fetus' welfare is equal to the mother's protected liberty."[29]

In other words, a father might act to save the life of his child, which would be an infringement on the mother's right to kill the child. This decision represents a reversal of the wisdom of Solomon's famous judgment in the Old Testament, in which he discovered that the real parent was the one who was willing to forsake her child in order to save his life. For the Supreme Court, the real parent is no longer the one who wishes to preserve the life of the child, but the one who is willing to take it. On the south wall of the Supreme Court chamber, Solomon is depicted in a frieze of eighteen famous lawgivers. Might any of the justices have noted the irony?

This bizarre judgment also relied upon the dissolution of the common law understanding of marriage as the basic unit of society that was already undermined by *Eisenstadt*. The court proclaimed that its conclusion rests upon the nature of marriage and the nature of the Constitution as found in *Eisenstadt*. Quoting that decision the court said the marital couple is "not an independent entity with a mind and heart of its own, but an association of two individuals each with a separate intellectual and emotional makeup. If the right of privacy means anything, it is the right of the *individual*, married or single, to be free from unwarranted governmental intrusion into matters so fundamentally affecting a person as the decision whether to bear or beget a child" (emphasis in original).[30]

---

[29] Casey, 505 U.S. 833.
[30] Ibid.

What this really means is that there is no "one flesh" union in marriage that constitutes it as an independent entity, but simply "an association of two individuals". The family is *not*, as Aristotle and Founder James Wilson taught, the prepolitical, irreducible institution upon which the state relies for its existence. Rather, it is the individual, as Rousseau asserted, isolated in the state of nature, upon whom things devolve. Even marriage does not penetrate the Rousseauian isolation of the individual, who is unaltered by the "association of two individuals" into which he enters. This is because, like all associations for Rousseau, there is nothing *natural* about marriage. As it did not exist in the state of nature, it is completely artificial. Nothing obtains to the married couple, only to the *individual*, as the state directs. As constitutional scholar John S. Baker Jr. remarked, "*Casey*, it appears, relied on a Rousseauian general will in striking down Pennsylvania's requirement that a woman notify her husband of a planned abortion on the basis that the statute 'embodies a view of marriage concurrent with the common law status of married women but repugnant to our present understanding of marriage'."[31] Of course, the court found the common law understanding of marriage repugnant because it was based in natural law, which the Court had long ago abandoned. This ruling is an interpretation of a Constitution that the *Casey* court members may recognize, but that the Founders, who would no doubt have found it repugnant, would not.

How could something this unjust be justified? How could the notion of citizenry become so degraded that it is completely divorced from virtue? It requires a thorough misconstruing of the nature of liberty. Here is how it was done in *Casey* in a statement from the decision (quoted in part earlier) that will be given at greater length now because it will be discussed several times later: "These matters, involving the most intimate and personal choices a person may make in a lifetime, choices central to personal dignity and autonomy, are central to the liberty protected by the Fourteenth Amendment. At the heart of liberty is the right to define one's own concept of existence, of meaning, of the universe, and of the mystery of human life. Beliefs about these matters could not define the attributes of personhood were they formed under compulsion of the State."[32]

---

[31] "The Natural and the Positive in Law", in *Saints, Sovereigns, and Scholars: Studies in Honor of Frederick D. Wilhelmsen*, ed. John S. Baker Jr.; R. A. Herrera; James Lehrberger, O.Cist.; and M. E. Bradford (New York: Peter Lang Publishing, Inc., 1993), 157.

[32] Casey, 505 U.S. 833.

Now we see more fully the import of the "autonomy of self". Liberty does not mean freedom to choose what is right; it means becoming the *source* of what is right. It means not conforming oneself to what is good, but making up one's own good. As we shall see later, there is little that could not be justified by this process of moral privatization.

Demonstrating a grim consistency, the court, in *Stenberg v. Carhart* (2000), invalidated a Nebraska statute that prohibited partial-birth abortion, which the Nebraska law defined as a procedure which "partially delivers vaginally a living unborn child before killing the unborn child and completing the delivery".[33] In other words, the child is partially out of the womb when he is killed, leaving it only a matter of inches before the procedure legally becomes an act of infanticide. It is the most visibly gruesome form of abortion. Nonetheless, the court, true to its logic, did not flinch and found that any abortion law that imposed an undue burden on a woman's "right to choose" was unconstitutional.

In what did the undue burden consist? Chief Justice Stephen Breyer, in expressing the opinion of the court, said that causing those who procure or perform abortions to "fear prosecution, conviction, and imprisonment" was an undue burden, and therefore declared the law to be against the Constitution. One would have thought that the fear was well founded, as the abortionists were only a narrow margin away from committing murder. They therefore needed the court's reassurance that what was clearly a child was not yet a "person" since the child was still partially intrauterine and, consequently, without any rights at all. The court met this need. The burden was removed from them and placed on the child. In an Orwellian feat of semantic distortion, the court delivered its ruling without using the word *child*, other than in quotations from the Nebraska statute, except in the second sentence of the ruling, where it appears, but only in a speculative sense—as in, some people might think that this is a child. (In 2007, however, the court upheld the *federal* Partial-Birth Abortion Ban Act of 2003 in *Gonzales v. Carhart*.)

If even the existence of a child cannot stand in the way of the imperative of contraceptive sex, what can? Can the definition of marriage as being between a man and a woman withstand its logic? In a deliciously ironic line, Mary Eberstadt wrote, "Once heterosexuals start claiming the right to act as homosexuals, it would not be long before homosexuals started claiming the

[33] Stenberg v. Carhart, 530 U.S. 914 (2000), http://supreme.justia.com/cases/federal/us/530/914/case.html.

rights of heterosexuals."[34] In light of what it has already found, how can the court exclude from the privilege of marriage those who exclusively devote themselves to sodomitical acts, which by their nature are sterile? If there can no longer be laws against these acts, why can't there be laws for them—as the foundation for marriage? There are very good answers to these questions, but the majority members of the court in the cases cited above are unaware of them. The separation of sex from procreation logically leads to the legalization of contraception, then to abortion, and finally to homosexual marriage and beyond. The logic is compelling, in fact, inescapable. Only the premise is insane.

Back to Lawrence

The brief review of these cases brings us back full circle to the *Lawrence* decision, which cited them (except for *Stenberg*) as reference for its justification, and makes it easier to see why *Lawrence* invalidated laws against sodomy. The *Lawrence* ruling is rife with an implied equivalence between conjugal sex and sodomy, for which the judicial ground had been well prepared. The "right to privacy" apparently includes anything (of a sexual nature) done in private—about which one is, by consequence of the privacy, rendered powerless to judge morally. The dignity to which *Lawrence* so frequently refers does not inhere in behavior as such, but in the privacy and personal freedom of individuals to choose whatever behavior they wish. According to the logic of *Lawrence*, to impugn any sexual act is to impugn the privacy and freedom that protect it. With this bit of legerdemain, the court sought to make irrelevant, or at least disguise, the moral character of sexual acts—with the result that all sexual acts become equal. In other words, there is no basis at all for the moral opprobrium aimed at sodomy. Nor, indeed, would there seem to be a basis upon which to disapprove of incest or any other sexual variation performed privately. The *Lawrence* decision said, in effect, that the state is indifferent as to whether one succumbs to a disordered sexual appetite, so long as he does it privately and freely. Apparently, the free exercise of choice is self-justifying.

Therefore, what could account for the preceding legal bias against sodomitical acts? The court answered, "While it is true that the law applies

---

[34] Mary Eberstadt, *Adam and Eve after the Pill* (San Francisco: Ignatius Press, 2012), 150.

only to conduct, the conduct targeted by this law is conduct that is closely correlated with being homosexual. Under such circumstances, [the] sodomy law is targeted at more than conduct. It is instead directed toward gay persons as a class." There we have it: it is discrimination against a *class* of people, clearly something against the founding principle of the United States that "all men are created equal". But how, one wonders, is this different from laws against any type of behavior that is associated with the people who engage in it? For instance, laws against drunk driving or disorderly conduct are most likely to be transgressed by practicing alcoholics. Are, therefore, these laws "targeted at more than conduct", at alcoholics as a class? Were this so, it would be impossible to make laws against drunk driving or disorderly conduct, just as the *Lawrence* ruling now makes it impossible to make laws against sodomy. The thinking behind *Lawrence* is disabling to the rule of law in general.

But let us examine in greater detail the damage it does to the matter at hand in terms of the morality of sexual relations. "To say that the issue in *Bowers* [which upheld a state law against sodomy] was simply the right to engage in certain sexual conduct", *Lawrence* states, "demeans the claim the individual put forward, just as it would demean a married couple were it to be said marriage is simply about the right to have sexual intercourse."[35] This invites a very strange analogy between the "sexual conduct" (i.e., sodomy) in a homosexual relationship and the "sexual intercourse" in a matrimonial relationship. Is it just as demeaning to reduce both relationships to the right to engage in their respective sexual acts?

First of all, the whole point of the *Lawrence* case is to decide whether, in the first place, there *is* a right to engage in anal intercourse. Second, marriage *is*, in part, precisely about the right to have sexual intercourse in that it provides the only proper context for the performance of it—with a spouse. Professor Budziszewski writes that "sexual powers are good, but only when exercised by the right person, with the right person, for the right motives, in the right way, and in the right state, which is marriage."[36] Sexual intercourse "in the right way" consummates marriage in a unitive act of enormous worth, a mutual self-giving that contains a plenitude of rights and duties. There is nothing demeaning about it; it is enhancing and life-giving. What is demeaning is the court's dismissive attitude toward the

[35] Lawrence, 539 U.S. 558.
[36] Budziszewski, *On the Meaning of Sex*, 111.

huge significance of "the right to have sexual intercourse" in marriage by its implied comparison with sodomy. Marriage legitimizes sex, humanizes and celebrates it. Justice Kennedy trivializes it.

As Professor Budziszewski suggests, the moral dignity of the sexual act depends upon the human integrity with which it is performed. If either person is reduced to a sexual object, then the act demeans and dehumanizes; it destroys human integrity. Through its equivocation, the court attempts to dignify the very thing that demeans. *Freely* choosing to act in this demeaning way cannot rescue this behavior from the moral debasement inherent in it.

Outside of the marital context, sex is, as mentioned before, to some degree or other invariably demeaning. It lacks the marital commitment and context. Thus, the self-giving, if it exists at all, is always hedged. It is hard to imagine an act more demeaning than sodomy. However, the court was unwittingly correct in saying that the issue in *Bowers* was not simply about the right to engage in certain sexual conduct. It was really about the establishment of a rationalization for that conduct. *Bowers* refused to accept the rationalization for homosexual behavior as something *required* by the Constitution. The *Lawrence* court avoided these reflections because it looked away from whatever was done freely and privately toward a thoroughly ideological notion of individual autonomy.

But in what way, one might wonder, would the claims of the individuals in the *Lawrence* case be demeaned by saying they were only about "certain sexual conduct"? The court ruled that "when sexuality finds overt expression in intimate conduct with another person, the conduct can be but one element in a personal bond that is more enduring."[37] In marriage this is certainly so because that personal bond is also expressed in a legal, and often sacramental, covenantal way. But is this really so regarding sexual conduct outside of marriage? Is there necessarily a "more enduring" personal bond involved? And was it so in this case? In fact, the two men who admitted to anal intercourse in *Lawrence* had had a one-night stand.[38] There was no relationship between them before that evening, nor was there one afterward. Sex was not "but one element"; it was the *only* element, except perhaps for alcohol. There was no personal bond. So, it *was* "simply [about] the right to engage in certain sexual conduct". Would it not, therefore, according to the court's own criteria, have met the definition of demeaning? What might

[37] Lawrence, 539 U.S. 558.

[38] Dahlia Lithwick, "Extreme Makeover: The Story Behind the Story of Lawrence v. Texas", *The New Yorker*, March 12, 2012.

have been the "more transcendent dimensions" of this encounter to which Justice Kennedy referred? Of course, the court was silent on these matters.

The sentence following the quote above states that "the liberty protected by the Constitution allows homosexual persons the right to make this choice", presumably, as it states earlier in the same paragraph, to "choose to enter upon this relationship in the confines of their homes and their own private lives and still retain their dignity as free persons." This is a bold assertion in light of the fact that all thirteen states, as Chief Justice Burger mentioned in *Bowers*, had statutes against sodomy at the time they ratified the Bill of Rights.

Why did it take more than two centuries for the court to discover the right to sodomy? Because, the *Lawrence* court claimed, those who drew up and ratified the Bill of Rights had not in any specificity "known the components of liberty and its manifold possibilities". (Neither, apparently, did the court in *Bowers* only seventeen years earlier, when it declared that there is no constitutional right to sodomy.) What's more, "they knew times can blind us to certain truths and later generations can see that laws once thought necessary and proper in fact serve only to oppress."[39] The Founders did, in fact, leave in place an amendment process by which to address such situations. They did not envisage a Supreme Court that could divine new "truths" on its own and impose them upon the nation.

In 1878 the Supreme Court was offered an opportunity similar to that of *Lawrence* to change the sexual mores and laws of the country by judicial fiat. In *Reynolds v. United States*, a Mormon who had broken the law against bigamy made the claim that his action was protected under the constitutional free exercise of religion. The court did not find this convincing because "polygamy has always been odious among the northern and western nations of Europe." While the Constitution may be silent on marriage, the court asserted that

> marriage, while from its very nature a sacred obligation, is nevertheless, in most civilized nations, a civil contract, and usually regulated by law. Upon it society may be said to be built, and out of its fruits spring social relations and social obligations and duties with which government is necessarily required to deal. In fact, according as monogamous or polygamous marriages are allowed, do we find the principles on which the government of the people, to a greater or less extent, rests.

[39] Lawrence, 539 U.S. 558.

In other words, the very character of a society and the nature of its government will depend on the makeup of the family. Monogamy is an essential precondition for democratic rule and is necessary in order to *shape* its citizens in their disposition toward it. Polygamy, to quote the court, "leads to the patriarchal principle and which, when applied to large communities, fetters the people in stationary despotism". In its profoundly Aristotelian perspective, the court saw that, while the Constitution may not mention the family directly, it *presupposes* the family and could not exist without it. Therefore, concluded the court, "There cannot be a doubt that ... it is within the legitimate scope of the power of every civil government to determine whether polygamy or monogamy shall be the law of social life under its dominion."

Such was the case during the ratification of the Bill of Rights, when, in 1788, at the very time the Commonwealth of Virginia was proposing an amendment guaranteeing the free exercise of religion, its legislature adopted the death penalty for bigamy. "From that day to this", the *Reynolds* court said, "we think it may safely be said there never has been a time in any State of the Union when polygamy has not been an offence against society, cognizable by the civil courts and punishable with more or less severity. In the face of all this evidence, it is impossible to believe that the constitutional guaranty of religious freedom was intended to prohibit legislation in respect to this most important feature of social life."[40]

In 1885, the court reaffirmed its view, again in respect to polygamy, on the central importance of family to social and political order. The *Murphy v. Ramsey* ruling declared that

> certainly no legislation can be supposed more wholesome and necessary in the founding of a free, self-governing commonwealth, fit to take rank as one of the coordinate states of the Union, than that which seeks to establish it on the basis of the idea of the family, as consisting in and springing from the union for life of one man and one woman in the holy estate of matrimony; the sure foundation of all that is stable and noble in our civilization; the best guarantee of that reverent morality which is the source of all beneficent progress in social and political improvement. And to this end, no means are more directly and immediately suitable than those provided by this act, which endeavors to withdraw all political influence from those who are practically hostile to its attainment.[41]

[40] Reynolds v. United States, 98 U.S. 145 (1878), http://supreme.justia.com/cases/federal/us/98/145/case.html.
[41] Murphy, 114 U.S. 15, 45 (1885).

What the *Reynolds* court found "impossible to believe"—that the Founders did not really know what they were doing because the times could blind them "to certain truths"—the *Lawrence* court found possible to believe. Who could know what these "certain truths" might be until, all of a sudden, one is no longer blind to them—as in a moment of illumination of the high court? Therefore, according to *Lawrence*, even though sodomy was forbidden in every state at the time of the ratification of the Fourteenth Amendment, its due process clause actually prohibits legislation against sodomy, even though no one knew it at the time or for a century and a half afterward. This is because we have come to understand in "later generations" that such laws "serve only to oppress".

But surely laws against sodomy are not the only ones that oppress. Do not laws against polygamy oppress polygamists? By the standards employed in *Lawrence*, what is to prevent the court from overruling *Reynolds* and *Murphy* the same way it overruled *Bowers*? In fact, it would seem to be inconsistent of the court not to do so.

Lawrence raised another matter of profound importance regarding the nature of law and its relationship to morality. The court stated that "the issue is whether the majority may use the power of the state to enforce these views on the whole society through the operation of criminal law."[42] The court implies here that right is not the rule of the stronger—which is certainly correct. The whole point of constitutional government is to prevent this kind of tyranny. Right is not constituted by strength, but by morality. The job of the legislature is to *reason* together over what is right and wrong and to arrive at laws that are good for the community. In so doing, the majority may not transgress the rights of the minority. Recall that rights are shared by all persons by virtue of their human Nature. They have these rights in common. *Only* what is held *in common* can possibly be a right. Rights do not inhere on the basis of an idiosyncrasy peculiar to a person or group of persons. There are not special, separate rights for thin people or for left-handed people. Human rights, to exist, must be universal.

In light of this, the majority may not simply decide anything it wishes—for instance, to enslave the minority, because that would be *unreasonable* and against the very notion of human rights from which the legislature derives its authority. One cannot on the basis of human rights advance a claim to deny the human rights of others. But the state may reasonably regulate

[42] Lawrence, 539 U.S. 558.

the life of all the individuals in a community for the sake of the common good. That is what the rule of law is for. Therefore, "the majority *may* use the power of the state to enforce" the rule of law "on the whole society through the operation of criminal law" quite legitimately (emphasis added). Is this not what *every* criminal law does or intends to do? How would law operate without enforcing its views on the whole of society? The rule of law, by definition, must do this. All one has to do is to insert in the sentence at the beginning of this paragraph a few words in brackets to see the point.

For instance, "The issue is whether the majority may use the power of the state to enforce these views [on murder or rape or kidnapping] on the whole society through the operation of criminal law." The answer then easily becomes, yes, it can—because murder, rape and kidnapping are still acknowledged as evil things. But whether the power of the state should be used to enforce any view will, or should, ultimately depend on the morality or immorality of the act it is proscribing. Thus, in this case, the answer would have to address the goodness or evil of sodomy. As we have already noted, the court refused to do this. (Note: Even if the court admitted to the immorality of sodomy, it would not necessarily follow that a criminal law against it should be supported. All laws enforce moral standards. But that does not mean all moral standards should be enforced by law. For various reasons, such a law might be imprudent. Take the case of prostitution, which is generally admitted to be an evil. Some states may forbid it, while other states may find it more prudent to control and limit it through regulation.)

Then *Lawrence* employs one of its several quotes from *Casey*: "Our obligation is to define the liberty of all, not to mandate our own moral code." If this is so, exactly *whose* moral code *is* being mandated in the *Lawrence* decision—for surely one is being imposed, as its invalidation of the *Bowers* ruling and the Texas state law is certainly based upon some understanding of what is right? Isn't it more appropriate to ask whether the ethical code in question is based on moral truths that flow from reason? To ask *whose* moral code or *whose* truth is to suggest that truth is relative—to the person whose it is. This is an extraordinarily dangerous teaching for the court to hold. The inability to make moral judgments based on reason finally corrupts the very idea of law itself. What's more, how can the court "define the liberty of all" without delineating the limits of liberty? Things are defined by their limits. If a thing is without limits, then it cannot be defined. If liberty is limited, it must be ordered to something. To what? The court seemed not to know.

The next quote from *Casey* used in *Lawrence* is regarding "the heart of liberty" as "the right to define one's own concept of existence, of meaning, of the universe, and of the mystery of human life". From this extraordinary statement, *Lawrence* concludes that "persons in a homosexual relationship may seek autonomy for these purposes, just as heterosexual persons do."[43] What could this sentence possibly mean? Its silliness becomes apparent with these substitutions: "Alcoholics may seek autonomy for these purposes, just as sober persons do"; or, "Kleptomaniacs may seek autonomy for these purposes, just as persons who respect private property do." If those substitutions seem too judgmental, here is a more neutral one: "Left-handed people may seek autonomy for these purposes, just as right-handed people do." Either way, the sentence is inane. What, by the way, could have caused the court to think that *homosexuals* are in some way constrained from thinking up their own idea of the universe, as apart from everyone else? If the court simply had meant to say that everyone has a right to make up anything they want—not a surprising view, given what the court itself does—then that's what it should have said, and not made it contingent on one's sexual proclivities.

What's more, does one go about defining the meaning of existence by entering into a sexual relationship (which is usually no time to think)? More accurately, one does this by *reasoning* about the Nature of things. One undertakes this effort as a *human being* endowed with reason, not specifically as a man or as a woman, or as a heterosexual or as a homosexual. As Jaffa said, "All moral obligation arises from the perception that another being is a human being"—not from the perception of their sexual inclinations, or from their race, or their class.[44] Does the court suppose that the universe has different meanings depending on gender or sexual orientation? If so, why can it not have a different meaning for an Aryan than it does for a Slav, or for a capitalist than it does for a member of the proletariat? If it does have these different meanings, how could one possibly arrive at an understanding of the *common* good, since the very meaning of the universe could not be held in common? And if there is no common good because of this, there could be no laws directed to achieving it. This would return us to right as the rule of the stronger—the very thing to which the court supposedly objects, but to which its logic inexorably leads.

43 Ibid.

44 Harry V. Jaffa, "Clarifying Homosexuality and Natural Law: Harry V. Jaffa Replies to Philip Dynia", Claremont Institute, August 19, 1993, http://www.claremont.org/publications /pubid.692/pub_detail.asp.

Also, what if one's "autonomy of self" defines "one's own concept of existence" based on the Nazi race-based theory of history that justifies the extermination of inferior peoples or on the communist class-based theory of history that justifies the elimination of the bourgeoisie? On what grounds might an objection be raised to these? Are there certain things to which one may *not* assent in one's autonomy—in other words, to which one does not have the *right* to assent? Both of these concepts of existence and meaning are inimical to the Declaration of Independence. On what basis can it be said that the Nazi and communist meanings of existence were wrong, and those of the Declaration right? The sex-based theory of history that the court is promoting here is also inimical to the principles of the Declaration. The court, as usual, is silent on this problem.

There is one way of reading this part of the decision, however, that makes sense of it. If by "the right to define one's own concept of existence, of meaning, of the universe", the court really meant to say that you, as a homosexual, have the right to rationalize your sodomitical behavior, even after a one-night stand, into something more pleasing and acceptable to your conscience—and you can not only do that but can also seek to enforce your rationalization upon other people and the state of Texas by revoking their laws—then it all becomes clear.

According to the court, freedom is without content, a void, and has nothing to do with *what* is chosen. There is no direction as to how you ought to use your freedom, or what you should or should not choose—no teleology. Defending freedom without explaining for what ends and by what right we are free, as Professor Angelo Codevilla has written, strips freedom of any moral seriousness. Ultimately, "Aimless freedom repels."[45] In this way, the court has endangered the very thing it should be protecting.

Furthermore, the court in *Lawrence* worries that "when homosexual conduct is made criminal by the law of the State, that declaration in and of itself is an invitation to subject homosexual persons to discrimination in the public and in the private spheres."[46] Also, "its stigma might remain even if it were not enforceable as drawn for equal protection reasons."[47] But how is this unlike any other criminal law that discriminates against those who do not observe it? The purpose of criminal law *is* to stigmatize the behavior it

[45] Angelo M. Codevilla, *Advice to War Presidents: A Remedial Course in Statecraft* (New York: Basic Books, 2009), 74.
[46] Lawrence, 539 U.S. 558.
[47] Ibid.

forbids. Why else penalize it? Yes, indeed, murderers and rapists do suffer discrimination for their crimes, once they have been caught, tried, found guilty, and then incarcerated or otherwise punished. Why should not the law work in this way concerning this case? Does not anal intercourse deserve the same "stigma of infamy" of which Aristotle spoke in regard to adultery? The court says that it does not because, "its continuance as precedent demeans the lives of homosexual persons." But the whole reason that the litigants had been arrested was because *they* had demeaned themselves in an act of anal intercourse. It is the act that demeans, not the prohibition against it.

Certainly, part of the purpose of the Texas law was to *teach* that sodomy is morally demeaning and that therefore one ought not to indulge in it. As Justice Scalia said in his dissenting opinion, "The Texas statute undeniably seeks to further the belief of its citizens that certain forms of sexual behavior are immoral and unacceptable."[48] Sodomy was only a minor misdemeanor offense in the Texas legal system, but even at this lenient level of penalty, the law's teaching was morally clear. Why, then, did the court insist that it is the *law*, rather than the act of sodomy, that demeans the "lives of homosexual persons"? If this is true, it would have to mean that the act of sodomy is *not* demeaning. The court never says this explicitly but makes clear that the choice of homosexual anal intercourse, under the protection of the right to privacy, is irreproachable. Contra the *Bowers* ruling, the Constitution apparently *does* confer "a fundamental right to engage in homosexual sodomy". This is the fundamental teaching of *Lawrence*.

The *Lawrence* opinion delivered a tremendous blow to the rule of law and its relationship to sexual morality. It concluded by saying, "The case does involve two adults who, with full and mutual consent from each other, engaged in sexual practices common to a homosexual lifestyle. The petitioners are entitled to respect for their private lives. The state cannot demean their existence or control their destiny by making their private sexual conduct a crime."[49] In his dissenting opinion, Justice Scalia pointed out the profound problem with this ruling: "State laws against bigamy, same-sex marriage, adult incest, prostitution, masturbation, adultery, fornication, bestiality, and obscenity are likewise sustainable only in light of *Bowers*' validation of laws based on moral choices. Every single one of these laws is called into question by today's decision; the Court makes no effort to cabin the scope of

[48] Ibid.
[49] Ibid.

its decision to exclude them from its holding."[50] Indeed, each of the actions mentioned by Justice Scalia can be part of a certain "lifestyle", and almost all of them constitute "private sexual conduct" performed with consent. The *Bowers* court had argued that "illegal conduct is not always immunized whenever it occurs in the home.... [Otherwise] it would be difficult, except by fiat, to limit the claimed right to homosexual conduct while leaving exposed to prosecution adultery, incest, and other sexual crimes even though they are committed in the home."[51] By overturning *Bowers*, did not the *Lawrence* court, by its own criteria, implicitly immunize each of those participating in these acts, as likewise they are "entitled to respect for their private lives"? Then on what basis could the court allow a state "to demean their existence or control their destiny by making their private sexual conduct a crime"?

Given that the state should *not* be demeaning the existence of homosexuals, should it also not be *affirming* their existence by showing "respect for their private lives"? Justice Kennedy claimed that this case did "not involve whether the government must give formal recognition to any relationship that homosexual persons seek to enter";[52] but, it did, except formally speaking. The logic *Lawrence* employed leads straight to it since the decision removed any moral reason to condemn sodomy. If there is nothing wrong with what homosexuals do in their private lives, why can't those lives go public? It does not seem to have occurred to Justice Kennedy that his ruling removed any basis upon which such formal recognition could in the future be withheld. But, as we shall see, he came to his senses ten years later in the *United States v. Windsor* decision, when he led the opinion overruling the Defense of Marriage Act because, he said, the state of New York had deemed homosexual marriage legally "worthy of dignity in the community equal with all other marriages".[53] He actually cited *Lawrence* to support his position, having finally realized its full implications.

Legislating Immorality from the Benches of State Courts

It took only a few months for the Massachusetts Supreme Judicial Court to catch on to this point and mandate same-sex marriage. In *Goodridge v.*

---

[50] Ibid.

[51] Bowers v. Hardwick (no. 85–140) 760 F.2d 1202, reversed.

[52] Lawrence, 539 U.S. 558.

[53] United States v. Windsor 417 F.2d 1131 (4th Cir. 1969), http://www.supremecourt.gov /opinions/12pdf/12-307_6j37.pdf.

Department of Public Health (2003), it found that the Commonwealth of Massachusetts could not "deny the protections, benefits and obligations conferred by civil marriage to two individuals of the same sex who wish to marry".[54] Why could it not—since it had done so since colonial times in the oldest state constitution in the country?

To support itself, the court cited *Lawrence* by saying that same-sex marriage "is a question the United States Supreme Court left open as a matter of Federal law in *Lawrence*." Therefore, on what basis could it be prohibited by Massachusetts state law? This is how the court expressed the quandary: "Many people hold deep-seated religious, moral, and ethical convictions that marriage should be limited to the union of one man and one woman, and that homosexual conduct is immoral. Many hold equally strong religious, moral, and ethical convictions that same-sex couples are entitled to be married, and that homosexual persons should be treated no differently than their heterosexual neighbors."[55] The court then washed its hands of this profound difference by declaring it irrelevant to the question before it. The court used Justice Kennedy's exact same rationalization by quoting from *Lawrence*: "Our obligation is to define the liberty of all, not to mandate our own moral code." Therefore, the court concluded that "exclusion is incompatible with the constitutional principles of respect for individual autonomy." Here we see exactly where Justice Kennedy's "autonomy of self" leads: to the rejection of the moral law. This is the morass into which *Lawrence* has led.

As a further presage of things to come, other state courts and some federal district courts extended the line of reasoning in these Supreme Court decisions to same-sex marriage. For instance, in 2009, in the *Varnum v. Brien* case, the Iowa Supreme Court decided to overturn state law in order to make same-sex marriage legal.[56] Not surprisingly, the court trotted out "equal protection of the law" as its excuse for the ruling. Equality before the law, however, does not mean that everyone gets to be affirmed in whatever he may choose to do. That is why laws have penalties. It means that the law applies equally to everyone, *despite* their personal desires. The court actually acted against this principle by saying that there should be a *special*

---

[54] Goodridge v. Department of Public Health, 798 N.E.2d 941 (Mass. 203), http://www2 .law.columbia.edu/faculty_franke/Gay_Marriage/Goodridge%20Decision%20edited%20 Fundamental%20Right.pdf.

[55] Ibid.

[56] Varnum v. Brien, 763 N.W.2d 862 (Iowa 2009), http://www.iowacourts.gov/wfData /files/Varnum/07-1499(1).pdf.

category of marriage for those disposed to the act of sodomy, who, for whatever reason or indisposition, refuse to comply with the laws for marriage passed by the Iowa legislature.

In Iowa, no doubt, there are also laws or regulations that define the qualifications for service in fire departments and police forces. If one cannot meet those qualifications through some physical or other infirmity, is the state then obliged to create a *special* kind of fire department or police force in which one can serve to meet the requirement of equality before the law? Of course not. It would defeat the very *purpose* of fire departments and police forces to have people serve on them who cannot perform the duties of firemen and police officers. They would therefore no longer be *real* police forces or fire departments. Likewise with marriage, a far more important institution than either the police or the fire department, creating faux marriage for those who cannot or will not perform the duties of real marriage defeats the purpose of the institution. The Iowa Supreme Court should at least have had the presence of mind to acknowledge what it was actually doing—denying that there *is* a real purpose to marriage—and to be ready to explain to others, such as polygamists, polyandrists, or those in man-boy or incestuous relationships, why it should not, by judicial fiat, also create a special kind of marriage for them.

In the *Wall Street Journal* op-ed "Why Gay Marriage Matters" (March 7, 2009), Michael Judge, whose brother is homosexual, celebrated the Iowa Supreme Court's decision to overturn the state law.[57] He confessed that he did not understand how anyone could oppose this enlightened decision—even if those opposing it included the majority of the people of Iowa, who supported the law against such "marriages" in the first place. Why, he asked, would anyone now wish to sponsor an amendment to the state constitution to define marriage as between a man and a woman?

Well, let's see. Mr. Judge quotes the court's complaint against "the disadvantages and fears they [homosexuals] face each day due to the inability to obtain a civil marriage in Iowa". The court then enumerates their legal disadvantages, which are all real—no sharing in health insurance, pension benefits, hospital visitation rights, and so on. The point, however, is not that there are disadvantages. The question is whether the disadvantages are based on a distinction made only by convention (and therefore changeable as a

[57] Michael Judge, "Why Gay Marriage Matters", *Wall Street Journal*, April 7, 2009, http://online.wsj.com/article/SB123906051568695003.html.

matter of custom) or by one that exists in Nature (and therefore normative and morally imperative). The exact same disadvantages exist for mistresses, unmarried heterosexual lovers, bigamists, polygamists, polyandrists, and those in man–boy relationships. If hardship is the criterion, should not all these be enfolded into the new definition of civil marriage? After all, they too, as the court said of homosexual couples, are "a historically disfavored class of persons [excluded] from a supremely important civil institution." Are they not also "kind-hearted people", like Mr. Judge's homosexual brother, on whose behalf he wrote?

Absent from the article or the court's decision is any explanation of why marriage is so important as a civil institution and why those other than monogamous men and women have normally been excluded from it. Before expanding upon the definition of marriage, or rather destroying it, one should at least have understood why it had existed for so long in the first place. There should at least have been some awareness as to why Aristotle began his *Politics*, not with a single individual, but with a description of a man and a woman together in the family, without which the rest of society cannot exist. Society can be said to exist only to the extent to which spousal relations remain intact. That is the "constitutionally sufficient justification" for marriage between a man and a woman that the Iowa Supreme Court, in an attack of aphasia, could not recall. The court also seems to have forgotten that the legal disadvantages against homosexual and other partnerships were put there exactly for the purpose of *shaping* behavior in a certain way to the general benefit of society and for discouraging behavior that undermines it.

Aside from the pecuniary penalties mentioned earlier, the court opined that "perhaps the ultimate disadvantage expressed in the testimony of the plaintiffs is the inability to obtain for themselves and for their children the personal and public affirmation that accompanies marriage."[58] Here, as we have seen before, is the real nub of the matter. The majority of homosexual relationships, as has been mentioned before, are largely based upon the act of sodomy. The plaintiffs ask for, and the court wishes to bestow, public affirmation, meaning moral approval, of this act as a foundation for marriage. Because law is inescapably based upon morality, this is what public affirmation *necessarily* means. Both the court and the plaintiffs claim that this change in the definition of marriage will make things *better*, which is a notion that has to be measured against an understanding of what is *good*.

---

[58] Varnum, 763 N.W.2d 862.

Those who consider sodomy an intrinsically disordered and morally corrupt act will now be unaffirmed and forced by law to acknowledge the opposite. This is, after all, a change in the public order, and that is what such changes mean.

This makes the court's statement that "the sanctity of all religious marriages celebrated in the future will have the same meaning as those celebrated in the past"[59] particularly disingenuous. How could they have the same meaning when the court has just changed the definition of what is morally acceptable as marriage? You cannot change the definition of what something is and at the same time claim that it remains unchanged. Was this deceit or ignorance on the court's part? You cannot introduce counterfeit currency and claim that the money supply is sound. You cannot water your wine and claim it is undiluted. Could it not have occurred to the court that, as philosopher Roger Scruton writes, real marriage "is rendered more difficult, the less society recognizes the uniqueness, the value, and the sacrificial character of what we do? Just as people are less disposed to assume the burdens of high office when the society withholds the dignities and privileges which those offices have previously signified, so are they are less disposed to enter real marriages when society acknowledges no distinction between marriages that deserve the name and relationships that merely borrow the title."[60]

Perry v. Schwarzenegger

In the spirit of the Iowa Court, superlawyers Theodore Olson and David Boies, from the inaptly named American Foundation for Equal Rights, filed a lawsuit in federal district court in 2009 on behalf of two California "gay" couples who alleged that their constitutional rights had been violated by their inability to wed according to Proposition 8, which added to the California Constitution the definition of marriage as only between a man and a woman. They apparently thought that their inability to wed was the result of California's prohibition against same-sex marriage, rather than their own unwillingness or inability to fulfill the requirements of marriage. By attempting to force their point of view into law through the courts, they insisted that everyone share in it.

[59] Ibid.
[60] George and Elshtain, *The Meaning of Marriage*, 20.

The original defendants in the case, Attorney General Jerry Brown and Governor Arnold Schwarzenegger, refused to defend their state constitution in court, even though Proposition 8 was passed by a majority of their citizens. Although the California attorney general has a statutory duty to "defend all causes to which the State ... is a party", Brown and Schwarzenegger decided to declare the initiative unconstitutional all on their very own. This seemed close to a dereliction of duty.

In deciding the *Perry v. Schwarzenegger* case in 2010, US District Chief Judge Vaughn R. Walker ruled that Proposition 8 is unconstitutionally discriminatory because marriage is not between a man and a woman. Where could he have gotten this idea? It turned out that the judge himself is a homosexual. It is more than a stretch to believe that his life as a homosexual did not affect his decision concerning homosexual rights. Would a person engaged in the very activity that is being questioned be the best judge of its legal character? One of the most elementary principles of justice is that one should not rule in a case in which one has an interest. But Judge Walker apparently did not feel the need to recuse himself, though it would seem obvious that he, as a homosexual, would have had a personal interest in the outcome. Frank Schubert, the manager of the successful Proposition 8 campaign in 2008, commented that "Walker was a judge in a long-term committed relationship with another man—in other words, he was in exactly the type of relationship as the plaintiffs who were bringing suit. Walker never disclosed this critical fact to Prop 8 supporters, or to the public, despite judicial rules requiring such disclosure if even the *appearance* of impropriety was present."[61]

A motion was raised to this effect. District Court Judge James Ware heard arguments on the motion and denied it. In the decision, Ware explained that "requiring recusal because a court issued an injunction that could provide some speculative future benefit to the presiding judge solely on the basis of the fact that the judge belongs to the class against whom the unconstitutional law was directed would lead to a Section 455(b) (4) standard that required recusal of minority judges in most, if not all, civil rights cases."

There is a profound problem with this ruling. It prejudges the case as a "civil rights" issue. It is not the "class" to which Walker belonged, but the *behavior* in which he engaged that was at issue in his conflict of interest. Do

---

[61] Frank Schubert, "The Legal Circus That Killed Proposition 8", Witherspoon Institute, July 22, 2013, http://www.thepublicdiscourse.com/2013/07/10603/.

laws against murder discriminate against a "class" of murderers? Acts do not constitute class. They are performed by individuals. It is the moral and legal character of an act that constitutes the matter at hand, not the class of the person performing the act.

Let us say that the constitutionality of Prohibition was being decided. Would it be relevant to the judge's competence to hear the case if he were an active alcoholic? Or would he be excused from recusal because he belonged to a "class" of alcoholics? Why, then, is it less relevant in this case—which was to decide the constitutionality of same-sex marriage—that Judge Walker was in a ten-year relationship with a partner, as he later admitted?

In fact, the judge was a beneficiary of his own ruling—not only in the direct sense that he could now marry his "partner" if he so wished (a relationship disclosed after the trial), but in the legal establishment of the larger rationalization of homosexual acts as being morally normative. His 136-page ruling can be seen as a bald act of self-justification, which he enforced upon the broader public as legally mandatory. This, of course, is a major misuse of law. People who live morally disordered lives—and a life centered on homosexual acts is morally disordered—must always search for rationalizations that permit them to continue their behavior. Otherwise, as indicated earlier, conscience rebels. Judge Walker's revolutionary 2010 ruling was indubitably tied to his private life, the rationalization for which he then required everyone to accept—according to the US Constitution, no less.

Judicial Rationalizations

As with the *Lawrence* decision, it is worth examining the rationalizations proffered in the *Perry v. Schwarzenegger* judgment, because they were then partially shared by the Ninth Circuit Court appeals panel, which supported Judge Walker's ruling in a split (2–1) decision in February 2012, and by the Supreme Court in June 2013. They are also widely shared among same-sex-marriage proponents.

Judge Walker declared that "Proposition 8 fails to advance any rational basis in singling out gay men and lesbians for denial of a marriage license."[62]

---

[62] Perry v. Schwarzenegger, 704 F. Supp. 2d 921 (N.D. Calif. 2010), http://s3.amazonaws.com/nytdocs/docs/450/450.pdf.

This, he contended, is wrong because marriage is a basic right. As mentioned earlier, however, one has a "right" or is "free" to marry only insofar as one is capable of being married. One does not have a right to a vocation in life whose duties one cannot perform. Does one have a "right" to serve in the military if one cannot physically meet its demands?

What, then, might be the minimal demands of marriage that one must be capable of performing? One of those marital duties, as in the two examples above, is actually physical, though its implications and true meaning extend far beyond the merely physical. Common law holds that a marriage is not fully valid until it is consummated. What does consummating a marriage mean? It means and has always meant by law an act of vaginal intercourse between the husband and wife. If this act does not take place, the marriage can be legally declared a nullity. Until consummation, it is subject to annulment. Therefore, becoming "one flesh" is, or at least was, not optional for a legally valid marriage. If one is incapable of consummating a marriage or simply unwilling to do so for any reason, there can be no marriage, and therefore the "right" to it is irrelevant. Similarly, if one cannot perform as a fireman, the right to be a fireman is also irrelevant.

How did Judge Walker get around this? By ignoring it—with this bit of legerdemain: he stated that the ability to produce offspring has never been a prerequisite for granting heterosexual couples marriage licenses. This, of course, is true, but he segues from it to the clear implication that an act of sodomy can therefore replace vaginal intercourse to consummate a marriage. He implies this, though the word *sodomy*, the elephant in the room, is *never* mentioned in his decision. He was wise, if not entirely honest, in not using the word, because it has never before been thought that sodomy could legally consummate a marriage, regardless of the fertility or infertility of the couple. Many state laws forbade sodomy. Since some even included prohibitions of it within marriage, it was inconceivable that marital consummation could have meant anything but vaginal intercourse.

For homosexual couples, the marital act is physically impossible—the pieces don't fit—and the attempt to ape it through sodomy is hygienically compromised and incapable in any circumstances of generating new life. For these reasons, among many others, common law has held *through the centuries* that marriage can be only between a man and a woman. In light of this, it is astonishing that Judge Walker could state in his conclusion that "Proposition 8 fails to advance any *rational* basis in singling out gay men and lesbians for denial of a marriage license" (emphasis added).[63] Is it not rational to state that those incapable of consummating a marriage cannot in fact be married? It seems quite irrational to say otherwise.

Regarding the matter of infertility, Judge Walker and the pro-homosexual movement use it in an attempt to gain traction for same-sex marriage by pointing out that certain heterosexual couples are infertile but may still marry. Therefore, they argue, the ability to procreate cannot be a prerequisite for marriage. They implicitly claim that there is no distinction between the infertility of homosexual relations and those of an infertile heterosexual couple. Consequently, homosexuals should be allowed to marry. All infertilities are equal, it would seem. But they are not. Homosexual relations are *essentially* sterile, intrinsically unfit for generation, while heterosexual relations are intrinsically generative and only *accidentally* infertile. In other words, there is nothing a same-sex couple could do at any time or in any way that would render their relations fertile. The opposite is true of the vast majority of heterosexual couples, who would actively have to do something to render their relations infertile.

In his essay "The Essence of Marriage", Ryan Sorba neatly summarized this issue in respect to natural law:

> Privations such as infertility, blindness, a missing arm, leg, etc. are accidental properties, not substantial. Accidental properties, such as privations, do not change the formal aspect of the subject. Just because a man is blind does not change the fact that he is a man, nor does it change the fact that the primary intelligible end of the eye is color and light.... The whole is self-evidently greater than the sum of its parts and even when one or more parts fail to function properly, the whole remains what it is. The existence of privation does not change the form or intelligible end of the whole, it simply blocks the whole from successfully realizing its full potential. We understand this and as a result we seek to cure blindness and other ailments when and wherever we can. This agreement is implicit in the whole field of medicine. When a part fails to function properly we attempt to correct it rather than change our conceptualization of what it is altogether.[64]

However, when the reproductive power of sex fails to function in marriage, Judge Walker uses this privation as an excuse to reconceptualize what marriage is altogether and to pretend that it is something other than what it is.

---

[63] Ibid.

[64] "The Essence of Marriage", *Ryan Sorba's Blog*, September 30, 2010, http://ryansorba .blogspot.com/2010/09/essence-of-marriage.html.

This is how he ends up equating infertility in some heterosexual marriages with the sterility in all same-sex couples.

They are not even both infertilities, properly speaking. This is a smoke-screen used to deflect attention from the real underlying matter. Infertility is an issue *only* in respect to those whose exercise of their procreative powers in heterosexual intercourse has failed for some reason that may be due to congenital or temporary health problems—the accidental properties or privations of which Sorba speaks. This is the only proper use of this word. One would not, for instance, refer to baseball playing or to a rock as an infertile act or thing because it would be gratuitous. Baseball does not have the potential to be fertile, nor do rocks, so why would anyone call them infertile? Things or acts that do not possess procreative powers are not called infertile, because they could not possibly *be* fertile. Likewise, homosexual liaisons do not possess procreative powers. They are, therefore, not properly called infertile, but more accurately, impotent.

Judge Walker's position also presumes that there is no distinction between the *kinds* of acts in an infertile heterosexual union and in an impotent homosexual one. Regardless of its fertility or infertility on any specific occasion, the coital act is procreative by its *nature* or *essence*—as only it can produce life—even when and if procreation does not result, as it does not in the vast majority of cases during a couple's fertile life. Is the Nature of marital relations fundamentally different during the frequent instances when pregnancy does not occur? Are those acts, then, equivalent in kind to sodomy? To suppose so would be like saying that when you are asleep with your eyes shut, your eyes are no longer organs of sight—since they do not see all the time. Nonetheless, the eye retains its Nature as an organ of sight even when it is not seeing. Likewise, reproductive powers and acts remain reproductive even when they are not reproducing. At a certain point, all heterosexual couples become permanently infertile due to age, but does this make the character of their acts sodomitical? They are no less marital or generative in their Nature because of this condition and, indeed, always remain, in their "one flesh" aspect, unitive. Unitive coition is obviously the necessary precondition for procreation, which is why these acts remain generative in their essence, even if accidentally they are not.

Sodomy, however, by its Nature and in all circumstances, is a nonprocreative act. One might even say that it is an antiprocreative act. An infertile heterosexual couple can still consummate a marriage; an impotent one cannot—and, on those grounds alone, as mentioned above, a marriage could be said not to exist. Therefore, since homosexual couples have no procreative potential, they should be called not infertile, but impotent. In other words, Judge Walker should not have equated infertility in heterosexual marriages with infertility in homosexual relationships. Rather, he should have contrasted heterosexual infertility with homosexual impotence. The former allows marriage; the latter does not. In legal terms, the spouse requesting an annulment of marriage on the grounds of impotency must prove that the impotence or physical incapacity in the partner is permanent and incurable and was so at the time of the marriage. Any attempted union between two males or two females easily meets these criteria for annulment. (Infertility, on the other hand, is not a ground for annulment.)

Sodomy and coition have never been treated as the same before because they are not the same. Judge Walker's whole ruling rests on a denial of this—on his deliberate confusion of what Sorba would call the substantial and the accidental. If these two acts can be equated, then treating them differently would be wrong. In the law, like must be treated alike. It is with this implicit conflation of sodomy and the marital act that Judge Walker tries to manufacture the charges of inequality and discrimination against same-sex couples. This is how he attempts to pull it off: "Like opposite-sex couples, same-sex couples have happy, satisfying relationships and form deep emotional bonds and strong commitments to their partners."[65] Therefore, "same-sex couples are identical to opposite-sex couples in the characteristics relevant to the ability to form successful marital unions." Consequently, denying same-sex couples the right to marriage *must* be a form of discrimination and a denial of equal protection.

Everyone *is* equal before this law, however, because no man and woman can be denied marriage for reasons of race, creed, or color. No extraneous issues can be brought to bear outside of the qualification that it takes a man and a woman to marry—certainly not matters of *class*, as was alleged by the Ninth Circuit review panel. Homosexuals and lesbians are also equal before this law insofar as they are willing, respectively, to find a woman or a man to marry (as those who leave the homosexual "lifestyle" often do). This makes specious Judge Stephen Reinhardt's claim on the appeals panel that "Proposition 8 singles out same-sex couples for unequal treatment by taking away from them alone the right to marry."[66] But they are not alone. Contrary

---

[65] Perry v. Schwarzenegger, 704 F. Supp. 2d 921.

[66] Perry v. Brown, 671 F.3d 1052 (9th Cir. 2012), http://www.danpinello.com/Perry.htm.

to effusions that everyone should have the right "to marry the person they love", relevant disqualifications for marriage include consanguinity—brothers and sisters, fathers and daughters, cannot marry, no matter how much they love each other. Neither can children, the insane, or those who are already married. Could anyone reasonably argue that children, the insane, brothers and sisters, or the already married are not equal before the law regarding marriage? How about a bisexual person who might require both a male and a female spouse simultaneously for his fulfillment? Such a prospect is already upon us. The North Dakota state attorney general Wayne Stenehjem delivered an opinion on December 12, 2013, stating that a male who was already married to a man in another state could apply for and receive a marriage license with a woman without breaking any North Dakota laws.[67]

Similarly, because of the principle of equality, everyone has the right to consent in the manner in which he is governed; but to exercise this right—expressed as the right to vote—one must meet the qualifications of voter registration as to age, residence, and so forth. If one is unwilling to register or has not reached the proper age, one cannot exercise the right. A child cannot; neither can an insane person. In some states, neither can felons.

Likewise, the law that forbids drunk driving applies equally to everyone, including alcoholics. Because an alcoholic is more likely to break this law, or because this law may be harder or perhaps even impossible for him to observe, does this mean the law is a violation of his due process and equality before the law? What would Judges Walker and Reinhardt say? If they employed the same logic as in their Proposition 8 rulings, they would say that alcoholics are being discriminated against as a "class" and that therefore the law against drunk driving is unconstitutional. The remedy, of course, would be a special statute or ruling to allow alcoholics to drive drunk. Why is this any less absurd than setting up a special class of marriage for those who refuse or are unable to perform the marital act?

Upon examination, however, Judge Walker's criteria for marriage are not as special as he might think. Why would not any of the relationships between brothers and sisters, between parents and children, or between married and unmarried not likewise qualify for marriage by the criteria that he set forth? Simply replace the words "opposite-sex couples" in the following sentence

[67] Eric M. Johnson, "North Dakota Says Man in Same-Sex Marriage May Wed Woman Too", Reuters, December 18, 2013, http://www.Reuters.Com/Article/2013/12/19/us-usa-northdakota-marriage-idUSBRE9BH1I520131219.

with those of any other loving relationship—say, "brother and sister" or "father and daughter"—and then continue with "couples have happy, satisfying relationships and form deep emotional bonds and strong commitments to their partners." Why should Judge Walker's ruling not apply to them as well?

Judge Walker, however, took greatest umbrage at the "belief that opposite-sex couples are *morally* superior to same-sex couples" and "the belief that a relationship between a man and a woman is inherently better than a relationship between two men or two women". On what could such a "belief" be based? He suggested either "animus toward gays and lesbians", which, of course, is inadmissible, or "moral disapproval of homosexuality", which very well might be admissible, depending on its relationship to the common good.[68]

More importantly, Judge Walker, like the *Lawrence* ruling, dismissed morality altogether as an insufficient basis for legislation. This was in sync with his purported libertarian beliefs. He concluded that "Proposition 8 finds support only in such [moral] disapproval"[69] and is therefore unconstitutional. Law is by its Nature moral, however, as it stakes its claim to make something better, rather than worse. *Better* and *worse* are relative terms ultimately measured against what Aristotle called "the good", the end toward which the human soul is ordered. If you do not think in terms of what is good for man, you cannot persuade others about what society's political order ought to be or how man's behavior should be legitimately regulated. Without morality, as mentioned earlier, law is reduced to the rule of the stronger.

While dismissing the morality of his opponents as inadmissible, Judge Walker went on to legislate his own stealth morality. He averred, in effect, that it is wrong—in other words, *immoral*—to deny homosexuals and lesbians a right to marry, because this is a violation of the principle of equality. Now, equality is a *moral* principle. Therefore, Judge Walker completely contradicted himself in asserting that morality is an insufficient basis for the law, when morality is exactly what he used to justify his decision in changing the law.

On the other hand, Judge Walker never addressed what might be immoral in the acts of homosexuals that leads others to the conclusion that heterosexual marriage is "morally superior" to same-sex marriage. He put it

[68] Ibid.
[69] Perry v. Schwarzenegger, 704 F. Supp. 2d 921.

all down to changing attitudes. He called the exclusion of same-sex couples from marriage "an artifact of a time when the genders were seen as having distinct roles in society and marriage".[70] Being a good historicist, he stated, "That time has passed." In fact, he insisted that same-sex partners can do anything in marriage (except consummate it?) as well as heterosexual couples, including child rearing.

As a parent, I wonder about this. When my children were younger, they used to think that they would disappear if my wife and I removed our wedding rings. We never told them that, yet they intuitively understood that their very existence depended upon the love between my wife and me. They felt in their bones that they were incarnations of this love, and they therefore concluded that if it were broken, they would disappear. To this day, immediate excitement is generated in our home if my wife and I start hugging and kissing in front of them. The children spontaneously celebrate as if they sense in our affection the reaffirmation of their existence. They move toward us for a group hug as if they wish to share in the love of which they know they are the product.

For all of Judge Walker's fulminations about the absolute equivalency of heterosexual and homosexual parenting, the children raised by two males or two females would never have that instinctive sense about the beginnings of their existence in the love of their parents—for the obvious reason that they could not originate in the relationship between two males or two females. If you are supposed to be the incarnation of the love between two people, but at least one of those people is missing, of what then are you the product? Can that incarnational love be replaced, or are your origins compromised? Here is the bitter reflection of one bisexual man who was raised by lesbians. Robert Oscar Lopez said, "It's disturbingly classist and elitist for gay men to think they can love their children unreservedly after treating their surrogate mother like an incubator, or for lesbians to think they can love their children unconditionally after treating their sperm-donor father like a tube of toothpaste."[71] Unconditional love, morally at least, was supposed to be there between the spouses as a condition for the creation of a new person. If it was not there (and it cannot be if one spouse is deliberately missing), how can the child be its incarnation? Is the child the result of one person and a petri dish?

[70] Ibid.
[71] Lopez, "What Do the Children Say?".

This terrible dilemma will leave these children with the lifelong quest for their real origins or will leave them suffering from their being unable to discover them and wondering why at least one of their real parents did not want them. Even the laudable love of adoptive parents cannot overcome this profound instinctual problem. (The subject will be dealt with more extensively in the chapter on same-sex parenting.)

Another of Judge Walker's extraordinary rationalizations is that "the evidence shows conclusively that moral and religious views form the *only* basis for a belief that same-sex couples are different from opposite-sex couples" (emphasis added). This is a startling claim. Is this true of a biologist? Can he tell the difference? Or a proctologist? How about a gynecologist? Might they not notice some slight difference between the two? To say that the *only* relationship that is procreative is the same as one that never is, or ever can be, is a leap into the void.

Judge Walker's decision was not only irrational; it was a denial of reality. Socrates said that the worst thing a person could do was to lie in his soul about *what is*. This is such a lie. It denies *what is* between a man and a woman in marriage. As bad as this is for the poor souls who have organized their lives around it, it is even worse for the political order that publicly adopts it for its own—since it is marriage properly understood that is essential for civilization's survival. Publicly enforced lies about *what is* are evil.

Judge Walker's rationalizations were allowed to stand in the *Hollingsworth v. Perry* decision by the US Supreme Court, issued June 26, 2013. Chief Justice John Roberts said that the Proposition 8 sponsors had no standing to defend the California Constitution in federal Court because they were mere "bystanders" under federal precedents. Therefore, a homosexual California federal judge, with the complicity of the California governor and attorney general, was able to disenfranchise California's voters by enforcing the rationalization for his own sexual misbehavior on them as a matter of law. On June 28, the US Ninth Circuit Court of Appeals hastily lifted the stay that had been in place preventing "gay" marriages until the Supreme Court decision. Apparently the judges acted quickly in order to allow the "marriages" to begin in time for Gay Pride weekend.[72]

---

[72] Dan Levine, "Gay Marriages Resume in California after Five-Year Hiatus", *Reuters*, June 29, 2013, http://www.reuters.com/article/2013/06/29/us-usa-court-gaymarriage-california -idUSBRE95R15N20130629?feedType=RSS&feedName=domesticNews&rpc=76.

Windsor Madness

On June 26, 2013, in the *United States v. Windsor* case, Justice Anthony Kennedy delivered the opinion of the court that the federal Defense of Marriage Act (DOMA), which defined marriage as between a man and a woman, was unconstitutional. Within hours, the decision, which affects more than one thousand federal statutes and a whole realm of federal regulations, began ricocheting through the federal government. "The Department of Defense welcomes the Supreme Court's decision today on the Defense of Marriage Act", said an eager Secretary of Defense Hagel. "The department will immediately begin the process of implementing the Supreme Court's decision in consultation with the Department of Justice and other executive branch agencies. The Department of Defense intends to make the same benefits available to all military spouses—regardless of sexual orientation—as soon as possible. That is now the law and it is the right thing to do." "Right" as in the "moral" thing to do? Let us consider.

In the history of the United States, only heterosexual married couples have ever received federal marriage benefits. In 1996, confirming what had always been the practice, Congress passed DOMA to provide a formal definition of *marriage* and *spouse* for the purposes of all acts of Congress and any federal regulations. How did this become a problem?

In 2009 Edith Windsor, who had "married" her lesbian partner in Ontario, Canada, in 2007, sought to claim the federal estate tax exemption for surviving spouses when her partner died. In compliance with DOMA, the Internal Revenue Service denied the exemption for the $363,053 that she was required to pay. Windsor, a New York resident, sued, contending that the principles of equal protection incorporated in the Fifth Amendment were violated since her marriage was recognized by the state of New York. The federal district court found in her favor, as did the Second Circuit Court. The House of Representatives was allowed to intervene in the case to defend the constitutionality of DOMA when the Obama administration withdrew its defense of the law. Thus, the case arrived at the Supreme Court in the spring of 2013.

The *Windsor* decision, delivered on the tenth anniversary of the *Lawrence v. Texas* ruling, was every bit as bad as one would expect from its predecessors. It simply followed their logic. In fact, it was so predictable as to make specious Justice Kennedy's preceding claim in *Lawrence* that that decision "does not involve whether the government must give formal recognition to any relationship that homosexual persons seek to enter". Of course, it did. In retrospect, his remark sounds almost hilariously naive or disingenuous. In fact, in certain aspects, the *Windsor* case reads as if Justice Kennedy is having a conversation with himself over the span of a decade. Finally, ten years after *Lawrence*, he closes the loop. He even quotes himself: "Private, consensual sexual intimacy between two adult persons of the same sex may not be punished by the State, and it can form 'but one element in a personal bond that is more enduring.' "

That's the setup: then Justice Kennedy knocks it down: "By its recognition of the validity of same-sex marriages performed in other jurisdictions and then by authorizing same-sex unions and same-sex marriages, New York sought to give further protection and dignity to that bond. For same-sex couples who wished to be married, the State acted to give their lawful conduct a lawful status. This status is a far-reaching legal acknowledgment of the intimate relationship between two people, a relationship deemed by the State worthy of dignity in the community equal with all other marriages."[73]

That bridge from "lawful conduct" to "lawful status", conferring equal dignity upon same-sex marriage, had been there to cross ever since Justice Kennedy lifted the starting gate in *Lawrence*. Once he and his confreres had found a constitutional right to sodomy, there was almost no way to stop enshrining the act as the basis for marriage. All the preceding judicial groundwork that we have reviewed is brought to fruition here, though it leaves one step yet remaining—to declare unconstitutional all remaining state laws that restrict marriage to a man and a woman.

In his dissent, Justice Antonin Scalia predicted that this will be the next shoe to drop, just as he predicted this decision in his *Lawrence* dissent. In fact, he brilliantly illustrated how this will happen by taking several paragraphs of the *Windsor* decision and simply substituting the words "this state law" for "DOMA". Voilà: there was the case ready made for voiding all state prohibitions of same-sex marriage. Justice Scalia also stated that "by formally declaring anyone opposed to same-sex marriage an enemy of human decency, the majority arms well every challenger to state law restricting marriage to its traditional definition. Henceforth those challengers will lead with this Court's declaration that there is 'no legitimate purpose' served by such a law, and will claim that the traditional definition has 'the purpose and effect to disparage and to injure' the 'personhood

---

[73] Windsor, 417 F.2d 1131 (4th Cir. 1969).

and dignity' of same sex couples."[74] And how will the court deal with the dilemma this decision has created when a same-sex couple from the state which allows such a marriage moves to a state that does not. Does the couple retain their federal benefits?

In *Windsor*, we see nearly complete the results of the denial of marriage as a fundamental institution natural to man, and the redefinition of it as an artificial construction, à la Jean-Jacques Rousseau, that can be remolded to his will and whim. "The federal statute is invalid", Kennedy wrote, "for no legitimate purpose overcomes the purpose and effect to disparage and to injure those whom the state, by its marriage laws, sought to protect in personhood and dignity."[75] If marriage is an artificial fabrication, Justice Kennedy is right. The state can redefine the convention of marriage and assign it to whom it will, and no one can gainsay it. In fact, to deny marriage to anyone would seem to be arbitrary.

Yet this is not what the Supreme Court said in the past. Recall that in 1885 the *Murphy v. Ramsey* ruling declared that "certainly no legislation can be supposed more wholesome and necessary in the founding of a free, self-governing commonwealth, fit to take rank as one of the coordinate states of the Union, than that which seeks to establish it on the basis of the idea of the family, as consisting in and springing from the union for life of one man and one woman in the holy estate of matrimony; the sure foundation of all that is stable and noble in our civilization; the best guarantee of that reverent morality which is the source of all beneficent progress in social and political improvement."[76] This seems a rather eloquent enunciation of a "legitimate purpose" in the definition of marriage as between a man and a woman, one that Aristotle would easily recognize. How could it not have occurred to Justice Kennedy, who seemed completely unaware of it—to the point that he dismisses its possible existence as a legitimate purpose?

Of all the misconceived nonsense in the *Windsor* ruling, perhaps the most egregious was Justice Kennedy's insinuation that "the children made me do it". Why was DOMA a problem for children? Justice Kennedy said that by denying same-sex couples legitimacy, DOMA "humiliates tens of thousands of children now being raised by same-sex couples". The act "makes it even more difficult for the children to understand the integrity and closeness of their own family and its concord with other families in their community

[74] Ibid.
[75] Ibid.
[76] Murphy, 114 U.S. 15, 45 (1885).

and in their daily lives". Thus, Justice Kennedy portrayed himself as riding to the children's rescue.

This strategy is reminiscent of President Obama's misuse of the military to justify same-sex marriage. First, as we mentioned before, he forced the repeal of Don't Ask, Don't Tell on the reluctant military and then used that very same military as the excuse for endorsing homosexual marriage, as if it were the military asking for it. Justice Kennedy's similar strategy goes like this: first, allow same-sex couples to adopt children; then do not blame the humiliation of the children on the situation into which they have been placed, through no fault of their own, but on the people who objected to it in the first place. Do not fault those who created the problem through the fabrication of faux marriage; fault those who warned that the fabrication of faux marriage, along with attendant adoptions, would create this problem. In other words, first exploit children by placing them in this situation, and then exploit them again in order to justify it.

Because they are broken by definition, same-sex "families" with children cannot have the integrity of which Justice Kennedy spoke. As mentioned earlier, such "families" are made to be broken, or rather broken to be made, *by design*. A parent must be removed to make them possible. This makes complete nonsense of Justice Kennedy's bizarre remark about how "difficult [it is] for the children to understand the integrity and closeness of their own family" if the same-sex "family" is not accorded full legitimacy. It is difficult for the children to understand, not because of any animus or lack of respect from others, but because that "integrity and closeness" is compromised by the very Nature of same-sex relationships. In light of this, who is really responsible for any lack of "concord with other families in their community" that same-sex families may experience? Justice Kennedy would have us believe that the humiliation and injustice that children suffer in same-sex "families" are not inherent to their situation, but exist as the result of America's tardy recognition of same-sex marriage.

Another interesting point is the repeated emphasis in *Windsor* on the authority of state law to define marriage. Indeed, no constitutional scholar would dispute this authority. But does it include the power to define it as *anything*? The *Murphy* ruling did not hold so. In *Reynolds v. United States* (1878), the court also did not consider that it included polygamy because, in part, "polygamy leads to the patriarchal principle ... which, when applied to large communities, fetters the people in stationary despotism, while that principle cannot long exist in connection with monogamy." Apparently, there is a relationship between the sort of marriage you allow and the freedom you exercise. Was Justice Kennedy aware of this connection? Also, did not the prohibition of polygamy have "the purpose and effect to disparage and to injure" those who practiced it?

Justice Kennedy said that DOMA's message to "married" homosexuals and lesbians was "that their marriage is less worthy than the marriages of others" and imposed "a stigma upon all who enter into same-sex marriages".[77] If that was his main objection, when Justice Kennedy is confronted with cases of polygamy or polyandry, as surely he will be if he stays on the court long enough, what criteria has he left in place to object to them?

If he did not get the connection, others immediately did. "We're very happy with it", said Joe Darger, a Utah-based polygamist who has three wives. "I think [the court] has taken a step in correcting some inequality, and that's certainly something that's going to trickle down and impact us.... I think the government needs to now recognize that we have a right to live free as much as anyone else."[78] How could Justice Kennedy object to this? We may soon find out because the "trickle down" is trickling very quickly. On December 13, 2013, in *Brown v. Buhman*, US District Court Judge Clark Waddoups found key parts of Utah's antipolygamy law to be unconstitutional according to the First and Fourteenth Amendments.[79] Therefore, litigant Kody Brown, a Utah resident, can keep his four wives. What did Judge Waddoups find wrong with the 1973 Utah state law that says a "person is guilty of bigamy when, knowing he has a husband or wife or knowing the other person has a husband or wife, the person purports to marry another person or cohabits with another person"? Straight from Justice Kennedy's ruling in *Lawrence v. Texas*, Judge Waddoups found that "consensual sexual privacy is the touchstone of the rational basis review analysis in this case, as in *Lawrence*."

Vindicated, Brown issued a statement after the ruling that could have been written by Justice Kennedy: "While we know that many people do not approve of plural families, it is our family and based on our beliefs. Just as we respect the personal and religious choices of other families, we hope that in time all of our neighbors and fellow citizens will come to respect our

[77] Windsor, 417 F.2d 1131.

[78] McKay Coppins, "Polygamists Celebrate Supreme Court's Marriage Rulings", BuzzFeed Politics, June 26, 2013, http://www.buzzfeed.com/mckaycoppins/polygamists-celebrate-supreme-courts-marriage-rulings.

[79] *Brown v. Buhman*, 2:11-CV-652.

own choices as part of this wonderful country of different faiths and beliefs." Indeed, as Justice Kennedy asked in the *Windsor* case in respect to same-sex marriages, is Brown's marriage any "less worthy than the marriages of others"? Justice Kennedy may still not realize the full implications of his *Lawrence* decision, but Judge Waddoups and Mr. Brown do.

What DOMA did was refuse to subsidize the redefinition of marriage in those states that chose to redefine it by not extending federal benefits to same-sex couples. This, of course, was completely within the legitimate power of Congress to do and did not in any way constitutionally impinge upon the power of the states. The *Windsor* decision proposes the novel notion that definitions in state law preempt definitions in federal law that concern federal law. Since when?

The philosophical and moral nub of the matter, however, was reached with Justice Kennedy's statement that "what the State of New York treats as alike the federal law deems unlike by a law designed to injure the same class the State seeks to protect." In other words, are heterosexual marriages like or unlike same-sex "marriages"? Are sodomitical "marriages", as *Windsor* asserts, "equal with all other marriages"? And, therefore, was the problem with DOMA that it strove to take what was equal and "make them unequal", and that its "principal purpose is to impose inequality"? Was DOMA imposing inequality or simply recognizing it? Is sodomy really the same as conjugal coition? Obviously, the *Windsor* ruling rests upon the astonishing proposition that marriage, as it has been understood throughout recorded history, is the same as a sodomitical relationship, which was unheard of until the Netherlands introduced the idea in 2000. Is it really irrelevant to the state of marriage "that men are in potentiality to be fathers, and women in potentiality to be mothers"?[80] The *Windsor* teaching is that it is. And this teaching measures the extraordinary distance from reality that it has achieved.

To claim that homosexual marriage is equivalent to the family, the sine qua non of the enduring existence of any political order, is to deny the foundations of society. To claim that a type of behavior on which the polis is founded is equivalent to a type of behavior inimical to a polity's foundation is to deny the principle of noncontradiction.

It has been clear, however, since at least Aristotle that the interest of the state in marriage is in its essential role for the propagation of society.

---

[80] Budziszewski, *On the Meaning of Sex*, 97.

Homosexual "marriages" play no such part, as they are neither unitive nor procreative; so what would be the interest of the state in recognizing them? Why is homosexual marriage morally or politically worthy of institutional protection? The price for providing it is the evacuation of the unitive and procreative meaning of marriage, and its replacement with "pretend" marriage. So as not to hurt the feelings of homosexuals, let them pretend they are married. In fact, let's pretend with them. Even more, let's make everyone pretend together by forcing the federal government to extend full marital benefits to them. Then the illusion will be complete, and no one will be hurt, right?

Not quite. This is a betrayal of the nuptial meaning of the body and a denial of reality. Sodomy is an act opposed to the good of marriage. How then can it be its foundation? Something cannot be its opposite. But the Supreme Court said that it can and that the federal government and we as taxpayers must agree. "Thinking against nature", wrote Irenaeus in *Against Heresies* (A.D. 180), "you will become foolish. And if you persist you will fall into insanity."

Part 2

Marching through the Institutions

Having seen its inexorable progress through the courts, we will now examine how the rationalization for homosexual misbehavior has been advanced
through other key institutions of learning and society until they have been
overtaken by it. No political or social institution can be allowed to remain
outside of it; otherwise the rationalization will be vulnerable.

7

Sodomy and Science

There are two fundamentally different conceptions of science—one that is scientific and one that is not. In the first, science properly deals with reality, mostly in its physical manifestations. It tries to understand the things that *are*—what they are, how they work and why, in term of efficient causes. Science is not metaphysics, but, in order to work, it must assume that things have ends. Otherwise, what would be the point of investigating them, and how would one go about doing it? It is not science that gives to things their ends; those exist already as part of themselves. Science works with the already existing ends in Nature to help bring them about, to fulfill them. Science is not so much the mastery of Nature as an alliance with it. To succeed, it must work with Nature, not against it. This is particularly true in practical sciences. You cannot heal people if you do not know what health is. As Dr. Leon Kass said, "The doctor is the cooperative ally of nature, not its master."

The other notion of science—the unscientific one—is an endeavor not so much to understand what exists and how to bring it to fruition, but to gain power over and fundamentally transform it. Man becomes the ultimate master through the exercise of his will by the instrument of science; he makes all things new according to his desires. Man's will ignores the ends of things and assigns to them his purposes, and they have purposes only insofar as he assigns them. They are nothing in themselves. Nor is man something in himself but only what he makes himself to be. This is science as ideology, as the construction of a false reality. Its spirit was reflected in this remark from an article in the *New England Journal of Medicine* (July 2003) regarding the prospects of embryonic stem cell research: "The Promethean prospect of eternal regeneration awaits us."

Psychiatry

Within the genuine notion of science, the endeavor of psychiatry is to understand how the psyche works when it is working rightly and then to help the
individual psyche to conform to its proper function. This, of course, would
have to include knowledge of what the proper sexual function is, and why.

The purpose of addressing the subject of homosexuality and psychiatry
is not to arrive upon a definitive understanding of the subject in this field,
because no such understanding has been conclusively reached. It is, rather,
to look at the dramatic changes that have taken place in the attitudes toward
the subject of homosexuality and the reasons for them. One can then judge
whether these changes are the result of genuine scientific endeavor or of
ideological demands.

Psychiatry purports to be and is recognized by law as a branch of medicine—that is, as a source of objective truth. Over the past forty years, it has
been used to justify and even to promote homosexual behavior. As will be
seen, this change from the diagnosis of a disorder to a symptom of health had
nothing to do with science in the genuine sense. It has been the result not
of any discovery, but rather of purely political processes—indeed, of power
plays in meeting halls, restaurants, and bedrooms. The two sets of judgments
stand on very different levels of science—one genuine and one not.

All of this becomes evident in the story of how these judgments changed.
This is especially important because the authority of psychiatry is being used
in legal cases to establish the normality of homosexual behavior and to make
the case for same-sex marriage and adoption.

Until 1973 homosexuality was defined as a mental illness in the *Diagnostic and Statistical Manual* (DSM) of the American Psychiatric Association,
the authoritative classification of mental disorders. In the first edition of
the DSM in 1953, homosexuality was listed as a "sociopathic personality
disturbance". The DSM-II, published in 1968, dropped the "sociopathic"
designation but still listed homosexuality as a "sexual deviation". DSM-II,
section 302, said, in part: "This category is for individuals whose sexual
interests are directed primarily towards objects other than people of the opposite sex, toward sexual acts ... performed under bizarre circumstances....
Even though many find their practices distasteful, they remain unable to
substitute normal sexual behavior for them."

These psychiatric classifications created an enormous obstacle for the na-
scent "gay rights" movement. Homosexual activist Franklin Kameny, the
man whom President Obama singled out for special praise at a 2009 White

House meeting, vigorously campaigned against the DSM classification. He said, "I feel that the entire homophile movement ... is going to stand or fall upon the question of whether or not homosexuality is a sickness, and upon our taking a firm stand on it."[1] Lesbian activist Barbara Gittings remarked that "it's difficult to explain to anyone who didn't live through that time how much homosexuality was under the thumb of psychiatry. The sickness label was an albatross around the neck of our early gay rights groups—it infected all our work on other issues."[2] As she said elsewhere, "The sickness issue was paramount."[3] Indeed, it would be hard to promote a mental illness or pathology as a human right. Therefore, it was absolutely necessary to remove the "thumb of psychiatry" in order to liberate homosexuality and give it a status as psychologically healthy as heterosexuality. How could this be done? By eliminating its classification as a mental illness from the DSM.

One would suppose that this would first require the scientific examination of evidence. Only afterward could a conclusion be drawn on whether homosexuality is a psychological problem. This is not what happened, however. Demanding change, homosexual militants began disrupting meetings of the American Psychiatric Association (APA). The following was reported by *Psychiatric News*, a publication of the APA:

> Melvin Sabshin, M.D., a member of the APA Board of Trustees in the early 1970s and chair of the Scientific Program Committee at that time, described how the alienation gay psychiatrists felt from their APA colleagues led in 1970 to the start of a concerted push for APA to include them in decision making and address their concerns and those of gay patients. If there was an official kickoff for APA's newly energized gay psychiatrists, it was the 1970 annual meeting in San Francisco, Sabshin suggested, where Gay Liberation Front activists along with political protesters in support of other social and political causes disrupted the meeting. "It was guerilla theater" at that meeting and the one held in Washington, D.C., the next year, he said.[4]

---

[1] Kay Tobin and Randy Wicker, *The Gay Crusaders* (New York: Arno Press, 1972), 98, cited in Ryan Sorba, "Homosexuality and Mental Health", Ryan Sorba's Blog, January 12, 2012, http://ryansorba.blogspot.com/.

[2] Cited in Brown, *A Queer Thing Happened to America*, 457.

[3] Eric Marcus, *Making History: The Struggle for Gay and Lesbian Equal Rights, 1945–1990: An Oral History* (New York: HarperCollins, 1992), 221; cited by Ryan Sorba, *Ryan Sorba's Blog*, January 12, 2012.

[4] "Panelists Recount Events Leading to Deleting Homosexuality as a Psychiatric Disorder from DSM", *Psychiatric News*, accessed July 31, 2013, http://www.psychiatricnews.org/pnews/98-07-17/dsm.html.

In *The Gay Militants*, Donn Teal gave this report on the same San Francisco meeting:

On May 14, 1970, psychiatrists became the hunted. An invasion by the coalition of "gay" and woman's liberationists interrupted the national convention of the American Psychiatric Association in San Francisco to protest the reading of a paper by an Australian psychiatrist on the subject of "aversion therapy," a system of treatment which attempts to change gay orientation by keying unpleasant sensations (such as electric shocks) to homosexual stimuli. By the time the meeting was over, the feminists and their gay cohorts were in charge ... and the doctors were heckling from the audience.[5]

One of the homosexuals who disrupted the San Francisco meeting, Garry Allender, later told the ABC radio program *All in the Mind*: "We were not polite, we were not quiet, we were not asking for favours, we were just trying to de-legitimise their authority and we felt they were oppressing us, and it was finally a chance to talk back to them."[6]

At the 1971 Washington meeting to which Sabshin referred, Kameny led a group of thirty protesters into the conference, shouting, "We are here to denounce your authority to call us sick or mentally disordered. For us, as homosexuals, your profession is the enemy incarnate. We demand that psychiatrists treat us as human beings, not as patients to be cured!"[7] Then Kameny sent a letter to the *Psychiatric News* in which he warned, "Our presence there was only the beginning of an increasingly intensive campaign by homosexuals to change the approach of psychiatry toward homosexuality or, failing that, to discredit psychiatry."[8]

This demand was obviously not inspired by scientific inquiry. It was the product of the homosexual activists' need to remove the "sickness label" so that the rationalization of their behavior could proceed unimpeded by this "albatross around the neck of our early gay rights groups", as Barbara Gittings expressed it.

If the measures employed sound like storm trooper tactics, there is a reason. They were inspired by them. In 1991, Eric Pollard, former member

[5] Donn Teal, *The Gay Militants* (New York: Stein and Day, 1971), 272–73.

[6] "81 Words: The Inside Story of Psychiatry and Homosexuality (Part 1 of 2)", on the Australian Broadcasting Corporation's Radio National program *All in the Mind*, August 4, 2007, http://www.abc.net.au/radionational/programs/allinthemind/81-words-the-inside-story-of-psychiatry-and/3246684#transcript.

[7] "The Militant Homosexual", *Newsweek*, August 23, 1971, 47.

[8] Tobin and Wicker, *The Gay Crusaders*, 130–31.

and cofounder of the militant homosexual organization ACT-UP/DC, admitted that, "I have helped to create a truly fascist organization. We conspired to bring into existence an activist group that ... could effectively exploit the media for its own ends, and that would work covertly and break the law with impunity.... [W]e subscribed to consciously subversive modes, drawn largely from the voluminous *Mein Kampf*, which some of us studied as a working model. As ACT-UP/DC grew, we struck intently and surgically into whatever institutions we believed to stand in our way".[9]

But why would members of the APA give in to this pressure, particularly since there was no scientific basis to justify the change in classification? One reason is that some APA members were heavily invested in the rationalization for reasons in their personal lives. One of the most striking of these was revealed in an *All in the Mind* radio interview on August 4, 2007, with journalist Alix Spiegel, granddaughter of Dr. John P. Spiegel, who was president-elect of the American Psychiatric Association in 1973. She said:

> To hear my family tell it, it was my grandfather alone who banished those 81 words from the DSM. When I was young the family legend was that my grandfather, president of the American Psychiatric Association, single handedly changed the DSM because he was a big-hearted visionary, a man unfettered by prejudice who worked on behalf of the downtrodden. This story was wrong on two counts (a) my grandfather was not president of the American Psychiatric Association in 1973, he was president elect; (b) he didn't single handedly change anything. But never mind because this version of events was discarded anyway. Discarded after the family went on vacation to the Bahamas to celebrate my grandfather's 70th birthday. I remember it well. I also remember my grandfather stepping out from his beach front bungalow on that first day followed by a small well-built man, a man that later during dinner my grandfather introduced to a shocked family as his lover, David. David was the first of a long line of very young men that my grandfather took up with after my grandmother's death. It turned out that my grandfather had had gay lovers throughout his life, had even told his wife-to-be that he was homosexual, two weeks before their wedding. And so in 1981 the story that my family told about the definition in the DSM changed dramatically. My grandfather was no

---

[9] Eric Pollard, "Time to Give Up Fascist Tactics", Letters to the Editor, *Washington Blade*, January 31, 1992.

longer seen as a purely enlightened visionary but as a closeted homosexual with a very particular agenda.[10]

As Aristotle said, "Men start revolutionary changes for reasons connected
with their private lives." Dr. Spiegel needed to rationalize his own sexual
misbehavior, and he used his profession to do it. Nor was Dr. Spiegel alone.
In his book *Homosexuality and the Politics of Truth,* Dr. Jeffrey Satinover
writes about attending a conference in England in 1994 and meeting a man
who told him something he had told no one else: "He had been in the gay
life for years but had left the lifestyle. He recounted how after the 1973 APA
decision he and his lover, along with a certain very highly placed officer of
the APA Board of Trustees and his lover, all sat around the officer's apart-
ment celebrating their victory. For among the gay activists placed high in
the APA who maneuvered to ensure a victory was this man—suborning
from the top what was presented to both the membership and the public as
a disinterested search for truth."[11]

According to Alix Spiegel, a small group of psychiatrists, "the young
turks", began to gather in Dr. Spiegel's Cambridge, Massachusetts, home:

> The young turks were all psychiatrists, all members of the APA and all
> liberal-minded easterners who had decided to reform the American Psy-
> chiatric Association from the inside. Specifically they had decided to re-
> place all the grey haired conservatives who ran the organisation with a
> new breed of psychiatrist; more sensitive to the social issues of the day
> with liberal opinions on Kent State, Vietnam, feminism. They figured
> that once they got this new breed into office they could fundamentally
> transform American psychiatry. And one of the things this group was keen
> to transform was American psychiatry's approach to homosexuality.[12]

This was the "inside" group working for change, apparently sometimes
in coordination with the "outside" group of homosexual agitators. According to Garry Allender, one of the homosexual activists who infiltrated the
1970 APA convention: "As I recall there were evidently closeted gay and
lesbian people who were inside the APA who wanted something to happen
and I think they just passed along information to us—and somebody got us
press passes, I guess, so that we could get through the front door."[13]

---

[10] "81 Words: The Inside Story of Psychiatry and Homosexuality (Part 1 of 2)".
[11] Satinover, *Homosexuality and the Politics of Truth,* 35.
[12] "81 Words: The Inside Story of Psychiatry and Homosexuality (Part 1 of 2)".
[13] Ibid.

Alix Spiegel's radio program "81 Words: The Inside Story of Psychiatry and Homosexuality" provides a fascinating record of what finally turned the tables on the DSM definition. (First, for background, it is necessary to know that open homosexuals were not allowed to practice psychiatry at the time, so they remained "in the closet". They began associating informally at APA conventions, however, calling themselves the GayPA. Dr. Robert Spitzer was a member of the APA's committee on nomenclature, which oversaw the definitions in the DSM. He held the then-orthodox psychiatric view of homosexuality as a disorder. He met Ronald Gold, a member of the Gay Activists Alliance, when Gold disrupted a behavioral therapy conference. Dr. Spitzer decided to listen to his grievances and later sponsored Gold's appearance at an APA convention. This led to a decisive meeting outside of the APA Honolulu meeting in 1973.)

This is the account from the transcript of the radio program:

ALIX SPIEGEL: According to Ronald Gold, [what] finally convinced Robert Spitzer to sit down and redraft the 81 words in the *Diagnostic and Statistics Manual* ... took place in a bar later that night in one of those campy Hawaiian lounges with bamboo furniture, grass skirted waitresses and a three page menu of exotically coloured drinks. This is where the GayPA had decided to hold its annual party, naturally after his speech at the conference Ron Gold got an invitation.

RONALD GOLD: I got invited to it but I was told, you know, keep it all very quiet and don't say anything and just come to this bar and we'll all be there. So I decided to invite Spitzer to come to this because he had told me essentially that he didn't know any gay psychiatrists and wasn't quite sure there were any. And I said, you just come along.

ALIX SPIEGEL: Ron warned Spitzer not to say anything, he was instructed not to speak, or stare, or indicate in any way that he was anything other than a closeted gay man.

RONALD GOLD: But once he got there and saw that the head of the Transaction Analysis Association and the guy who handed out all the training money in the United States, and the heads of various prestigious psychiatry departments at various universities were all there, he couldn't believe it. And he started asking all these dimwitted questions.

ALIX SPIEGEL: At the time members of the GayPA were still completely hidden. They hadn't been active in the struggle to change the DSM; they were too fearful of losing their jobs to identify themselves publicly. So when Robert Spitzer, an obviously straight man in a position of power at the APA, appeared at the bar the men of the GayPA were completely unnerved.

RONALD GOLD: So the grand dragon of the GayPA, whoever he was I can't remember now, came up to me and said, "Get rid of him, get him out of here! You've got to get rid of him." And I said, "I'm doing nothing of a kind, he's here to help us and you are not doing anything."

ALIX SPIEGEL: And that's when it happened. There in front of Robert Spitzer and the grand dragon of the GayPA. There in the midst of neon coloured drinks and grass skirted waitresses a young man in full army uniform walked into the bar. He looked at Robert Spitzer, he looked at Ronald Gold, he looked at the grand dragon of the GayPA. And then the young man in uniform burst into tears. He threw himself into Ron's arms and remained there, sobbing.

RONALD GOLD: Well I had no idea who he was. It turned out he was a psychiatrist, an army psychiatrist based in Hawaii who was so moved by my speech, he told me, that he decided he had to go to a gay bar for the first time in his life. And somehow or other he got directed to this particular bar and saw me and all the gay psychiatrists and it was too much for him, he just cracked up. And it was a very moving event, I mean this man was awash in tears. And I believe that that was what decided Spitzer, right then and there, let's go. Because it was right after that that he said, "Let's go write the resolution." And so we went back to Spitzer's hotel room and wrote the resolution.

ALIX SPIEGEL: That night?

RONALD GOLD: That night.[14]

[14] "81 Words: The Inside Story of Psychiatry and Homosexuality (Part 2 of 2)", on the Australian Broadcasting Corporation's Radio National program *All in the Mind*, August 11, 2007, http://www.abc.net.au/radionational/programs/allinthemind/81-words-the-inside-story -of-psychiatry-and/3228820#transcript.

The resolution was presented and passed, although not finally until it was submitted to the entire membership in a referendum. A minority of the membership, although a majority of those responding to the referendum, gave final approval to the resolution. So much for science as the basis for delisting homosexuality as a mental illness. Obviously, this was not the result of scientific advances, nor was the change in the DSM made by those psychologically expert in the subject of homosexuality. It was the result of sheer advocacy. Homosexuals themselves admit as much. Gay activist and author Jeffrey Weeks wrote that "the decision of the American Psychiatric Association to delete homosexuality from its published list of sexual disorders in 1973 was scarcely a cool, scientific decision. It was a response to a political campaign fueled by the belief that its original inclusion as a disorder was a reflection of an oppressive politico-medical definition of homosexuality as a problem."[15] Homosexual activist and neuroscientist Dr. Simon LeVay stated that "gay activism was clearly the force that propelled the APA to declassify homosexuality."[16]

In the book *Making History: The Struggle for Gay and Lesbian Equal Rights: 1945–1990: An Oral History*, lesbian partners Kay Lahusen and Barbara Gittings are equally candid about what occurred:

LAHUSEN: This was always more of a political decision than a medical decision.

GITTINGS: It never was a medical decision—and that's why I think the action came so fast. After all, it was only three years from the time that feminists and gays first zapped the APA at a behavior therapy session to the time that the Board of Trustees voted in 1973 to approve removing homosexuality from the list of mental disorders. It was a political move.[17]

That it was a political move discomfited some members—even very liberal ones—who thought that the standards of science had been traduced.

---

[15] Jeffrey Weeks, *Sexuality and Its Discontents: Meanings, Myths, and Modern Sexualities* (London: Routledge and Kegan Paul, 1988), 213, cited in "Chapter Seven: Stonewall and the American Psychiatric Association", banap.net, February 18, 2013, http://www.banap.net/spip.php?article70.

[16] Simon LeVay, *Queer Science: The Use and Abuse of Research into Homosexuality* (Cambridge, MA: MIT Press, 1996), 224.

[17] Cited in Ryan Sorba, "Homosexuality and Mental Health", *Ryan Sorba's Blog*, January 12, 2012, http://ryansorba.blogspot.com/2012/01/homosexuality-and-mental-health.html.

Two lifelong liberal psychologists, Rogers H. Wright and Nicholas A. Cummings, objected:

> The Diagnostic and Statistical Manual of the American Psychiatric Association yielded suddenly and completely to political pressure when in 1973 it removed homosexuality as a treatable aberrant condition. A political firestorm had been created by gay activists within psychiatry, with intense opposition to normalizing homosexuality coming from a few outspoken psychiatrists who were demonized and even threatened, rather than scientifically refuted. Psychiatry's House of Delegates sidestepped the conflict by putting the matter to a vote of the membership, marking the first time in the history of healthcare that a diagnosis or lack of diagnosis was decided by popular vote rather than scientific evidence.[18]

In *Homosexuality and American Psychiatry*, Professor Ronald Bayer, who was sympathetic to the homosexual cause, also gave an account and a critique of the change in classification:

> The entire process, from the first confrontation organized by gay demonstrators at psychiatric conventions to the referendum demanded by Orthodox psychiatrists, seemed to violate the most basic expectations about how questions of science should be resolved. Instead of being engaged in a sober consideration of data, psychiatrists were swept up in a political controversy.... The result was not a conclusion based on an approximation of the scientific truth as dictated by reason, but was instead an action demanded by the ideological temper of the times.[19]

Here is what advocacy succeeded in doing to the DSM-III classification of homosexuality, which, as a result of the change, stated:

> This category is for individuals whose sexual interests are directed primarily toward people of the same sex and who are either disturbed by, in conflict with, or wish to change their sexual orientation. This diagnostic category is distinguished from homosexuality, which by itself does not constitute a psychiatric disorder. Homosexuality *per se* is one form of sexual behavior and, like other forms of sexual behavior which are not by themselves psychiatric disorders, is not listed in this nomenclature of mental disorders.

[18] Rogers H. Wright and Nicolas A. Cummings, eds., *Destructive Trends in Mental Health: The Well-Intentioned Path to Harm* (New York: Routledge, 2005), 9.

[19] Ronald Bayer, *Homosexuality and American Psychiatry* (Princeton, NJ: Princeton University Press, 1987), 3–4.

Homosexuals who were unhappy with being homosexual, however, could still be diagnosed with "ego-dystonic homosexuality".

But that was not all. Further changes were afoot. In the *Journal of Psychohistory* (Winter 1992), Dr. Charles W. Socarides, then the clinical professor of psychiatry at Albert Einstein College of Medicine/Montefiore Medical Center, New York, said, "This diagnostic category underwent several metamorphoses in several editions of the DSM III, including establishing a separate category of 'ego-dystonic homosexuality' (for those who were 'unhappy' that they were homosexual) to the ultimate elimination of the word 'homosexual' from the DSM III Revised 1987 as a scientific category."[20]

As Alix Spiegel reported, "Today there's no entry in the DSM on homosexuality, no entry at all. In 1987 the 237 words that Robert Spitzer wrote about ego-dystonic homosexuality were quietly removed."[21] The victory was complete. The disorder had disappeared. No treatment required or welcome.

In 1975 the American Psychological Association followed suit and on its website now declares that "being gay is just as healthy as being straight."[22] The 2009 American Psychological Association Task Force on Appropriate Therapeutic Responses to Sexual Orientation proclaimed as "scientific fact" that "same-sex sexual attractions, behavior, and orientations per se are normal and positive variance of human sexuality."[23] The problem is that there is no credible science to substantiate this assertion.

To the American Psychiatric Association changes, Dr. Socarides, a member of the organization, gave this scathing rebuke:

> By declaring a condition a "non-condition," a group of practitioners had removed it from our list of serious psychosexual disorders. The action was all the more remarkable when one considers that it involved the out-of-hand and peremptory disregard and dismissal not only of hundreds of psychiatric and psychoanalytic research papers and reports but also of a number of other serious studies by groups of psychiatrists, psychologists,

---

[20] Charles W. Socarides, "Sexual Politics and Scientific Logic: The Issue of Homosexuality", *The Journal of Psychohistory* (Winter 1992), http://www.kidhistory.org/homopolo.html.

[21] "81 Words: The Inside Story of Psychiatry and Homosexuality (Part 1 of 2)".

[22] American Psychological Association, "Being Gay Is Just as Healthy as Being Straight", American Psychological Association website, May 28, 2003, http://www.apa.org/research /action/gay.aspx.

[23] American Psychological Association, *Report of the APA Task Force on Appropriate Therapeutic Responses to Sexual Orientation* (Washington, D.C.: American Psychological Association, 2009), 2, http://www.apa.org/pi/lgbt/resources/therapeutic-response.pdf.

and educators over the past seventy years, for example, the Report of the Committee of Cooperation with Governmental (Federal) Agencies of the Group for the Advancement of Psychiatry (1955); the New York Academy of Medicine Report (1964); the Task Force Report of the New York County District Branch of the APA done in 1970–72 (Socarides, et al., 1973). To the psychoanalyst, this was psychiatric folly. Psychoanalysts comprehend the meaning of a particular act of human behavior by delving into the motivational state from which it issues. Obviously these decision makers had not viewed individuals in this manner.[24]

Socarides continued: "For the next 18 years, the APA decision served as a Trojan horse, opening the gates to widespread psychological and social change in sexual customs and mores. The decision was to be used on numerous occasions for numerous purposes with the goal of normalizing homosexuality and elevating it to an esteemed status."[25]

Perhaps the most devastating indictment was delivered by one of the most prestigious psychiatrists in the profession, Dr. Abram Kardiner, a co-founder of the first psychoanalytic training school in the United States and former professor of psychiatry at Columbia University. He wrote that

> there is an epidemic form of homosexuality, which is more than the usual incidence, which generally occurs in social crises or in declining cultures when license and boundless permissiveness dulls the pain of ceaseless anxiety, universal hostility and divisiveness.... Supporting the claims of the homosexuals and regarding homosexuality as a normal variant of sexual activity is to deny the social significance of homosexuality. To do this is to give support to the divisive elements in the community. Above all it militates against the family and destroys the function of the latter as the last place in our society where affectivity can still be cultivated. Homosexuals cannot make a society, nor keep ours going for very long. Homosexuality operates against the cohesive elements in society in the name of fictitious freedom. It drives the opposite sex into a similar direction. And no society can long endure when either the child is neglected or when the sexes war upon each other.[26]

Dr. Kardiner went on to express his disapproval in a letter to the editors of *Psychiatric News*: "Those who reinforce the disintegrative elements in our society will get no thanks from future generations. The family becomes

---

[24] Socarides, "Sexual Politics and Scientific Logic".
[25] Ibid.
[26] Ibid., 315.

the ultimate victim of homosexuality, a result which any society can tolerate only within certain limits. If the American Psychiatric Association endorses one of the symptoms of social distress as a normal phenomenon it demonstrates to the public its ignorance of social dynamics, of the relation of personal maladaptation to social disharmony, and thereby acquires a responsibility for aggravating the already existing chaos."[27] Dr. Kardiner died in 1981. One can only imagine his reflections on the institutionalization of this maladaptation in same-sex marriage today.

It should be noted that the National Association for Research and Therapy of Homosexuality (NARTH), begun in the wake of the APA delisting decision in 1973, continues to maintain that homosexuality is a dysfunction and can be corrected. The late Dr. Socarides was one of its founders.

Immutability

Other areas of science enlisted to depathologize homosexuality are genetics and biology—insofar as they can lend credence to the assertion that homosexuality is an immutable condition. Many who think that homosexuality is a genetic condition believe that this, in and of itself, justifies homosexual marriage. That is why a great deal has been invested in the argument over whether homosexuality is a genetic trait or a learned behavior. As mentioned earlier, this issue is immaterial to the morality of homosexual acts. As Aristotle said of human actions in his *Ethics*, "It is only when they are voluntary that they have the character of just or unjust" (5.8). There is actually an element of condescension toward homosexuals here, as if they do not actually choose their behavior: the poor fellows can't act otherwise. Their actions are involuntary and therefore beyond morality. Compulsive behavior also means they are incapable of self-rule. To be in the grip of a compulsion means precisely the inability to choose not to engage in the compulsion. To admit to oneself that one is in the grip of such a condition must be particularly onerous. Therefore, the rationalization that one is "born that way" and has no means of resistance becomes all the more attractive the more necessary it becomes.

The same kind of argument, however, as we have suggested, could be made about alcoholism. The City of Hope National Medical Center

---

[27] Cited in Brown, *A Queer Thing Happened to America*, 460–61.

researchers discovered a certain gene in 77 percent of the alcoholic patients they studied. There may be a missing chromosome that predisposes certain people to alcoholism; others seem to acquire alcoholism through their behavior. In either case, drunkenness is no less evil because of an inherent predisposition to it. Likewise, sodomy. Of course, it is very hard to live with such predispositions, and profound sympathy and assistance is due to those who suffer from them. The worst disservice that could be done in either case, however, would be to encourage or participate in the celebration of the afflictions, as in Gay Pride Day. Why is Gay Pride Day any less absurd than an Alcoholic Pride Day would be? Both conditions exist as aberrations, as abnormalities in the light of what is normal by Nature. To substitute an abnormality for normality destroys the distinction between the two and closes off the path to recovery.

Alcoholics, by definition, are alcoholics for life. If they wish to remain sober, they must never drink again. Are homosexuals like this also? Will they forever suffer from (or celebrate) their inclination? There is mixed evidence regarding this. Of those wanting to change, some have been able to; some have not. Except in the very real terms of personal hardship, however, it does not really matter. After all, *everyone* is disposed to some moral disorder or another. The immutability of the condition or of the inclination is irrelevant to the moral character of the acts to which they are predisposed. Of course, some homosexual apologists find the genetic excuse exculpatory. Therefore, they need it for the rationalization of their behavior: If I am this way by Nature, how can I help what I do? The alcoholic could use the same justification for his drunkenness. In neither case does the inclination neuter free will or remove responsibility for actions. To say otherwise robs the human actor of moral dignity.

This issue is also extremely important because homosexual activists wish to establish the immutability of their condition in order to constitute themselves as a "class". Legally, a class can be determined only by accident of birth, by such traits as race or sex. This explains the enormous interest in establishing sexual *orientation* as genetic or biological. Homosexuals want to be designated a "class" so that they can game the legal system for the spoils of discrimination. Therefore, this issue has huge legal and financial consequences.

Nonetheless, it is at least worth stating that the immutability theory cannot be sustained by the supposed existence of a "gay gene". There is no scientific evidence for it, which is not to say there may not be genetic influences on sexual orientation. This is the conclusion of some homosexual scientists, such as Dr. Richard Pillard or neuroscientist Dr. Simon LeVay at the Salk Institute in San Diego, who have gone searching for it or for innate brain differences. Dr. Pillard, who was supposedly the first openly homosexual psychiatrist in the United States, has avidly sought for a genetic cause for homosexuality. In a 2010 Boston University interview, he admitted that "it's really hard to come up with any definite statement about the situation. I think some sort of genetic influence seems very likely, but beyond that, what really can we say? And the answer is: not a lot."[28]

Dr. LeVay conducted a study of hypothalamic structures in men, which supposedly confirmed innate brain differences between homosexuals and heterosexuals, but he warned against misinterpreting his findings in a 1994 interview: "It's important to stress what I didn't find. I did not prove that homosexuality is genetic, or find a genetic cause for being gay. I didn't show that gay men are born that way, the most common mistake people make in interpreting my work. Nor did I locate a gay center in the brain."[29]

Dr. Marc Breedlove, professor of neuroscience at Michigan State University, said, "Have we found a gene, where when a person inherits it, they will for certain be gay? No, we haven't found such a gene", though he stresses there are genetic influences on sexual orientation. Intriguingly, he stated in regard to his own research: "[My] findings give us proof for what we theoretically know to be the case—that sexual experience can alter the structure of the brain, just as genes can alter it. [I]t is possible that differences in sexual behavior cause (rather than are caused by) differences in the brain."[30]

Dr. LeVay also stated that "it is possible to construct a hypothesis whereby both 'gay genes' and a desire to be homosexual are necessary for a person actually to become homosexual." From where might that desire to become homosexual come? Dr. Jeffrey Satinover mused that "the incidence of homosexuality is clearly influenced by mores. Where people endorse and encourage homosexuality, the incidence increases; where they reject it, it decreases. These factors have nothing to do with genetics."[31]

---

[28] Kimberly Cornuelle, "Nature vs. Nurture: The Biology of Sexuality", *BU Today*, November 16, 2010, http://www.bu.edu/today/2010/nature-vs-nurture-the-biology-of-sexuality/.

[29] Cited on Simon LeVay's home page at Golden Map, accessed August 1, 2013, http://en.goldenmap.com/Simon_LeVay.

[30] "Real Scientists Debunk JONAH's Junk Science", video, 2:35, posted by Wayne Besen, September 25, 2012, http://www.truthwinsout.org/opinion/2012/09/29888/.

[31] Satinover, *Homosexuality and the Politics of Truth*, 116.

If there is no science to support it, the immutability theory nonetheless has generated significant political support. We can see the burgeoning significance of the matter in Attorney General Eric Holder's 2011 letter to the US Congress, explaining why the Obama administration would no longer defend the Defense of Marriage Act (which defined marriage as being between one man and one woman) in court. A group can be defined as a "class", explained Mr. Holder, if individuals "exhibit obvious, immutable, or distinguishing characteristics that define them as a discrete group". Therefore, everything hinges upon whether homosexuality is an *unchangeable* characteristic. Mr. Holder announced that "a growing scientific consensus accepts that sexual orientation is a characteristic that is immutable." So great is this consensus that, according to him, "we do not believe [claims to the contrary] can be reconciled with more recent social scientific understandings".[32]

This bestows upon homosexuals the privilege of being a class, just as are blacks, Hispanics, or women. As a class, they can be discriminated against. Has there been such discrimination? Mr. Holder answers that "there is, regrettably, a significant history of purposeful discrimination against gay and lesbian people, by governmental as well as private entities, based on prejudice and stereotypes that continue to have ramifications today." One of those ongoing ramifications was the restriction of marriage to one man and one woman by the Defense of Marriage Act. Thus, he concluded, this law was discriminatory against homosexuals as a class and therefore unconstitutional and indefensible.

But let us try to put these claims in perspective. Let us say that in cannibals, cannibalism is an immutable characteristic. They simply can't stop eating people. Identifiable as cannibals, they could be discriminated against as a class. But this begs the question as to whether discrimination against them would be justified or not. Surely, one would think, it would be warranted because eating other people is wrong. Therefore, the discrimination against them is based not so much on cannibals as people, but on their activity of eating other people. If there were nothing wrong with eating other people, there would be no moral basis for discrimination against cannibals.

Likewise, even if homosexuality is an immutable characteristic, what distinguishes homosexuals is their sexual activity. Therefore, like cannibals,

---

[32] Attorney General Eric Holder, "Letter from the Attorney General to Congress on Litigation Involving the Defense of Marriage Act", February 23, 2011, United States Department of Justice website, http://www.justice.gov/opa/pr/2011/February/11-ag-223.html.

discrimination against them would be based not so much on who they are, as on what they do. The whole question, then, turns upon whether what they do is right or wrong. Mr. Holder's letter clearly assumes that this question has been settled, and in his answer we see the profound ramifications of the *Lawrence v. Texas* case and its vindication of sodomy. Using *Lawrence*, Mr. Holder declares, in an opprobrious tone, that "indeed, until very recently, states have 'demean[ed] the existence' of gays and lesbians 'by making their private sexual conduct a crime' "—meaning, of course, that it was wrong to do so.

Mutability

However, even if one were to grant that sodomy is a morally fine act, the contention that homosexuals are a class is indefensible because sexual orientation is not an immutable characteristic—even if some are unable to change it. There is simply too much clinical and other evidence that proves otherwise. A black man has never become a white man, or a Hispanic an Asian. A woman has never become a man, or a man a woman—without massive surgical and hormonal intervention. There is ample fluidity, however, particularly in younger years, in sexual orientation. Straight men have become homosexuals, and homosexuals have become straight. The mutable cannot be immutable.

In 2003 Dr. Jeffrey Satinover testified before the Massachusetts Senate Judicial Committee on this subject. He said that the National Health and Social Life Survey (NHSLS) study of sexuality

> was completed in 1994 by a large research team from the University of Chicago and funded by almost every large government agency and NGO with an interest in the AIDS epidemic. They studied every aspect of sexuality, but among their findings is the following, which I'm going to quote for you directly: "7.1 [to as much as 9.1] percent of the men [we studied, more than 1,500] had at least one same-gender partner since puberty.... [But] almost 4 percent of the men [we studied] had sex with another male before turning eighteen but not after. These men ... constitute 42 percent of the total number of men who report ever having a same gender experience." Let me put this in context: Roughly ten out of every 100 men have had sex with another man at some time—the origin of the 10 percent gay myth. Most of these will have

identified themselves as gay before turning eighteen and will have acted on it. But by age 18, a full half of them no longer identify themselves as gay and will never again have a male sexual partner. And this is not a population of people selected because they went into therapy; it's just the general population. Furthermore, by age twenty-five, the percentage of gay identified men drops to 2.8 percent. This means that without any intervention whatsoever, three out of four boys who think they're gay at age 16 aren't by 25.[33]

In their article "Homosexuality and the Truth", former homosexuals Sy Rogers and Alan Medinger provide the following quotes from experts who disagree with the contention that homosexuality is immutable:

> Dr. Reuben Fine, Director for the New York Centre for Psychoanalytic Training, in his 1987 book, *Psychoanalytic Theory, Male and Female Homosexuality: Psychological Approaches*: "I have recently had occasion to review the result of psychotherapy with homosexuals, and been surprised by the findings. It is paradoxical that even though politically active homosexual groups deny the possibility of change, all studies from Schrenck-Notzing on have found positive effects, virtually regardless of the kind of treatment used ... a considerable percentage of overt homosexuals became heterosexual ... If the patients were motivated, whatever procedure is adopted, a large percentage will give up their homosexuality. In this connection, public information is of the greatest importance. The misinformation spread by certain circles that 'homosexuality is untreatable by psychotherapy' does incalculable harm to thousands of men and women."

> Dr. Irving Bieber and his colleagues: "The therapeutic results of our study provide reason for an optimistic outlook. Many homosexuals become exclusively heterosexual in psychoanalytic treatment. Although this change may be more easily accomplished by some than others, in our judgment, a heterosexual shift is a possibility for all homosexuals who are strongly motivated to change." Bieber stated seventeen years later: "We have followed some patients for as long as ten years who have remained exclusively heterosexual."

[33] Dr. Jeffrey Satinover, "Testimony before the Massachusetts Senate Committee Studying Gay Marriage", Catholic Education Resource Center, April 28, 2003, http://catholiceducation .org/articles/sexuality/h00092.html.

Dr. Robert Kronemeyer, in his 1980 book, *Overcoming Homosexuality*: "For those homosexuals who are unhappy with their life and find effective therapy, it is 'curable'."

Dr. Edmund Bergler in his book *Homosexuality: Disease or Way of Life?*: "The homosexual's real enemy is ... his ignorance of the possibility that he can be helped."[34]

In his 2003 testimony Dr. Satinover added: "A review of the research over many years demonstrates a consistent 30–52 percent success rate in the treatment of unwanted homosexual attraction. Masters and Johnson reported a 65 percent success rate after a five-year follow-up. Other professionals report success rates ranging from 30 percent to 70 percent."[35]

Stanton L. Jones, provost and professor of psychology at Wheaton College, conducted a more recent study of people seeking change in sexual orientation "through their involvement in the cluster of ministries organized under Exodus International". The span of the study was six to seven years. His reported results are as follows: "Of these 61 subjects, 53 percent were categorized as successful outcomes by the standards of Exodus Ministries. Specifically, 23 percent of the subjects reported success in the form of 'conversion' to heterosexual orientation and functioning, while an additional 30 percent reported stable behavioral chastity with substantive disidentification with homosexual orientation. On the other hand, 20 percent of the subjects reported giving up on the change process and fully embracing gay identity."[36] Dr. Jones said, "I conclude from these data and years of study that homosexual orientation is sometimes mutable."[37]

Extraordinarily, Dr. Robert Spitzer, who was largely responsible for removing homosexuality as a disorder from the DSM in 1973, did his own study of two hundred subjects on whether homosexuality is mutable and concluded that it is: "There is evidence that change in sexual orientation following some form of reparative therapy does occur in some gay men and

[34] Sy Rogers and Alan Medinger, "Homosexuality and the Truth", Exodus Global Alliance, accessed August 1, 2013, http://www.exodusglobalalliance.org/homosexualityandthe truthp37.php.

[35] Dr. Jeffrey Satinover "Testimony before the Massachusetts Senate Committee".

[36] Stanton L. Jones, "Sexual Orientation and Reason: On the Implications of False Beliefs about Homosexuality", Wheaton College, January 2012, accessed August 1, 2013, http://www .wheaton.edu/CACE/CACE-Print-Resources/~/media/Files/Centers-and-Institutes /CACE/articles/Sexual%20Orientation%20and%20Reason%20%201-9-20122.pdf.

[37] Ibid.

lesbians." His 2001 paper stated that "the majority of participants gave reports of change from a predominantly or exclusively homosexual orientation before therapy to a predominantly or exclusively heterosexual orientation in the past year."[38] He admitted, "I approached this quite skeptical, and I've been convinced otherwise."[39] In 2004 he said: "The gay activists have taken the viewpoint that, from a political strategic point of view, they do better if they can convince society at large that once you are homosexual, you can never change, and I can appreciate it that that helps them politically, and I am sympathetic towards their political goals, but I think it's just not true."[40] He had been warned of the dangers he would encounter by even raising this question. "People at the time did say to me, 'Bob, you're messing with your career, don't do it'", Dr. Spitzer said. "But I just didn't feel vulnerable."[41]

Indeed, there was a storm of intense criticism and accusations of betrayal. Dr. Christopher H. Rosik exclaimed, "It is hard to imagine the fall from professional grace that Spitzer took due to this study."[42] One commentator on his paper actually cited the Nuremberg Code of ethics to condemn the study as not only defective but immoral.

Dutch psychologist Dr. Gerard van den Aardweg wrote of Dr. Spitzer's reaction, as a result of all this, when he tried to encourage him to go further in his treatment of homosexuals:

> Sometime after his 2003 article I had a conversation with him on the telephone. I asked him if he would continue his research, or even if he would try to guide a few people with homosexual problems and who sought "alternative" professional help, that is, help and support to change as much as possible from homosexual to heterosexual interests. In his interviews with people who had walked along that path, he certainly had learned a lot, among other things, the great need among many homosexually

---

[38] Benedict Carey, "Psychiatry Giant Sorry for Backing Gay 'Cure'", *New York Times*, May 18, 2012, http://www.nytimes.com/2012/05/19/health/dr-robert-l-spitzer-noted-psychiatrist-apologizes-for-study-on-gay-cure.html?pagewanted=all&_r=1&.

[39] Phillip L. Hamilton, "Activists Know Study Could Change Public Policy", *Lubbock Avalanche-Journal*, May 18, 2001, http://lubbockonline.com/stories/051801/phi_075-2617.shtml.

[40] "Dr. Robert Spitzer—Homosexuals Can Change", YouTube video, 5:45, of 2004 statement by Dr. Robert Spitzer, posted by "exgaypfox", April 8, 2009, http://www.youtube.com/watch?v=wr6T4ka7TxU&list=PLF62A308EBC192AC5&index=1.

[41] Carey, "Psychiatry Giant Sorry for Backing Gay 'Cure'".

[42] Christopher H. Rosik, "Spitzer's 'Retraction': What Does It Really Mean?", NARTH, June 1, 2012, http://narth.com/2012/06/2532/.

inclined persons for this kind of help. I felt that Dr. Spitzer was the kind of psychiatrist who could do much good for some of these persons. So why not give it a try? His reply was adamant. No, he would never touch the whole subject ever again. He had nearly broken down emotionally after terrible personal attacks from militant gays and their supporters. There was an outpouring of hatred.[43]

In 2012, after having undergone years of disparagement, the nearly eighty-year-old Dr. Spitzer, ill with Parkinson's, issued a retraction in which he said, "I believe I owe the gay community an apology for my study making unproven claims of the efficacy of reparative therapy."[44]

The retraction does not seem to have been based on any new science. In fact, the conclusion from his study, whatever its flaws, stands unrefuted. In an affidavit, Dr. Michelle A. Cretella testified that "despite Dr. Spitzer's 'apology' to the homosexual community for publishing this study, there has been no new data to contradict his original results. Dr. Spitzer's research remains scientifically sound, and his original conclusion—that some highly motivated individuals with unwanted homosexual attractions can change—still stands. This is why Dr. Kenneth Zucker, editor of the *Archives of Sexual Behavior*, never published an official retraction of Spitzer's study."[45] Unless *all* two hundred subjects in his interviews were lying or delusional, which is highly unlikely, Dr. Spitzer's study is still pertinent as proof that change is sometimes possible.

Why was Dr. Spitzer, heretofore a hero in the homosexual world, subjected to such vituperation? Because his study was seen as the foundation for a moral judgment that could compromise the rationalization for homosexual behavior—which is why it was called immoral. If homosexuals can change, it raises the unpleasant question as to whether they *should* change. Of course, there can be no change if a person does not accept responsibility for his actions. It is exactly the goal of the immutability movement to evade responsibility by denying that change is possible, or even desirable, through bogus genetic or biological claims.

[43]Gerard van den Aardweg, "Frail and Aged, a Giant Apologizes", *MercatorNet*, May 31, 2012, http://www.mercatornet.com/articles/view/frail_and_aged_a_giant_apologizes.

[44]Dave Rattigan, "Spitzer: 'I Owe the Gay Community an Apology' ", *Ex-Gay Watch* (blog), April 26, 2012, http://www.exgaywatch.com/2012/04/spitzer-i-owe-the-gay-community-an-apology/.

[45]Affidavit of Michelle A. Cretella, MD, in Ferguson v. JONAH, May 18, 2013, http://www.consciencedefense.org/contents/media/Cretella_Declaration.pdf.

Psychologist Dr. Douglas Haldeman has argued that change therapies are unethical because they are "predicated on a devaluation of homosexual identity and behavior". Of course they are. The whole point of change is to make things better, based on the assumption that it is better *not* to engage in homosexual behavior than it is to do so. Therefore, the homosexuals trying to change *should* be helped. Dr. Haldeman thinks that, whether they work or not, "change of orientation therapy programs should be eliminated" because, morally, one should not engage in them.[46] This is obviously based upon a moral judgment, not a scientific one, and it remarkably ignores the wishes of homosexual patients.

Here is further evidence against the immutability theory from Dr. van den Aardweg, who, through his therapeutic work, helped to demonstrate that change is possible. In *Homosexuality and Hope: A Psychologist Talks about Treatment and Change*, he wrote:

> From extensive analysis of a series of 101 persons I had in treatment, I have derived the following summarizing statements about the effectiveness of our therapy. Of those who continued treatment—60 percent of the total group—about two-thirds reached at least a satisfactory state of affairs for a long period of time. By this is meant that the homosexual feelings had been reduced to occasional impulses at most while the sexual orientation had turned predominately heterosexual, or that the homosexual feelings were completely absent, with or without predominance of heterosexual interests. Of this group, however, about one-third could be regarded as having been changed "radically". By this is meant that they did not have any more homosexual feelings, and in addition that they showed a fundamental change in overall emotionality from negative to positive—from instability to reasonable, normal stability—with a follow-up period of at least two years.[47]

On a more personal level, journalist Janneke Pieters wrote in 2009 that

> twenty years ago, Greg Quinlan was living as a homosexual and was a homosexual-rights grassroots lobbyist. He had no doubt he was born homosexual. Advocacy groups like the Human Rights Campaign, for which Quinlan worked, claim that homosexuals have the right to marry

---

[46] G. C. Davison, (1982) "Politics, Ethics and Therapy for Homosexuality", in *Homosexuality and Psychotherapy*, ed. John C. Gonsiorek (New York: Haworth Press, 1982), 89–96.

[47] Gerard van den Aardweg, *Homosexuality and Hope: A Psychologist Talks about Treatment and Change* (Ann Arbor, Mich.: Servant Books, 1986) 105–6.

and adopt children. These rights are presumably based on the idea that sexual orientation cannot be changed.... Quinlan made the decision to quit the homosexual lifestyle cold turkey not because his feelings toward men changed, but because he was deeply unhappy. "I was sick of it, and I knew what I was doing was wrong", he said. He eventually deepened his relationship with God, which led to forgiving his abusive father. That burden released, his same-sex attraction diminished. Today, Quinlan is a pro-family lobbyist. "I am doing for the Lord what I used to do for the gay-rights movement," he says. "I hope I can make up for some of it."[48]

If homosexuality is even sometimes mutable, then it cannot be immutable. The evidence for this is often disregarded or treated with tremendous hostility by homosexual activists because it imperils their class designation and all that goes with it. Therefore, tremendous pressure has been exerted within and on the APA and other professional associations to declare that such change is impossible and, in fact, undesirable. Homosexuals who have made the change are viciously attacked and attempts are being made, and have so far succeeded in places like California and New Jersey, to pass legislation prohibiting reparative therapy for youth.

The Enforcement of Dysfunction

In 2012 California Governor Jerry Brown signed into law Senate Bill 1172, which "prohibit[s] a mental health provider, as defined, from engaging in sexual orientation change efforts, as defined, with a patient under 18 years of age. The bill would provide that any sexual orientation change efforts attempted on a patient under 18 years of age by a mental health provider shall be considered unprofessional conduct and shall subject the provider to discipline by the provider's licensing entity."[49] Therefore, it is now illegal in California for therapists to aid teenagers struggling with same-sex attractions by performing any type of reorientation therapy on them—even though, as Dr. Santinover reported, this is the age group in which sexual inclinations are especially mutable. The bill announces the premise upon which it is based: "An individual's sexual orientation,

---

[48] Janneke Pieters, "Scientists 'Outing' Gay Gene Myth", *National Catholic Register*, July 17, 2009, http://www.ncregister.com/site/article/scientists_outing_gay_gene_myth.

[49] Sexual Orientation Change Efforts, S. 1172 (2011–2012), http://leginfo.legislature.ca.gov /faces/billNavClient.xhtml?bill_id=201120120SB1172.

whether homosexual, bisexual, or heterosexual, is not a disease, disorder, illness, deficiency, or shortcoming." The bill also quotes a 2012 article in the *Journal of the American Academy of Child and Adolescent Psychiatry* that states, "Indeed, there is no medically valid basis for attempting to prevent homosexuality, which is not an illness."[50] While the bill speaks volubly about the dangers of conversion therapy, for which there is only anecdotal evidence, it never once mentions the far greater dangers of the homosexual life, for which there is ample scientific evidence. Dr. Richard Fitzgibbons protested, "This law demonstrates a profound disregard for the medical and psychological health of youth. It is an egregious act of deliberately denying to youth the knowledge of the homosexual lifestyle and the serious health risks associated with it."[51]

Perhaps the reason is that its principal sponsor was a homosexual legislator, which also helps explain why the bill seems not to prohibit therapists from helping straight youths to become homosexual—only the other way around. Similar bills to ban conversion or reparative therapy for minors have been, or are being, introduced in New York, and Pennsylvania. The bill's sponsor in Pennsylvania, Philadelphia Democratic State Representative Babette Josephs, announced that "as homosexuality is not a disorder, so attempts to 'convert' the sexual orientation of anyone, particularly a minor, threatens the individual's short- and long-term health and well-being."[52] First comes the denial of reality, and then comes the enforcement of the denial to the point at which those who wish to return to reality, and quite possibly save their lives, will be prevented from doing so. The totalitarian impulse underlying the rationalization of homosexual behavior is here revealed in the attempt to forbid those seeking help from obtaining it.

Even some pro–homosexual rights scientists are appalled. Dr. Nicholas Cummings said:

> I have been a lifelong champion of civil rights, including lesbian and gay rights. I [was] appointed as president (1979) [of] the APA's first Task

50 Ibid.

51 Richard Fitzgibbons, MD, "California Law Places Youth at Risk: An Interview with Rick Fitzgibbons, MD", Truth and Charity Forum.org, November 26, 2012, http://www .truthandcharityforum.org/california-law-places-youth-at-risk-an-interview-with-rick -fitzgibbons-m-d/.

52 State Rep. Babette Josephs, "Josephs Bill Would Ban Gay-to-Straight Conversion Therapy for Minors", news release, October 5, 2012, http://www.pahouse.com/PR/182100512.asp.

Force on Lesbian and Gay Issues, which eventually became an APA division. In that era the issue was a person's right to choose a gay life style, whereas now an individual's choice not to be gay is called into question because the leadership of the APA seems to have concluded that all homosexuality is hard-wired and same-sex attraction is unchangeable. My experience has demonstrated that there are as many different kinds of homosexuals as there are heterosexuals. Relegating all same sex-attraction as an unchangeable—an oppressed group akin to African-Americans and other minorities—distorts reality. And past attempts to make sexual reorientation therapy "unethical" violates patient choice and makes the APA the de facto determiner of therapeutic goals.... The APA has permitted political correctness to triumph over science, clinical knowledge and professional integrity. The public can no longer trust organized psychology to speak from evidence rather than from what it regards to be politically correct.[53]

The effect of this political correctness on those seeking help was poignantly related by former homosexual Rich Wyler. His therapist's name was Matt. "The first order of business on my first visit with Matt was for me to sign a release form required by the American Psychological Association. Reparative therapy was unproven, the form said; the APA's official stance was that it didn't believe it was possible to change sexual orientation; attempting to do so might even cause psychological harm. Yeah, right, I thought, as if the double life I was living was not causing psychological harm enough."[54]

In fact, the *Journal of Human Sexuality* (vol. 1, 2009) has reported:

> Those who have received help from reorientation therapists have collectively stood up to be counted—as once did their openly gay counterparts in the 1970s. On May 22, 1994, in Philadelphia, the American Psychiatric Association was protested against for the first time in history—not by pro-gay activists, but by a group of people reporting that they had substantially changed their sexual orientation and that change is possible for others (Davis, 1994). The same thing happened at the 2000 Psychiatric Association convention in Chicago (Gorner, 2000), and again at the 2006 APA convention in New Orleans (Foust, 2006).

[53] Nicholas Cummings, "Former APA President Dr. Nicholas Cummings Describes His Work with SSA Clients", interview with NARTH, accessed August 1, 2013, http://narth.com /docs/cummings.html.
[54] Cited in Brown, *A Queer Thing Happened to America*, 470.

As mentioned before, some homosexuals who wish to change their orientation have been unable to do so, but many others have. By itself this is substantial and incontrovertible evidence against the theory that homosexuality is an immutable characteristic. (If it were immutable, where has this class been throughout thousands of years of recorded history? As Justice Kennedy said in *Lawrence v. Texas*, "The concept of the homosexual as a distinct category of person did not emerge until the late 19th century.") As such, the case for constituting homosexuals as a class falls apart and, with it, all the legal and financial benefits from having been discriminated against.

Nonetheless, society as a whole is now being invited, or rather coerced, into the double life of the big lie—to pretend that what is, is not and that what is not, is. There is something worse than disease; there is the denial of its existence. This is all part of what Fr. James Schall calls the "systematic effort not to name things what they really are so that we are never faced with what we are actually doing". A double life, however, leads to a double death. One is physical, the other spiritual. The worst thing, Socrates warned, is the lie in the soul about *what is*.

8

Same-Sex Parenting

If homosexual orientation and behavior are nonproblems, what, aside from the inability to have children, could possibly prevent same-sex couples from performing as parents as well as heterosexual couples? According to the American Psychological Association, apparently nothing. In an official publication in 2005, the association claimed that "the evidence to date suggests that home environments provided by lesbian and gay parents are as likely as those provided by heterosexual parents to support and enable children's pyschosocial growth" and that "there is no scientific evidence that parenting effectiveness is related to parental sexual orientation."[1] This point of view has been echoed throughout the court system.

For instance, in the 2009 *Varnum v. Brien* decision of the Iowa Supreme Court, Justice Mark Cady embraced the proposition that "sexual orientation and gender have no effect on children raised by same-sex couples, and same-sex couples can raise children as well as opposite-sex couples." He condescended to those who believe "dual-gender parenting is the optimal environment for children" as "thoughtful and sincere", but declared that this opinion was "largely unsupported by reliable scientific studies".[2] A footnote in the decision explained: "The research appears to strongly support the conclusion that same-sex couples foster the same wholesome environment as opposite-sex couples and suggests that the traditional notion that children need a mother and a father to be raised into healthy, well-adjusted adults is based more on stereotype than anything else."[3]

[1] American Psychological Association, *Lesbian and Gay Parenting*, 2005 ed., 15, http://www.apa.org/pi/lgbt/resources/parenting-full.pdf.

[2] Varnum, 763 N.W.2d 862 (Iowa 2009).

[3] Ibid.

In 2010, the Third District Court of Appeal in Florida entertained a case concerning the constitutionality of homosexual adoption. It declared that "based on the robust nature of the evidence available in the field, this Court is satisfied that the issue is so far beyond dispute that it would be irrational to hold otherwise."[4]

In the 2010 *Perry v. Schwarzenegger* case, Judge Walker stated, "Children raised by gay or lesbian parents are as likely as children raised by heterosexual parents to be healthy, successful and well-adjusted. The research supporting this conclusion is accepted beyond serious debate in the field of developmental psychology." One of the sources he cited, however, was a brochure published by the American Psychological Association, which said, "Few studies are available regarding children of gay fathers." How, then, could it have been "beyond serious debate"?

In a footnote to his 2011 letter to Congress, Eric Holder noted, "As the Department has explained in numerous filings, since the enactment of DOMA, many leading medical, psychological, and social welfare organizations have concluded, based on numerous studies, that children raised by gay and lesbian parents are as likely to be well-adjusted as children raised by heterosexual parents."[5]

As with the prior assertions as to the immutability and normality of homosexual orientation and behavior, these statements have no credible science to substantiate them. One can begin with the commonsense observation of Dr. Satinover: "What is known, from decades of research on family structure, studying literally thousands of children, is that every departure from the traditional, stable, mother-father family has severe detrimental effects upon children; and these effects persist not only into adulthood but into the next generation as well. In short, the central problem with mother-mother or father-father families is that they deliberately institute, and intend to keep in place indefinitely, a family structure known to be deficient in being obligatorily and permanently either fatherless or motherless."[6] An American College of Pediatricians paper from January 2012 seconded this judgment: "Clearly, apart from rare situations, depriving a child of one

---

[4] "Opinion of Third District Court of Appeal in Florida Department of Children and Families v. In re: Matter of Adoption of X.X.G. and N.R.G.", September 22, 2010, http://www.3dca.flcourts.org/opinions/3D08-3044.pdf.

[5] Attorney General Eric Holder, "Letter from the Attorney General to Congress on Litigation Involving the Defense of Marriage Act", February 23, 2011.

[6] Dr. Jeffrey Satinover, "Testimony before the Massachusetts Senate Committee".

or both biological parents, as same-sex parenting requires in every case, is unhealthy."[7]

Also, in an Australian research and policy paper, published in July 2011, titled *For Kids' Sake: Repairing the Social Environment for Australian Children and Young People*, Patrick Parkinson, professor of law at the University of Sydney, said, "In the last twenty years or so, the dominant policy direction has been to treat all families alike without reference to family structure. Yet the overwhelming evidence from research is that children do best in two-parent married families, and this is not just the result of selection effects."[8]

Nonetheless, the 2005 American Psychological Association publication asserted that "not a single study has found children of lesbian or gay parents to be disadvantaged in any significant respect relative to children of heterosexual parents." At the time it was made, this claim was not accurate, and it is even less accurate today. First of all, in 1996, Australian researcher Sotirios Sarantakos did a study in which he compared fifty-eight children of heterosexual married parents, fifty-eight children of heterosexual cohabiting couples, and fifty-eight children living with homosexual couples. Sarantakos found that "children of married couples are more likely to do well at school in academic and social terms, than children of cohabiting and homosexual couples."[9] The American Psychological Association largely ignored this study, only bothering to denigrate it in a footnote as not coming from a "source [the journal *Children Australia*] upon which one should rely for understanding the state of scientific knowledge in this field".

As it turns out, however, it is the American Psychological Association that is not to be relied upon for scientific knowledge. In a devastating appraisal of the studies on which the association depended for its conclusion, Professor Loren Marks of Louisiana State University pointed out that "not one of the 59 studies referenced in the 2005 APA Brief compares a large, random, representative sample of lesbian or gay parents and their children, with a large,

---

[7] American College of Pediatricians, "Same-Sex Parenting: Is It Time for Change?", January 22, 2004, http://www.liberty.edu/media/9980/attachments/pr_wegner_shawano _acpeds_ss_parenting_detrimental_013012.pdf.

[8] Professor Patrick Parkinson, AM, *For Kids' Sake: Repairing the Social Environment for Australian Children and Young People* (Sydney: University of Sydney, 2011), 14, http://sydney.edu .au/law/news/docs_pdfs_images/2011/Sep/FKS-ResearchReport.pdf.

[9] Sotirios Sarantakos, "Children in Three Contexts: Family, Education and Social Development," *Children Australia* 21, no. 3 (1996); quoted in Michael Cook, "'The Kids Are All Right'? Think Again", *Mercator.Net*, June 15, 2012, http://www.mercatornet.com/articles /view/the_kids_are_all_right_think_again.

random, representative sample of married parents and their children."[10] As a result, Dr. Marks concluded that "the jury is still out on whether being raised by same-sex parents disadvantages children. [...] However, the available data on which the APA draws its conclusions, derived primarily from small convenience samples, are insufficient to support a strong generalized claim either way."[11]

In their 2001 review of homosexual-parenting studies for the Ethics and Public Policy Center, Robert Lerner and Althea K. Nagai reached a conclusion that could apply as well to the studies cited in the 2005 American Psychological Association paper: "The methods used in these studies are so flawed that these studies prove nothing. Therefore, they should not be used in legal cases to make any argument about 'homosexual vs. heterosexual' parenting. Their claims have no basis."[12]

There is now, however, a basis for disputing the American Psychological Association's contention of parental equivalence, not only because of the ineptitude of the fifty-nine studies upon which it relied, but because of the findings of the New Family Structures Study, led by Professor Mark Regnerus at the University of Texas, published in the July 2012 issue of *Social Science Research*. Dr. Regnerus used data that met the standards for research in social science in a way that now makes it impossible to continue making the American Psychological Association's claims with any real authority. According to its author,

> This study, based on a rare large probability sample, reveals far greater diversity in the experience of lesbian motherhood (and to a lesser extent, gay fatherhood) than has been previously acknowledged or understood.... The most significant story in this study is arguably that children appear most apt to succeed well as adults—on multiple counts and across a variety of domains—when they spend their entire childhood with their married mother and father, and especially when the parents remain married to the present day. Insofar as the share of intact, biological mother/father families continues to shrink in the United States, as it has, this portends growing challenges within families, but also heightened dependence on

---

[10] Loren Marks, "Same-Sex Parenting and Children's Outcomes: A Closer Examination of the American Psychological Association's Brief on Lesbian and Gay Parenting", *Social Science Research* 41 (2012): 735–51; quote on 748.

[11] Ibid.

[12] Robert Lerner and Althea K. Nagai, *No Basis: What the Studies Don't Tell Us about Same-Sex Parenting* (Washington, DC: Ethics and Public Policy Center, 2001), 6.

public health organizations, federal and state public assistance, psycho-therapeutic resources, substance use programs, and the criminal justice system.[13]

In a *Slate* article about his research, Dr. Regnerus said:

The basic results call into question simplistic notions of "no differences," at least with the generation that is out of the house. On 25 of 40 different outcomes evaluated, the children of women who've had same-sex relationships fare quite differently than those in stable, biologically-intact mom-and-pop families, displaying numbers more comparable to those from heterosexual stepfamilies and single parents. Even after including controls for age, race, gender, and things like being bullied as a youth, or the gay-friendliness of the state in which they live, such respondents were more apt to report being unemployed, less healthy, more depressed, more likely to have cheated on a spouse or partner, smoke more pot, had trouble with the law, report more male and female sex partners, more sexual victimization, and were more likely to reflect negatively on their childhood family life, among other things. Why such dramatic differences? I can only speculate, since the data are not poised to pinpoint causes. One notable theme among the adult children of same-sex parents, however, is household instability, and plenty of it. The children of fathers who have had same-sex relationships fare a bit better, but they seldom reported living with their father for very long, and never with his partner for more than three years.[14]

This points to a chronic problem for comparability studies of child rearing under heterosexual couples compared with homosexual couples. As we have seen in part 1, lesbian and homosexual couples simply do not last that long. Dr. Regnerus reported that "there are limitations to this study, of course. We didn't have as many intact lesbian and gay families as we hoped to evaluate, even though they are the face of much public deliberation about marriage equality."[15] As noted earlier, infidelity and brief duration are the norms with same-sex relationships. The data-gathering group that

[13] Mark Regnerus, "How Different Are the Adult Children of Parents Who Have Same-Sex Relationships? Findings from the New Family Structures Study", *Social Science Research* 41, no. 4 (July 2012), http://www.sciencedirect.com/science/article/pii/S0049089X12000610.

[14] Mark Regnerus, "Queers as Folk: Does It Really Make No Difference if Your Parents Are Straight or Gay?", *Slate*, June 11, 2012, http://www.slate.com/articles/double_x/doublex/2012/06/gay_parents_are_they_really_no_different_.single.html.

[15] Ibid.

screened fifteen thousand young adults for the Regnerus study discovered only two who had been reared by a same-sex couple from birth to age eighteen, and both were by lesbian couples. Not one had been raised by a male same-sex couple from birth.

Dr. Jennifer Roback Morse, president of the Ruth Institute, wrote that the Regnerus results also show that

> these young adults [brought up by same-sex parents] are more likely to report having been sexually touched by a parent or adult caregiver, that they had been forced to have sex against their will, than those who had been brought up in intact biological families. Twenty-three percent of young adults whose mothers had a same sex relationship had been touched sexually by a parent or adult care-giver, compared with 2 percent of those whose parents were continuously married, 10 percent of those whose parents were divorced or never married, and 12 percent of those who lived in a stepfamily. Thirty-one percent of young adults whose mothers had had a same sex relationship and 25 percent of those whose father had had a same sex relationship reported that they had ever been forced to have sex against their will, compared with 8 percent of those whose parents were continuously married, 23 percent of those who had been adopted, 24 percent of those whose parents had divorced, 16 percent of those who lived with stepparents and 16 percent of those whose parents were never married. While 90 percent of those whose parents were continuously married reported themselves as "entirely heterosexual," only 61 percent of those whose mother had a same sex relationship and 71 percent of those whose father had a same sex relationship reported themselves as "entirely heterosexual." Just over 80 percent of young adults who grew up in all other family forms, including adopted, divorced, stepfamily and never married parents, reported themselves as "entirely heterosexual."[16]

Further evidence, with even more research to support it, comes from a 2013 study by Douglas W. Allen, professor of economics at Simon Fraser University in British Columbia, who utilized a large and representative sample from 2006 Canadian census data to reach his conclusions. The abstract to the study, titled "High School Graduation Rates among Children of Same-sex Households", states: "Children living with gay and lesbian families in

---

[16] "Prepared Remarks for the Illinois State Legislature, Hearings on SB 10", Ruth Institute, February 27, 2013, http://www.ruthblog.org/2013/02/27/prepared-remarks-for-the-illinois-state-legislature-hearings-on-sb-10/.

2006 were about 65 percent as likely to graduate compared to children living in opposite sex marriage families. Daughters of same-sex parents do considerably worse than sons."[17]

The American College of Pediatricians summarizes the risks to children from same-sex parents as follows:

> Research has demonstrated considerable risks to children exposed to the homosexual lifestyle. Violence between same-sex partners is two to three times more common than among married heterosexual couples. Same-sex partnerships are significantly more prone to dissolution than heterosexual marriages, with the average homosexual relationship lasting only two to three years. Homosexual men and women are reported to be promiscuous, with serial partners, even within what are loosely termed "committed relationships." Individuals who practice a homosexual lifestyle are more likely than heterosexuals to experience mental illness, substance abuse, suicidal tendencies and shortened lifespans. Although some would claim that these dysfunctions are a result of societal pressures in America, the same dysfunctions exist at inordinately high levels among homosexuals in cultures where the preferable practice is more widely accepted.... Given the current body of evidence, the American College of Pediatricians believes it is inappropriate, potentially hazardous to children, and dangerously irresponsible to change the age-old prohibition on same-sex parenting, whether by adoption, foster care, or reproductive manipulation. This position is rooted in the best available science.[18]

The statement is supported by thirty-six references to scientific studies.

At its finest, social science seems to provide statistical confirmation of common sense. The relationships it points to—such as poorer outcomes for children of same-sex couples than for those in stable homes of heterosexual parents—are only correlative, not causative. Social scientists are unable to say *why* the correlations exist. They can only say that they *do* exist. The limitation is a necessary by-product of this kind of quantitative approach. This

---

[17] Douglas W. Allen, "High School Graduation Rates among Children of Same-Sex Households", *Review of Economics of the Household* 11, no. 4 (December 2013): 635–58, http://link.springer.com/article/10.1007/s11150-013-9220-y; see also http://www.cultureoflife.org/e-brief/no-difference-thesis-household-built-sand.

[18] Michelle Cretella, MD, FCP, and Den Trumbull, MD, FCP, "Homosexual Parenting: Is It Time for a Change?", American College of Pediatricians, January 22, 2004, revised March 2013, http://www.acpeds.org/the-college-speaks/position-statements/parenting-issues/homosexual-parenting-is-it-time-for-change.

does not mean that the research is not useful, because, if done correctly, it can provoke the right questions; but the answers were given long ago. As Aristotle taught, bad examples lead to bad behavior, and bad behavior corrupts the soul.

There is also ample human testimony from those who have endured same-sex upbringing and the price they have paid for it. Here is a *cri de coeur* from Jean-Dominique Bunel, a sixty-six-year-old French man who was raised by two women: "I suffered from the lack of a father, a daily presence, a character and a properly masculine example, some counterweight to the relationship of my mother to her lover. I was aware of it at a very early age. I lived that absence of a father, experienced it, as an amputation."[19] Creating same-sex marriage would be "institutionalizing a situation that had scarred me considerably. In that there is an injustice that I can in no way allow." If the women who raised him had been married, he said, he would "have jumped into the fray and would have brought a complaint before the French state and before the European Court of Human Rights, for the violation of [his] right to a mom and a dad."

Here are several other anecdotal accounts of the costs incurred by children from same-sex parental upbringing, the first three taken from a Family Research Council publication on whether homosexual parenting poses risks to children:

> Kyneret Hope (twenty-five years old): "I experienced [lesbian] separatism as a constant level of anger and negativity.... That was part of the lifestyle I knew, but there was also a down side: men were called mutants, straight women were considered disowned sisters who wasted woman-energy on men, and other lesbians were sometimes accused of being government spies sent to infiltrate and undermine the community. Anyone who was not like us was evil, and I had to be careful not to cross over to the enemy's camp."[20]

> Carey Conley (twenty-one years old): "I built up a great deal of fear and frustration. I was angry that I was not part of a 'normal' family and could not live with a 'normal' mother. I wondered what I did to

---

[19] Quoted by Wendy Wright in "French Homosexuals Demonstrate against Same-Sex 'Marriage'", *LifeSiteNews*, January 18, 2013, http://www.lifesitenews.com/news/french-homosexuals-demonstrate-against-same-sex-marriage/.

[20] Kyneret Hope, "Of Lesbian Descent", in Louise Rafkin, ed., *Different Mothers: Sons and Daughters of Lesbians Talk about Their Lives* (Pittsburg: Cleis Press, 1990), 59.

deserve this. Why did my biological mother let a lesbian adopt me? How could she think that this life was better than what she could have given me? ... During these years I talked with my sister about my feelings and problems. We discussed how we didn't understand my mother and her lifestyle. We talked of how we resented her for placing us in such a situation, all the while knowing how hard it would be for us."[21]

Jakii Edwards, who was raised by a lesbian mother and has written an entire book about it: "We constantly wonder if we will eventually become gay. There is humiliation when other kids see our parents kissing a same-sex lover in front of us. Trust me, it's hard on the children, no matter how much they love their gay parent. The homosexual community may never admit it, but the damage stemming from their actions can be profound."[22]

Robert Oscar Lopez: "Quite simply, growing up with gay parents was very difficult, and not because of prejudice from neighbors. People in our community didn't really know what was going on in the house. To most outside observers, I was a well-raised, high-achieving child, finishing high school with straight A's. Inside, however, I was confused. When your home life is so drastically different from everyone around you, in a fundamental way striking at basic physical relations, you grow up weird. I have no mental health disorders or biological conditions. I just grew up in a house so unusual that I was destined to exist as a social outcast. My peers learned all the unwritten rules of decorum and body language in their homes; they understood what was appropriate to say in certain settings and what wasn't; they learned both traditionally masculine and traditionally feminine social mechanisms.... I had no male figure at all to follow, and my mother and her partner were both unlike traditional fathers or traditional mothers. As a result, I had very few recognizable social cues to offer potential male or female friends, since I was neither confident nor sensitive to others. Thus I befriended people rarely and alienated others easily....

---

[21] Carey Conley, "Always Changes" in ibid., 157–59.
[22] Jakii Edwards with Nancy Kurrack, *Like Mother, Like Daughter? The Effects of Growing Up in a Homosexual Home* (Vienna, VA: Xulon Press, 2001), 8, http://downloads.frc.org/EF/EF08L45.pdf.

My home life was not traditional nor conventional. I suffered because of it, in ways that are difficult for sociologists to index."[23]

One does not really need a sociological study to confirm the import of what Lopez is saying. One needs only to acknowledge reality. To deny it, one needs to refuse that acknowledgement, with all the assistance that the faux science mentioned above can bring to the denial. Once the rationalization for homosexuality is established, the circle of pain spreads out to embrace more and more of society—to include its most innocent and vulnerable members, the children. Rationalizations are oblivious to the damage they cause, as they are self-justifying and self-righteous.

Aside from the immensely important legal ramifications involved in the immutability and class issues discussed earlier, there is also the matter of culpability. If homosexuals are not intrinsically disordered—and are as well-adjusted and as normal as heterosexuals—then the suffering and alienation they experience must be caused by others, by the rejection of the society around them. It is, then, not the homosexuals who need to change or be changed, but the society. *It* is at fault. As the late Enrique Rueda noted in *The Homosexual Network*, "The problem with homosexuality came to be presented more as a question of society's way of dealing with homosexuals than with anything they did."[24] This projection of their problems upon society is what drove the rationalization from the beginning: you are not going to change us; we are going to change you. And we will do that by taking from you your very notion of the family and conforming it to ourselves. At a Human Rights Campaign dinner, which celebrated him as an LGBT (lesbian, gay, bisexual, and transgender) civil rights hero, the late Franklin Kameny said, "I have tended not to adjust myself to society, but with considerable success have adjusted society to me, and society is much the better off for the adjustments I have administered."[25] Those who object to this transmogrification become the problem. As the table turns, we begin to hear things like this from Dr. Richard Isay, a homosexual activist and psychoanalyst who wrote in a letter to the *New York Times* that

[23] Robert Oscar Lopez, "Growing Up with Two Moms: The Untold Children's View," Witherspoon Institute, August 6, 2012, http://www.thepublicdiscourse.com/2012/08/6065/.

[24] Enrique T. Rueda, *The Homosexual Network* (Old Greenwich, CN: The Devon-Adair Company, 1982), 106.

[25] "LGBT Civil Rights Hero Frank Kameny at HRC National Dinner", YouTube video, 2:06, posted by Human Rights Campaign, October 13, 2006, http://www.youtube.com/watch?v=j_4S_iQ3fEo.

"homophobia ... is a psychological abnormality. Those afflicted should be quarantined and denied employment."[26]

The Isay remark is refreshing in its naked acknowledgment of the culture war. Psychiatry, psychology, and social science are being used as weapons in this war. There are two contending views of reality in which homosexual acts are seen either as disordered and immoral or as well-ordered and ethical. These two views are immiscible. They cannot both be right, and they cannot both prevail. Either the one or the other will succeed and be enforced. Dr. Isay was at least honest in putting forth the terms of enforcement from his side.

---

[26] Cited in Jeffrey Satinover, *Homosexuality and the Politics of Truth*, 182.

9

Sodomy and Education

As mentioned at the beginning of this book, if homosexual acts are moral, as so many insist, then they should be normative. If they are normative, they should be taught in our schools as a standard. If they are a standard, they should be enforced. And so it has come, and is coming, to be. Education is an essential part of the drive to universalize the rationalization for homosexual behavior; so it must become a mandatory part of the curriculum, as it now is in California. What began as a plea for diversity ends with a demand for conformity. Seizure of the educational establishment is necessary for its success.

It is hardly news that scores of colleges and universities now offer courses in LGBT studies. We will first provide a sample of the kind of courses being offered and then concentrate on the effort at the high school and elementary school levels, which illustrate even more dramatically that there are no lengths to which the homosexual propagandists are not willing to go to justify themselves—in this case to children.

How much of this kind of thing in higher education is there? In an online resource guide to "University LGBT/Queer Programs", last updated in 2012, the following colleges and universities in the United States and Canada offering "LGBTQ/Sexuality/Sexualities undergraduate majors, minors, certificates, concentrations" were listed as follows:

> Majors are offered by Wesleyan (2003), U. Chicago, Brown, Hobart and William Smith Colleges, York University (Sexuality Studies, 2009), University of Toronto, Miami University (Ohio, 2010), Ohio State (2011), San Diego State (2012), Otterbein (2012)
>
> Minors are offered by Ohio State, San Francisco State, Stanford, Berkeley, UCLA?, UC Riverside, Towson (proposal, Nov. 96, still online), Cornell, SUNY, Purchase, Allegheny, Hobart and William Smith Colleges, George Mason, Concordia University (Canada), Western

Washington University, Bowdoin College, Humboldt State University (Aug 2004), University of Minnesota (fall 2004), Kent State University (fall 2001), University of North Carolina-Chapel Hill (2004), University of North Texas (2004), University of Delaware (Fall 2006), Hofstra (2006), Nebraska-Lincoln (2006), Syracuse (2006), McGill (2006), University California at Santa Barbara (2006), Northern Illinois University (both undergraduate and graduate certificates), University of Kansas (2008), University of Houston (2008), York University (Sexuality Studies, 2004), UC-Davis (2009, Sexuality Studies), University of Toronto, University of British Columbia, DePaul (2007?), University of New Hampshire, Carleton University (Ottawa), University of Michigan, Colgate University (2009), University of Oregon (2009?), Bridgewater State College (2009), Illinois-Urbana-Champaign (Fall 2009), Brooklyn College (approved 2008, inaugurated Fall 2009), Washington State (approved 2009), Miami University (Ohio, 2010), University of Vermont (2006), University of Louisville (2010), Brandeis (2011), Metropolitan State College of Denver (2012), Sonoma State College (California, 2010), Sarah Lawrence (2000??), San Diego State (2005?), Otterbein (2012)

Certificates or Concentrations are offered by Arizona State U., U. Iowa, Yale, Brandeis?, Denison U., Duke, U. Wisconsin-Madison (2003), U. Wisconsin-Milwaukee, U. of Maryland, U. of Colorado at Boulder, York University (Sexuality Studies, 2004).[1]

Here is the fall 2013 curriculum offered by the University of Maryland, College Park, Maryland, in its Lesbian, Gay, Bisexual, and Transgender Studies Program, in which one can receive either a minor or a certificate:

LGBT 200 Introduction to Lesbian, Gay, Bisexual, and Transgender Studies

LGBT 265 Lesbian, Gay, Bisexual, and Transgender Literatures (also offered as ENGL 265)

LGBT 298R Lesbian, Gay, Bisexual, and Transgender Art and Culture (also offered as WMST 298I)

LGBT 350 Lesbian, Gay, Bisexual, and Transgender People and Communication

LGBT 386 Lesbian, Gay, Bisexual, and Transgender Community Organization Internship

[1] "University LGBT / Queer Programs" University of Kansas website, last updated October 31, 2012, http://www.people.ki.edu/~jyounger/lbgtqprogs.html.

LGBT 448C Sex and the City

LGBT 448Q Queer Citizenship: Perspectives on Bodies, Sexualities, and Performances

LGBT 465 Theories of Sexuality and Literature (also offered as ENGL 465)

LGBT 499 Independent Study

Also being offered are the following approved LGBT electives:

AMST 498D—Black Masculinities

CMLT 398L/CMLT 498L/ENGL 329C—Sexuality in the Cinema

EDHI 338N—Teaching and Learning about Cultural Diversity through Intergroup Dialogue: LGBT/Heterosexual

FMSC 330—Family Theories and Patterns

HIST 213—History of Sexuality in America

HLTH 377—Human Sexuality

HONR 258W—Exploring Homophobia: Demystifying Lesbian, Gay, and Bisexual Issues

SOCY 325/WMST 325—The Sociology of Gender

WMST 400—Theories of Feminism

Graduate level courses of interest:

AMST 629M—Cultural Politics of Neoliberalism

EDCI 697—Embracing Diversity in Classroom Communities[2]

Then there is, of course, the LGBT Equity Center, a unit of the University of Maryland, reporting to the chief diversity officer. (This is not a parody.) The center's website says, "We envision the University of Maryland as a fully equitable community that empowers innovators and agents of social justice for lesbian, gay, bisexual, transgender, and queer people."[3]

What kind of "social justice" issues might arise? Rachel Pepper, coauthor of *The Gay and Lesbian Guide to College Life*, has served as program coordinator for Lesbian, Gay, Bisexual, and Transgender Studies at Yale.

---

[2] "LGBT Studies", University of Maryland website, accessed August 1, 2013, http://www.lgbts.umd.edu/courses.html.

[3] "LGBT Equity Center", University of Maryland website, accessed August 1, 2013, http://www.lgbt.umd.edu/.

According to the *New York Times*, "Transgender students, Ms. Pepper says, would want to know if the health center provides hormone shots as part of the health plan."[4]

The online publication *Inside Higher Ed* reported that the University of Pennsylvania puts openly "gay" applicants in touch with "gay" students and organizations on campus. Eric J. Furda, the dean of admissions, saw nothing wrong with this kind of procurement and said that it was simply doing for "gay" applicants what it has done for other groups. He told the *New York Times*, "We are speaking to students on the areas they are most interested in."[5]

The University of Southern California also reaches out to applicants who identify themselves as gay or transgender. "Prospective students can have a 'Rainbow Floor Overnight Experience'—a night on the gay floor of a residence hall and a day visiting their host's classes and student organizations."[6]

Not even religiously affiliated schools are immune to the infiltration of activist homosexual student organizations. In 2011, after examining the official web sites of 244 Catholic universities and colleges in America, a Catholic organization found that 107—or 43 percent—recognize student clubs that favor the homosexual agenda. "Many of these clubs promote same-sex 'marriage,' open homosexuality in the military, and push for the mainstreaming of unnatural vice."[7]

The infiltration of higher education by LGBT studies is well known. Less attention seems to have been paid to the effort to spread LGBT propaganda in elementary schools and high schools. Because of the young ages of students in kindergarten through twelfth grade, the introduction of pro-homosexual materials has required a special sensitivity from those who are trying to get away with it. They must avoid the explicit nature of the LGBT courses offered at the college level and disguise the effort in terms of something other than what it really is. Therefore, they use a stealth approach under the cover of issues such as school safety, diversity, and bullying.

One of the primary organizations involved in spreading the rationalization for homosexual behavior in elementary and high schools is the Gay,

[4] John Schwartz, "Finding a Gay-Friendly Campus", *New York Times*, April 16, 2010, http://www.nytimes.com/2010/04/18/education/edlife/18guidance-t.html?pagewanted=all.

[5] Ibid.

[6] Ibid.

[7] TFP Student Action, "Pro-Homosexual Clubs Found at 107 Catholic Colleges: PROTEST NOW", TFP Student Action website, December 6, 2011, http://www.tfpstudentaction.org/get-involved/online-petitions/pro-homosexual-clubs-at-107-catholic-colleges.html.

Lesbian, and Straight Education Network (GLSEN), begun in 1990 in Massachusetts. According to its mission statement, GLSEN "strives to assure that each member of every school community is valued and respected regardless of sexual orientation or gender identity/expression. We believe that such an atmosphere engenders a positive sense of self, which is the basis of educational achievement and personal growth. Since homophobia and heterosexism undermine a healthy school climate, we work to educate teachers, students and the public at large about the damaging effects these forces have on youth and adults alike."

The statement sounds fairly anodyne, though its clear purpose is to make homosexuality acceptable, and for good reason. GLSEN's founder, homosexual activist Kevin Jennings, spoke at a homosexual conference on March 5, 1995, titled, "Winning the Culture War", in which he laid out the rhetorical strategy for success. Jennings is worth quoting at length for what he reveals about the agenda:

> If the Radical Right can succeed in portraying us as preying on children, we will lose. Their language—"promoting homosexuality" is one example—is laced with subtle and not-so-subtle innuendo that we are "after their kids." We must learn from the abortion struggle, where the clever claiming of the term "pro-life" allowed those who opposed abortion on demand to frame the issue to their advantage, to make sure that we do not allow ourselves to be painted into a corner before the debate even begins. In Massachusetts the effective reframing of this issue was the key to the success of the Governor's Commission on Gay and Lesbian Youth. We immediately seized upon the opponent's calling card—safety—and explained how homophobia represents a threat to students' safety by creating a climate where violence, name-calling, health problems, and suicide are common. Titling our report "Making Schools Safe for Gay and Lesbian Youth," we automatically threw our opponents onto the defensive and stole their best line of attack. This framing short-circuited their arguments and left them back-pedaling from day one. Finding the effective frame for your community is the key to victory. It must be linked to universal values that everyone in the community has in common. In Massachusetts, no one could speak up against our frame and say, "Why, yes, I do think students should kill themselves": this allowed us to set the terms for the debate.[8]

[8] " 'Governor's Commission for Gay Youth' Retreats to 'Safety' and 'Suicide' ", *Massachusetts News*, December 2000, http://www.massnews.com/past_issues/2000/12_Dec/1200fist3 .htm.

So successful was Mr. Jennings in his framing operation that he was appointed in the first Obama administration to the position of assistant deputy secretary for the Office of Safe and Drug-Free Schools in the Department of Education. The irony was not lost on fifty-two members of Congress, who wrote to President Obama requesting that he rescind the appointment because Mr. Jennings had, as the letter stated, "for more than 20 years, almost exclusively focused on promoting the homosexual agenda". Mr. Obama did not do so, and Mr. Jennings served in the position for two years.

GLSEN's mission of promoting a safe and supportive environment for students of all sexual orientations means providing the *approval* of those orientations. In the *Safe Space Kit: Guide to Being an Ally to LGBT Students*, GLSEN provides an examination of conscience for those wanting to be allies to LGBT students. Here are some of the searching questions: "If someone were to come out to you as LGBT, what would your first thought be? Have you ever been to an LGBT social event, march or worship service? Why or why not? Have you ever laughed at or made a joke at the expense of LGBT people?"[9]

The booklet advises that good allies "use LGBT-related terminology accurately and respectfully". Would that include the terminology that homosexuals use to describe their activities, such as "rimming" or "golden showers"? Apparently not. With an Orwellian touch, the *Safe Space Kit* advises that, during casual conversations and classroom time, one should "make sure the language you are using is inclusive of all people. When referring to people in general, try using words like 'partner' instead of 'boyfriend/girlfriend' or 'husband/wife', and avoid gendered pronouns, using 'they' instead of 'he/she'." What's wrong with referring to a man as "he" and to a woman as "she"? Well, the glossary helps us to understand the definition of gender as "a social construct based on a group of emotional, behavioral and cultural characteristics attached to a person's assigned biological sex". The whole point of GLSEN is that if you don't like the "gender construct" society has assigned you, you can construct another for yourself, and you have every right to expect that everyone should go along with you. If they don't, they should be brought into line, no doubt by a local LGBT Equity Center that will render "social justice".

[9] GLSEN, *Safe Space Kit: Guide to Being an Ally to LGBT Students* (New York: GLSEN, 2011), 7, https://safespace.glsen.org/about.cfm.

As far as students "coming out" are concerned, one should realize that "it can be a difficult and emotional process for an LGBT student to go through, which is why it is so important for a student to have support." In other words, encourage them by providing approval and support. Whatever you do, however, don't advise the student *not* to tell anyone. Why not? Because, the booklet answers, "this implies that there is something wrong and that being LGBT must be kept hidden."

To help carry out this work there are "Gay-Straight Alliances (GSAs), student clubs that work to improve school climate for all students, regardless of sexual orientation or gender identity/expression. 4,000 GSAs are registered with GLSEN." The number of GSAs should give some idea of the scope of this organization's influence. To date, GLSEN has covered the District of Columbia and thirty-one states.[10] "Our goal is to distribute a Safe Space Kit to every middle and high school in the United States by the end of 2013", said Dr. Eliza Byard, GLSEN's executive director. Now that California has mandated homosexual propaganda in its state schools, GLSEN has fixed up the curriculum for them.

Among the activities sponsored by GLSEN and its affiliates are the following: Day of Silence, National Coming Out Day, No Name Calling Week, Transgender Day of Remembrance, Harvey Milk Day, and GSA Day. On January 24, 2012, Secretary of Education Arne Duncan gave official government approval of the first GSA Day through a GSA public service announcement on YouTube commemorating the event and endorsing GSA clubs in schools.[11] So this is an officially endorsed event. GLSEN is able to afford its many publications and activities with corporate sponsors such as AT&T, Cisco Systems, Citibank, Google, Wells Fargo, HBO, American Express, Barclays Capital, Goldman Sachs, IBM, Pepsi, and Mass Mutual.[12]

On GLSEN's Day of Silence, students take a vow of silence to draw attention to the anti-LGBT harassment and discrimination in schools. "The Day of Silence has grown into one of the largest student-led actions in the world because of students' determination to directly address the

---

[10] GLSEN website, http://www.glsen.org/, accessed May 2013.

[11] "Message on National Gay-Straight Alliance Day from Secretary Arne Duncan", YouTube video, 2:10, posted by "usedgov", January 24, 2012, http://www.youtube.com /watch?feature=player_embedded&v=94NNqjxh58A.

[12] Partners page on GLSEN's website, accessed August 1, 2013, http://www.glsen.org /support/partners.

pervasive issue of anti-LGBT behavior and bias in our schools", said Eliza Byard. "Generations of students have organized and participated in the Day of Silence to express a collective call for schools to be safe and respectful places of learning. GLSEN is once again proud to stand behind these courageous students and their right to receive an education without the harmful disruptions of anti-LGBT name-calling, bullying and discrimination."[13]

GLSEN is also hard at work providing role models for LGBT students. On April 29, 2013, NBA player Jason Collins, who plays center for the Washington Wizards basketball team, announced he was a homosexual in an article for the *Sports Illustrated* website. Hardly a week had passed before GLSEN announced it would honor Collins with the Courage Award at the GLSEN Respect Awards in New York on May 20. "We are incredibly proud to honor Jason Collins with our Courage Award", said Dr. Byard. "His decision to come out is a game-changer for sports and will have a profound impact on the lives of lesbian, gay, bisexual and transgender youth, particularly those who participate in or want to participate in athletics. Jason's actions also send another clear message to young people that sexual orientation can no longer be the standard to unfairly judge an athlete's ability or potential."[14]

GLSEN has also helped to create "Unheard Voices, an oral history and curriculum project that will help educators integrate lesbian, gay, bisexual and transgender (LGBT) history, people and issues into their instructional programs. At the core of the program are brief audio interviews with individuals who bore witness to or helped shape LGBT history in some way. Each interview is accompanied by a backgrounder with discussion questions and activities for educators, and a student reading with biographical information about the interview subject and historical background on the era."

Here is the advice following the Phyllis Lyon interview, which celebrates her cofounding of the lesbian organization Daughters of Bilitis, the female counterpart to the male homosexual Mattachine Society, in 1955: "Get your students involved in advocating for LGBT rights. Assign them to research a local or national issue, such as bullying prevention measures, same-sex marriage, same-sex couples at prom, etc. Have students present

---

[13] GLSEN website, accessed May 2013.
[14] Ibid.

their findings to the class and brainstorm ways they can make a difference (e.g., writing letters to legislators or a local newspaper, having conversations with friends, standing up for someone who is being bullied, raising money for an organization, starting an awareness campaign, participating in GLSEN's Ally Week or Day of Silence). Then have small groups of students select one of their ideas to enact."[15]

What does this kind of thing actually translate into in the classroom? The film *It's Elementary: Talking about Gay Issues in School* was the first item recommended on the book link page on GLSEN's website.[16] *It's Elementary* is, according to its makers, "the groundbreaking film that addresses anti-gay prejudice by providing adults with practical lessons on how to talk with children about lesbian, gay, bisexual, and transgendered people". The filmmakers, Debra Chasnoff and Helen Cohen, visited six elementary and middle schools to film teachers and students discussing "gay and lesbian issues" in their classrooms. The purpose was to explore "what happens when experienced teachers talk about lesbians and gay men with their students". It aired on more than a hundred public television stations in 1999 and continues to be widely used.

This film is worth some detailed attention not only because of its wide circulation, but because it seems to incorporate what GLSEN advocates. In fact, GLSEN's founder, Kevin Jennings, said, "*It's Elementary* is the most important film dealing with LGBT issues and safe schools ever made. It took a topic that was mystifying to many people and made it real, inspiring an entire generation of educators to see how they could make a difference.... No other film has had a bigger impact on LGBT issues in the schools."[17]

Through means of a transcript, let us examine what the film presents. It should be noted that the film is a documentary. Though it obviously has its own pro-homosexual point of view, it is simply recording what is already taking place in classrooms from first through eighth grade to inculcate the acceptance of homosexuality as a norm.

At a filmed meeting of the faculty at Cambridge Friends School, a Quaker school in Cambridge, Massachusetts, a teacher declares, "What we're trying to have people do is to understand that people are. And we have to

---

[15] Ibid.

[16] Ibid.

[17] Kevin Jennings quoted on Ground Spark, http://groundspark.org/latest-news/presskits/elementary_kit/ie_kit_reviews, accessed December 12, 2013.

respect the right of all of us to just be, and be who we are, and we do that in the classroom when we teach so that everyone can learn. 'There isn't a right way, there isn't a wrong way, there isn't a good way, there isn't a bad way.'"[18] So much for Aristotle's *Nicomachean Ethics*. This teaching, however, comports perfectly with the *Space Safe Kit*'s advice to "show students that you understand there is no one way a person 'should' be." This sophistical message obviously works. A third grader summed it up by saying, "I don't get it. Who cares if you're gay? Do you care? It's like, duh, you're gay."[19] Who cares? The entire homosexual lobby, which has been pushing its rationalization to reach this exact point, cares.

At the Fourth Annual Gay Pride Assembly at Cambridge Friends School, a homosexual teacher makes a presentation. While kids are singing "This Little Light of Mine", he says: "Imagine if every time I went to play soccer, I had to hide my right shin. I might hide it like this. And then I would try to play soccer. It wouldn't be easy, but I could do it. It would take a lot of energy to play soccer and also hide my leg. Well, at CFS, I don't have to hide. So I can play soccer with two legs. At CFS, I can tell the truth that I'm a gay man. And that gives me so much more energy to be a better teacher, to be a better co-worker, and to be a better friend. I'll see you on the soccer pitch."[20] This is followed by applause.

The teacher neglected to tell the school assembly that going through life as a committed homosexual is very much like being a one-legged man. Part of his humanity is missing, or is disavowed, the part that could correspond with the other half of humanity in such a way that there might even be more humanity. How can you have more energy from being alienated from yourself? Why is accepting your self-alienation a good thing? Why should students be taught that it is?

In another episode from the same school, teachers are reading from a children's book, *Asha's Mums*, to promote the normality of same-sex "parents":

[18] "'It's Elementary' Hits the Airwaves", CNSNews.com, July 7, 2008, http://cnsnews .com/news/article/034ito39s-elementary034-hits-airwaves.

[19] Gerald Notaro, *It's Elementary: Talking about Gay Issues in School*, Educational Media Reviews Online, accessed August 1, 2013, http://libweb.lib.buffalo.edu/emro/emroDetail .asp?Number=13.

[20] Transcript of *It's Elementary: Talking about Gay Issues in School*, Ark TV website, June 17, 2009, http://livedash.ark.com/transcript/it's_elementary__talking_about_gay_issues_in_school /918/KQED/Wednesday_June_17_2009/59404/; portions of the film can be seen at "Homosexuals Brainwashing Our Children in Elementary Schools", *MassResistance* (blog), accessed August 1, 2013, http://www.massresistance.org/media/video/brainwashing.html.

TEACHER: Here we go. *Asha's Mums*: "My class has been talking all week about the trip we're going to take to the science center. Some of the children, like Terence and Elsie, have already been there. My teacher, Miss Samuels, gave us a form to take home. Our parents had to fill it out and sign it, so that we would have permission to go on the trip. I gave it back to her the next day. Just before break, she asked to see me. She wanted to know which of the names on the form was my mom's. I said both. 'It can't be both. You can't have two moms,' she said briskly. 'My brother and I have two mums,' I protested. Corrine and Judy were listening to me. 'Take the form back home and have it properly filled out,' said Miss Samuels."

TEACHER: Now, if you were Asha, how do you think you would feel?

STUDENTS: Bad.

TEACHER: Why is that, Camilla?

STUDENT 1: Because they said you shouldn't have two moms.

TEACHER: Because the teacher said you couldn't have two moms?

STUDENT 2: Well, the teacher probably wasn't like very open-minded or something the teacher knew about having two moms and being lesbian but she didn't like people like that.

TEACHER: Can you describe a little bit more what you mean by "open-minded"?

STUDENT 2: Well, like if you're not very open-minded, it's like you know, like—let's say there's like a new kind of vegetable or something. And if you're not very open-minded, then you won't try it. Cause you're not like, you know, like to try new things and stuff. And if you're you are open-minded, then you would like to try it. And then so, like, if she wasn't very open-minded, then she would be, like, she'd be prejudiced.[21]

[21] Ibid.

Apparently, the biology teacher at Cambridge Friends School was not available to explain that it is physically impossible to have more than one mother. How open-minded is it not to have mentioned this?

In another filmed venue, Emily, a first grader at Public School 87 in New York City, reads to the class from her Mother's Day essay:

> EMILY: My mothers mean so, so, so, so, so much to me. I have two mothers. Two moms is pretty nice. Well, it's more than pretty nice, it's really nice. You can't imagine. Although having two mothers is a problem to others, I respect that that's the way they think, and I can't do anything about it. I still think that those people think stupidly. This once happened with a boy in my class who couldn't come to my house because my parents were lesbians. One night I called their house and their mother told me their version of the Bible. I stood up for my mothers and knew that many kids in my class were supporting me and calling me to see how I was. I am proud of my moms and enjoy marching in the gay pride march every single year with my moms.
>
> TEACHER: Wasn't that a nice essay? Shouldn't we give Emily a round of applause? (*Applause.*)[22]

Evidently, no one has told poor Emily that one of her parents is a dad. This is followed by the same teacher introducing the subject of "gay marriage".

> TEACHER: Okay, let me tell you quickly the background. Today the law says that if you're the same sex, two men and two women, you can't get married. It is against the law. And I thought that it might be kind of fun for us to sort of be pretend judges for a few minutes. What I'm going to give each of you is a sheet that just tells you that some people think that it's wrong for gays to get married, that it's not natural and that it goes against what a family is. Other people think that the state should not decide these things, that it should just be up to two adults to decide what they want to do. What do you think the answer to these questions are [*sic*]? Should gays be allowed to marry, should they not? What I want you to do is have a discussion. And of course, when you have a discussion, not everybody agrees. But everybody does listen to one another and try to understand each other's positions.

[22] Ibid.

STUDENT 1: I don't see why they shouldn't get married. They love each other. It's just like any other people.

STUDENT 2: I think gay people should get married. God! If you love someone, let them get married. Let's say Andreas was going to get married to Erik. But I am the judge and I'm saying, no, you two can't get married. I don't care if you love them, you can't get married. How do you think you guys would feel? Mad.

STUDENTS: Yeah exactly.

STUDENT 3: Like now there—the majority is not gay or lesbian couples. I think they should think about what if the majority was gay or lesbian couples, and there was a law that said you had to be gay or lesbian, and you couldn't get married to the opposite sex. I think they should think about that and see how they would feel, and then they might know how the gays and lesbians feel. And then I think that they might—they should really think about that.

STUDENT 4: It's like they want to be the bosses of other people.

STUDENT 3: It's just like being prejudiced against blacks or Jews.[23]

The background song with the closing credits has these lyrics (taken from Khalil Gibran): "Your children are not your children; / They come through you, but they are not from you; / And though they are with you, they belong not to you; / You can house their bodies but not their souls."

Jean-Jacques Rousseau could not have said it better. It is a song to which Melissa Harris-Perry would be happy to sing along. Well, then, if not their parents', whose children are they? One may be sure that wherever same-sex marriage has been legally enshrined, it will be taught in schools with or without the permission of parents. In this respect, the children will belong to the state and its schools. Massachusetts, which legalized same-sex marriage in 2003, is exhibit A.

In 2005 kindergartners in Lexington, Massachusetts, were given a "diversity book bag" to take home, which is what the five-year-old son of David

---

[23] Ibid.

and Tonia Parker did. To the parents' shock, the bag contained a picture book titled *Who's in a Family?* In the book are approvingly displayed same-sex "parents" with descriptions such as: "Robin's family is made up of her dad, Clifford, her dad's partner, Henry, and Robin's cat, Sassy." The author of *Who's in a Family?*, Robert Skutch, explained in an interview on National Public Radio's *Here and Now,* May 3, 2005, "The whole purpose of the book was to get the subject [of same-sex-parent households] out into the minds and the awareness of children before they are old enough to have been convinced that there's another way of looking at life." As the responses of the children throughout *It's Elementary* illustrate, propaganda works. All you have to do is repeat it often enough before their minds are formed. Children can be easily exploited, as the film demonstrates.

The Parkers wrote a letter to the principal stating, "There is a book included entitled, *Who's in a Family* (with pictures) that include lesbian and homosexual couples with children—implicitly equating this family structure as a morally equal alternative to other family constructs. We stand firmly against this book or any other subject matter pertaining to homosexuality ever being indoctrinated to our child, discussed in school, or sent home. We don't believe gay parents constitute a spiritually healthy family and should not be celebrated."[24] The Parkers requested advance notification of the distribution of any such material in the future and indicated that they wanted their son excused from any future exposure "to any sexual orientation/ homosexual material/same sex unions between parents".

The principal responded: "I have confirmed with our Assistant Superintendent and our Director of Health Education that discussion of differing families, including gay-headed families, is not included in the parental notification policy."[25] On April 27 David Parker went to the school for a scheduled meeting and insisted that he would not leave until the issue was resolved. As a consequence he was arrested by the Lexington police and charged with trespassing. He spent the night in jail.

The next year, at the same school, a second grade teacher read the book *King and King* to the students as part of an educational unit on weddings. In the book, the queen is frustrated that she cannot interest her son in any of the princesses she presents to him as prospective brides. Then one day he

[24] Cited in "Timeline of Events and Email Correspondence Leading Up to April 17 Final Meeting and Arrest", *MassResistance* (blog), accessed August 1, 2013, http://www .massresistance.org/docs/parker/timeline_events.html.

[25] Ibid.

sees the brother of one of the princesses. "At last, the prince felt a stir in his heart.... It was love at first sight", the book exclaims. The pictorial depiction of the subsequent wedding shows the two "kings" holding hands. The last picture is of the two of them kissing.

Parents Robb and Robin Wirthlin complained that they had not been notified about the reading or its contents, to which they objected. Robin Wirthlin appeared on CNN, saying, "We felt like seven years old is not appropriate to introduce homosexual themes.... My problem is that this issue of romantic attraction between two men is being presented to my seven-year-old as wonderful, and good and the way things should be.... Let us know and let us excuse our child from the discussion."[26] They were told that the school was under no obligation to notify them or to allow their child to opt out.

In 2006, the Wirthlins and David and Tonia Parker filed a federal lawsuit against the school district of Estabrook Elementary School, claiming that the school was engaging in sex education without parental notification, in violation of their civil rights and state law. Chief Judge Mark L. Wolf of the US District Court dismissed the lawsuit, saying, "Diversity is a hallmark of our nation. It is increasingly evident that our diversity includes differences in sexual orientation.... [The Department of Education] also encourages instruction concerning different types of families.... Some families are headed by same-sex couples."[27] Here is the triumph of Kevin Jennings' rhetorical strategy.

The ramifications of Wolf's judgment became abundantly clear in 2008, when Dr. Paul B. Ash, the superintendent of Lexington Public Schools, announced the "new, formalized diversity curriculum in preparation for the next year, when we plan to pilot 4 to 5 short units in each elementary grade. Some units will focus on families, including families with single parents, foster parents, and gay and lesbian parents."[28] A parent, Shawn Landon, protested, demanding "prior notification to any discussion, education, training, reading or anything at all related (even remotely) to homosexuality".[29]

---

[26] Quoted in "King and King", *Wikipedia*, last modified July 6, 2013, http://en.wikipedia.org/wiki/King_%26_King.

[27] "Federal Judge Mark Wolf Dismisses David Parker's Civil Rights Lawsuit", *MassResistance* (blog), accessed August 1, 2013, http://www.massresistance.org/docs/parker_lawsuit/motion_to_dismiss_2007/order_to_dismiss.html.

[28] "David Parker's Elementary School Rolling Out New 'Gay' Curriculum in Wake of Court Decision", *MassResistance* (blog), April 4, 2008, http://www.massresistance.org/docs/gen/08b/ash_exchange_040308.html.

[29] Ibid.

Here is part of Dr. Ash's response to the father:

Perhaps you are not aware of the lawsuit decided by the United States Court of Appeals (*Parker vs. Hurley*). This case established Lexington's right to teach diversity units, including stories that show same gender parents. The court decided we are not required to inform parents in advance of teaching units that include same gender parents or required to release students when such topics are discussed. The Appeals Court dismissed the claim that parents have a right to require the school provide advance notice or the right to remove their children. In addition, the School Committee has decided that teachers must be able to teach topics they feel are appropriate without the requirement parents be notified in advance.[30]

Recall Rousseau's prescription for the replacement of the family by the state: "The public authority, in assuming the place of father and charging itself with this important function [should] acquire his [the father's] rights in the discharge of his duties." This prescription was filled in Massachusetts. One can expect its spread wherever same-sex marriage is mandated by the state. It is now being filled in California.

Back to the classroom, we have another GLSEN publication, *Ready, Set, Respect!*, an elementary-school toolkit to assist the state in its usurpation of parental duties. This booklet advises schools on how to deal with certain children being perceived as "not behaving 'enough' like a boy or 'enough' like a girl". It states: "As educators we have the opportunity to create environments that not only support students as they develop an awareness of gender but that also challenge the stereotypes that may impair healthy development."[31]

As if on cue, in May 2013 the Tippecanoe School for the Arts and Humanities, a Milwaukee elementary school, sponsored a "Gender Bender Day" for which the students were asked to dress as a member of the opposite sex. *National Review Online* reports:

"I think it's just teaching them the wrong lesson about gender", one parent told local Fox affiliate WITI. "If you're a boy, stay a boy. You shouldn't have something like that at school." Another parent said she was "speechless" about the school's decision. She, like some other parents, ended up keeping her son home from school that day. A school-board

---

[30] "David Parker's Elementary School Rolling Out New 'Gay' Curriculum".
[31] GLSEN website, accessed May 2013.

member dismissed parents' concerns, saying they were "using the kids for political purposes". In an effort to appease upset parents, the school changed the name to "Switch It Up Day." In fact, WITI couldn't find many students participating in the themed day when it finally came last Friday; it appears to be mostly teachers and other staffers.[32]

On Fox-6 News TV, one mother protested: "I don't want to send my son to school dressed as girl. He's only 7 years old."

This is clearly the age at which some homosexual ideologues and their allies would like to reach children with their propaganda, however. The extent to which this can go becomes, on occasion, unintentionally hilarious. In the *Ready, Set, Respect!* booklet, for instance, teachers are advised to "write math problems with contexts that include a variety of family structures and gender-expressions". For example, "Rosa and her dads were at the store and wanted to buy three boxes of pasta. If each costs $.75, how much will all three boxes cost?" This reads as if some now unemployed Soviet or Sandinista propagandist wrote it. If it were written during the Cold War, they would be buying Kalashnikovs, not pasta, but then, of course, there would have been only one dad, not two.

GLSEN also maintains its own Book Link. Before 2009, the list was extensive, with more than one hundred titles. Here are three of them. In *Reflections of a Rock Lobster*, the author graphically recounts his sexual adventures in first grade. In *Passages of Pride*, the author describes a fifteen-year-old boy's relationship with a much older man. In *Queer 13: Lesbian and Gay Writers Recall Seventh Grade*, a writer recounts how he, as a thirteen-year-old, went along with and enjoyed "near-rapes" by older men, one of whom he met on a bus.[33]

According to Linda Harvey of Mission:America, whose website contains brief excerpts from some of these books, they contain "unabashed support for children engaging in homosexuality and cross-dressing, anonymous restroom sex, pick-ups on the Internet, frequent porn viewing, and sex between adults and young teens".[34] GLSEN subsequently removed these

---

[32] Andrew Johnson, "Cross-Dressing Day at Elementary School Crosses Parents", *National Review Online*, May 28, 2013, http://www.nationalreview.com/corner/349467/cross-dressing-day-elementary-school-crosses-parents.

[33] Maxim Lott, "Obama's Safe Schools Czar Tied to Lewd Readings for 7th Graders", Fox News.com, December 14, 2009, http://www.foxnews.com/politics/2009/12/14/obamas-safe-schools-czar-tied-lewd-readings/.

[34] Linda Harvey, "The Sleazy History of GLSEN", Mission:America, accessed August 1, 2013, http://www.missionamerica.com/articletext.php?artnum=131.

books from its Book Link after public controversy developed over the list, associated with Jennings' appointment to the Department of Education in 2009. Mission:America has also made available the full GLSEN book list before it was scrubbed down to the current seven recommendations.[35]

The six remaining books include *Nothing Pink*, which the Book List summarizes as follows: "The first Sunday at his Father's new church, Vincent meets Robert, and what was previously a spiritual crisis becomes physical. Vincent's parents can't do much about the time Vincent spends with Robert, whatever their suspicions and fears. When Vincent's mother discovers a copy of a magazine in Vincent's room that makes the unacknowledged truth blatantly obvious, Vincent's nature and faith collide." Also recommended is *Mini Mia and Her Darling Uncle*: "Mini Mia loves her Uncle Tommy. They hang out in coffee bars, go for walks, swim, and do other fun stuff. But one day Fergus appears in her uncle's kitchen. Mini Mia does not want to share Tommy with his new boyfriend." *And Baby Makes 4* presents this subject matter: "One of her moms is pregnant! What will this mean for a child who is becoming an older sibling?"[36]

It is a measure of the depravity of the homosexual movement that it will not spare the innocence of children in the spread of its rationalization, which must embrace *everyone* at every age, regardless of cost. Innocence cannot be left to stand in its way. As shocking as some of the classroom and reading material may be, it is all part of the inexorable logic of the situation playing itself out. This is what *must* happen if homosexual acts are prescribed as moral goods. With candor and logic, Daniel Villarreal wrote at Queerty. com: "We want educators to teach future generations of children to accept queer sexuality. In fact, our very future depends on it.... Why would we push anti-bullying programs or social studies classes that teach kids about the historical contributions of famous queers unless we wanted to deliberately educate children to accept queer sexuality as normal? ... I and a lot of other people want to indoctrinate, recruit, teach, and expose children to queer sexuality AND THERE'S NOTHING WRONG WITH THAT" (emphasis in original).[37]

[35] GLSEN website, http://glsen-cloud.mediapolis.com/cgi-bin/iowa/all/booklink/index .html?state=tools&type=educator.

[36] "And Baby Makes 4", GSLEN, accessed August 1, 2013, http://glsen-cloud.mediapolis .com/cgi-bin/iowa/all/booklink/record/2594.html.

[37] Daniel Villarreal, "Can We Please Just Start Admitting That We Do Actually Want to Indoctrinate Kids?" Queerty, May 12, 2011, http://www.queerty.com/can-we-please-just -start-admitting-that-we-do-actually-want-to-indoctrinate-kids-20110512/.

Classroom presentations by homosexuals, or on the subject of homosexuality, are invitations to obscenity and inevitably lead to the question asked by one boy during the film *It's Elementary*: "How do you guys do it?" The response was, "We are not allowed to talk about our personal sex lives—we can't do that." Nevertheless, with the question implanted, curious young minds will ineluctably be drawn to the subject of sodomy. "So *that's* what those nice guys who talked with us do? There must not be anything wrong with it!" Mission accomplished—to make the *abnormative* normative before the children have developed their critical faculties of thought. Innocence is the most powerful rebuke to the rationalization for sexual misbehavior, and thus it cannot be allowed to stand outside its corruption. Otherwise, the corruption could not withstand itself. Innocence is a threat. So it must be brought down and pulled in, tainted and smeared, so it will be at home with the corruption around it.

Everyone who has an affliction deserves respect and consideration. But respect does not require calling the affliction something other than what it is—much less its opposite. One cannot teach about sickness and at the same time call it health. It is much worse to promote moral sickness as moral well-being—especially to children. To teach children that one's orientation, sexual or otherwise, gives one license to perform acts that are inherently immoral is an evil teaching. It scandalizes the children. It also degrades the dignity of human free will and responsibility to teach that these acts are inevitable outcomes of "who we are" rather than freely chosen deeds with consequences in terms of both moral and physical health.

10

Sodomy and the Boy Scouts

Since the Boy Scouts of America (BSA) have represented the exact opposite of the homosexual ethos that GLSEN and its allies foster, it is no surprise that the homosexual movement has concentrated on compromising it. The integrity of the Boy Scouts served as a living rebuke to the rationalization for homosexual misbehavior and therefore had to be brought to heel for the rationalization to succeed.

The Boy Scouts fought long and hard against being forced to include avowed homosexuals in its ranks as either scouts or scoutmasters. In *Boy Scouts of America v. Dale* (2000), the Supreme Court upheld the Boy Scouts' First Amendment right of expressive association in removing an assistant scoutmaster who was "an avowed homosexual and gay rights activist".

In writing for the majority, Chief Justice William Rehnquist said that the "presence [of the avowed homosexual] in the Boy Scouts would, at the very least, force the organization to send a message, both to the youth members and the world, that the Boy Scouts accepts homosexual conduct as a legitimate form of behavior". Forcing the Scouts to do this would have violated the First Amendment rights of its members, who, as the court noted, "teach that homosexual conduct is not morally straight" and do "not want to promote homosexual conduct as a legitimate form of behavior".[1]

On May 23, 2013, this changed. The Boy Scouts of America's national governing body voted to lift its long-standing ban on openly homosexual youth in the program. Effective January 1, 2014, "No youth may be denied membership in the Boy Scouts of America on the basis of sexual orientation

---

[1] Boy Scouts of America et al. v. Dale, 530 U.S. 640 (2000), http://caselaw.lp.findlaw.com/scripts/getcase.pl?court=US&vol=99-699.

or preference alone."[2] The organization, as Justice Rehnquist might express it, sent a message. It is the same message that the homosexual activist was trying to force the Scouts to send back in 2000—"that the Boy Scouts accepts homosexual conduct as a legitimate form of behavior". Does this seem too harsh an assessment of its new policy?

The official position of the Scouts had been not to "grant membership to individuals who are *open* or *avowed* homosexuals" (emphasis added). In other words, the Scouts had a rule somewhat similar to the Don't Ask, Don't Tell policy that the US military entertained, and, for the same reason, it was not allowed to stand. It interfered with the rationalization for homosexual behavior. In other words, by announcing their proclivities publicly, "open" homosexuals are not only telling others that they have accepted themselves as active homosexuals but also insisting that others accept them on that basis as well. What otherwise would be the point of openly declaring their sexual proclivities?

As late as June 2012 the Scouts' policy had been not to "grant membership to individuals who are open or avowed homosexuals or who engage in behavior that would become a distraction to the mission of the BSA. Scouting believes same-sex attraction should be introduced and discussed outside of its program with parents, caregivers, or spiritual advisers, at the appropriate time and in the right setting." Why, less than a year later, was this no longer true? This is a story worth telling because it demonstrates the implacable way in which the homosexual movement marches through the institutions of civil society to conform them to its self-justification.

The Boy Scouts were as American as apple pie, and they certainly tried to keep it that way. This earned them a lot of criticism. Typical was the censure of the *Washington Post*'s editorial page in "So Much for Brave and Kind" (July 20, 2012).[3] The Scouts' decision to reaffirm the policy to deny membership to "individuals who are open or avowed homosexuals" also earned the condemnation of President Obama, who said: "My attitude is that gays and lesbians should have access and opportunity the same way everybody else does in every institution and walk of life. The Scouts are a great institution that are promoting young people and exposing them to

---

[2] "Membership Standards Resolution", Boy Scouts of America website, last updated January 14, 2014, http://www.scouting.org/sitecore/content/MembershipStandards/Resolution/Resolution.aspx.

[3] Quoted in "So Much for Brave and Kind", *Hamilton Spectator*, July 21, 2012, http://www.thespec.com/opinion-story/2250565-so-much-for-brave-and-kind/.

opportunities and leadership that will serve people for the rest of their lives. And I think nobody should be barred from that."[4]

The *Post* obviously agreed with Mr. Obama when it opined that this was *un-American*, because the policy taught "young people that it seeks to empower that some of them are unequal, merely because of the way they were born". This "represents a sad embrace of intolerance", and it is "nothing if not an incitement to 'criticize' and 'condemn'" open or avowed homosexuals.

Did, in fact, the Boy Scouts organization deny the founding principle of the United States that all men are created equal? To the contrary, the Scouts have no social, economic, racial, class, or sectarian religious barriers to entry. If anything, they have been a shining example of the principle of equality. All you have to do to become a scout is to adhere to the principles expressed in the Boy Scout pledge: "On my honor, I will do my best / To do my duty to God and my country and to obey the Scout Law; / To help other people at all times; / To keep myself physically strong, mentally awake and morally straight."

Is there anything iniquitous in this pledge? The purpose of the Scouts was the physical and moral formation of young boys. The moral part of that formation excluded the open avowal and promotion of homosexual acts, which were considered inherently immoral. In 1991 the BSA stated: "We believe that homosexual conduct is inconsistent with the requirement in the Scout Oath that a Scout be morally straight and in the Scout Law that a Scout be clean in word and deed, and that homosexuals do not provide a desirable role model for Scouts."[5] This is the basis of the "exclusion" that the *Post* and Mr. Obama deplored.

This policy, however, had nothing to do with the way people are born, but everything to do with how they *behave* and what they openly *espouse*. It is not about *who* they are, but about what they *do* and, more importantly, how they justify what they do. A BSA June 28, 2000, press release stated that "scouting's message is compromised when prospective leaders present themselves as role models inconsistent with Boy Scouting's understanding of the Scout Oath and Law."

---

[4] Quoted in Laurie Higgins, "Obama's Obfuscation on Boy Scouts", *WND*, February 28, 2013, http://www.wnd.com/2013/02/obamas-obfuscation-on-boy-scouts/.

[5] "Morally Straight", Boy Scouts of America National Council website, accessed August 2, 2013, http://web.archive.org/web/20100206191637/http://www.bsalegal.org/morally-straight-cases-225.asp.

Until May 2013 the Scouts had bravely refused to be used as an instrument by the homosexual movement to advance its cause. What it could not achieve through direct assault, activist homosexuals had attempted to gain by unremitting attack through the court system. Here is a summation from the Boy Scouts of America National Council of some of the cases that have been brought against the Scouts by open homosexuals attempting to transform the nature of the organization. Each of these cases could be worn as a badge of honor for the Boy Scouts.

Boy Scouts of America v. Dale

An Assistant Scoutmaster who was an avowed homosexual and gay rights activist sued after his leadership was revoked, alleging that Boy Scouts violated the New Jersey Law Against Discrimination, which prohibits discrimination on the basis of sexual orientation in places of public accommodation. The New Jersey Superior Court, Chancery Division granted summary judgment in favor of Boy Scouts, but the Appellate Division and thereafter the New Jersey Supreme Court held that Boy Scouts had acted in violation of the State's public accommodations law. The United States Supreme Court reversed the New Jersey Supreme Court and held that a state may not, through its nondiscrimination statutes, prohibit the Boy Scouts from adhering to a moral viewpoint and expressing that viewpoint in internal leadership policy and that the New Jersey Supreme Court's decision violated Boy Scouts' First Amendment right of freedom of association.

Curran v. Mount Diablo Council of Boy Scouts of America

An open homosexual sued Mount Diablo Council under California's Unruh Civil Rights Act, challenging the council's refusal to approve him as an adult leader. After trial, the Los Angeles County Superior Court ruled in favor of the Boy Scout council. On appeal, the California Supreme Court granted review and held in a unanimous opinion that Boy Scouts is not a "business establishment" for purposes of the Unruh Civil Rights Act's requirement of equal rights to public accommodations.

*Boy Scouts of America v. District of Columbia
Commission on Human Rights*

Open homosexuals filed complaints in the DC Commission alleging that
they were denied privileges of a place of public accommodation when they
were rejected as volunteer Boy Scout leaders. On June 20, 2001, a year
after the Supreme Court issued its opinion in *Dale*, the District of Columbia Commission on Human Rights refused to apply *Dale* and instead held
that Boy Scouts of America and the National Capital Area Council violated the District of Columbia Human Rights Act of 1977. The District of
Columbia Court of Appeals reversed, holding that to force Boy Scouts to
appoint open homosexuals as Scout leaders would violate the Boy Scouts'
First Amendment freedom of expressive association.

*Chicago Area Council of Boy Scouts of America v. City
of Chicago Commission on Human Relations*

An open homosexual filed a claim under Chicago's human rights ordinance
alleging that he was denied employment with the local Boy Scouts council
because of his open homosexuality. Ultimately, an Illinois appellate court
held that the Boy Scouts were allowed to require job applicants to observe
the Scout Oath and Law when they were seeking to serve as professionals
acting in representative capacities for Scouting. The court remanded for a
determination as to whether the employment tester was seeking a nonrep-
resentative position from which he was improperly excluded, and the Commission determined that he had not been seeking such a position.[6]

The legal assault was only one front in the war against the Boy Scouts.
Another was the pressure brought to bear on American corporations
and nonprofit foundations to withdraw their financial support. This has
achieved significant success. Those refusing to contribute further include:
Chase Manhattan, Levi Strauss, CVS, Wells Fargo, Pew Charitable Trusts,
the UPS Foundation, Merck Foundation, Chipotle, Hewlett-Packard,
American Airlines, J.P. Morgan, some fifty of thirteen hundred local
United Way chapters, and, what had been BSA's largest corporate donor,

[6] Ibid.

Intel. A typical excuse for defunding the Scouts was given by Brian Grill, Merck Foundation executive vice president, who explained: "It is critical to honor and support a foundational policy of diversity and inclusion in all funding decisions.... The BSA's policy of exclusion directly conflicts with the Merck Foundation's giving guidelines ... [and] policies that prevent ... discrimination."[7]

Filmmaker Steven Spielberg resigned from the Boy Scouts Advisory Council in 2001. He said: "It has deeply saddened me to see the Boy Scouts of America actively and publicly participating in discrimination."[8] But wasn't Spielberg, in turn, discriminating by doing this? In March 2013 Microsoft founder Bill Gates, an advocate of same-sex marriage, agreed that the Boy Scouts should rescind its ban on homosexual members and leaders. When asked why, he simply responded, "Because it's 2013."[9] By this remark he proved to be a good Rousseauian. History, not Nature, makes man. Not only have times changed, but times have changed man. Therefore, thought Gates, it is adequate simply to give the date, rather than a reason.

The absurdity of the Post's, President Obama's, and Gates' attacks against the Boy Scouts can be understood as follows. Let us say there is a Temperance League to which some active and "open" alcoholics seek admittance. The whole point of the Temperance League is to teach the evils of overindulgence in spirits. If it accepts others who openly advocate and practice drunkenness, it would be denying the reason for its own existence. It would abandon the moral principle that it is evil to be drunken.

What would be the purpose of the "active" alcoholics in joining the Temperance League? They would not be joining in order to quit drinking or to be changed, but to change the Temperance League itself so that there would be one less societal organization in the way of their getting good and sozzled whenever they wanted to without public moral opprobrium. They would join to reverse the public teaching on drunkenness. Is it, then, a matter of intolerance to exclude active alcoholics? Yes, of course, it is, but it is based not on who the alcoholics are, but on what they do and how they

---

[7] Quoted in Ed Vitagliano, "The Breaking of the Boy Scouts", *American Family Association Journal* (April 2013): 14–15.

[8] Noah Davis, "Spielberg Resigns from Boy Scouts Board", Hollywood.com, April 26, 2001, http://www.hollywood.com/news/brief/386418/spielberg-resigns-from-boy-scouts-board.

[9] Meredith Bennett-Smith, "Bill Gates, Former Boy Scout, Wants Group to Lift Gay Ban 'Because It's 2013'", *Huffington Post*, March 15, 2013, http://www.huffingtonpost.com/2013/03/15/bill-gates-former-boy-scout-lift-gay-ban_n_2885325.html.

justify what they do. Any reformed alcoholic would be welcome to join the Temperance League.

Now, the *Post* might say that this is treating active alcoholics as unequal to non-alcoholics "merely because of the way they were born". And, in fact, there is a case to be made that certain people are afflicted with a genetic predisposition to alcoholism. Some people with this predisposition, however, choose not to drink, while others choose to imbibe. In other words, despite the predisposition, the act is still a matter of free will and therefore a moral issue. All acts are not equal. Moral acts are superior to immoral acts. Virtue is superior to vice. Truth is superior to falsehood.

Speaking of which, one ought to say that the *Post*'s editorial was simply one volley in its incessant barrage against sexual morality and marriage. Not only its editorial page, but the "Style" section and often even its news pages are dedicated to the overthrow of chastity and any notion of marriage as between a man and a woman. Like any good propagandist, the *Post* believes that if it repeats its mantra often enough, it will change reality or create a new one. The *Post* certainly feels itself free to "criticize" and "condemn" those like the Boy Scouts who would not go along with the program. If you do not embrace their unreality, you will be upbraided. How tolerant is that?

As already mentioned, the Boy Scouts finally flinched under this tremendous pressure, announcing a proposal to keep the ban on homosexual adult leaders but to allow homosexual youths until the age of eighteen to participate in its programs. An April 2013 statement said that "while perspectives and opinions vary significantly, parents, adults in the Scouting community and teens alike tend to agree that youth should not be denied the benefits of scouting." This compromise seemed slightly disingenuous since there had never been a sexual orientation litmus test for entering the Scouts, and the only thing disallowed was the *open* promotion of the homosexual cause. The Boy Scouts allowed its principles to be put up for a vote (some 61 percent of the voting council supported the proposal) and then, after the vote, caved. What, then, does this policy change mean, if not the abandonment of the prohibition of such promotion?

By now accepting openly homosexual members, the Boy Scouts are, at the very least, certainly going to be dealing with a major distraction (can homosexual scouts bunk together?). But what's much worse, the organization is implicitly accepting the rationalization for homosexual sexual behavior as part of its moral formation. In this, it will be complicit in corruption. It is avoiding doing this explicitly by continuing to insist on chastity from its scouts in its policy that "any sexual conduct, whether heterosexual or homosexual, by youth of Scouting age is contrary to the virtues of Scouting." If, however, it is accepting the homosexual inclination as legitimate, what, then, could be wrong with the thing toward which it is inclined, meaning homosexual behavior?

"I've waited 13 years for this", said Matt Comer, now twenty-seven, who had to leave his scout troop at age fourteen after he started a GLSEN Gay-Straight Alliance at his school. Since the fourth grade, he told the *New York Times*, he had dreamed of becoming an Eagle Scout and was crushed when he was denied the chance. "Today we finally have some justice for me and others", he said. "But gay youths will still be told they are no longer welcome when they turn 18."[10]

Indeed, the new BSA policy of allowing declared homosexuals only until the age of eighteen is logically untenable. If it is okay to be an open and declared homosexual at seventeen, why not at eighteen, or twenty-five? This line will not hold. And, of course, the *Washington Post* was hardly assuaged by the compromise. It was accurate, however, in declaring that "the Boy Scouts of America's national leaders have become morally incoherent." The *Post* further opined that "excluding openly gay adults suggests that they are dangerous, potential child abusers or brainwashers of such threat that they should be denied any place in the Boy Scouts of America. The logic is perverse: It's okay for gay teens to learn, grow and serve in the fellowship of Scouting without lying about who they are—but only until they're 18, after which they become a menace."[11] (The *Post* failed to explain why pederasty is a bad idea in the Catholic Church but a good idea in the Boy Scouts.)

What Mr. Comer had done by starting his Gay-Straight Alliance was directly to challenge the teachings and regulations of the Boy Scouts. In other words, rather than abide by the rules of the organization he had *voluntarily* joined, he insisted on his own rules to the extent that the Boy Scouts must be made to conform to them. That is Mr. Comer's idea of justice: to conform others to his will.

[10] Erik Eckholm, "Boy Scouts End Longtime Ban on Openly Gay Youths", *New York Times*, May 23, 2013, http://mobile.nytimes.com/2013/05/24/us/boy-scouts-to-admit-openly-gay-youths-as-members.html?from=global.home.
[11] Editorial board, "The Boy Scouts' Proposal on Gay Participation Goes the Wrong Way", *Washington Post*, April 27, 2013, http://articles.washingtonpost.com/2013-04-27/opinions/38859049_1_gay-scouts-boy-scouts-scout-oath.

It reminds me of a situation somewhat like this. Let us suppose that at a country club, a golfer decided all of a sudden to play the eighth hole in the opposite direction. In other words, he teed off at the green and aimed for the tee. Let us then suppose that he was approached and remonstrated with by the rules committee of the club and he responded: "Oh, but I was playing the hole by my own rules because of who I am." To which the rules committee could reasonably reply, "But you are a member of the club, and you're playing at the club." The rules committee could remind the errant member that he had agreed to the rules when he joined the club and that, if he no longer wished to abide by them, he should leave. Why are the Boy Scouts the only "club" whose rules may be traduced by those who still insist on the right to remain its member?

This is what makes it particularly hilarious to read the cant used by the homosexual movement to celebrate its victory. It is now all about inclusiveness. Founder of Scouts for Equality, Zach Wahls, an Eagle Scout raised by two lesbians, said the time had come for change. "There is nothing Scout-like about exclusion of other people, and there is nothing Scout-like about putting your own religious beliefs before someone else's."[12]

Apparently Wahls failed to notice that the new policy will lead to the exclusion of many more people than the policy excluding open homosexuals did and that he had just placed his beliefs before theirs. He also neglected to note that the Scouts have not yet been stripped of their requirement that Scouts must possess a belief in God in order to be a member. Why should the Scouts any longer be allowed to get away with this exclusive requirement? Think of all the atheists who want to go Scouting. Should they be denied this experience simply to uphold a belief in God? Why shouldn't the Scouts be forced to deny that principle so that the atheists can go camping? In fact, as a sign of things to come, the Girl Guides in Great Britain announced in June 2013 that they were abandoning the promise to "love my God". Beginning in September, they will pledge instead to "be true to myself and develop my beliefs".[13] To accommodate young atheists in the Scouts, the Scouting Association in Great Britain also plans to drop the

[12] Marice Richter, "Boy Scouts of America Set to Vote on Gay Youth Ban", *Reuters*, May 23, 2013, http://www.reuters.com/article/2013/05/23/usa-boyscouts-ban-idUSL2No E40WD20130523.

[13] Cole Moreton, "Scout Association Amends Vow to God in Bid to Appease Atheists and Other Faiths, *Telegraph*, June 23, 2013, http://www.telegraph.co.uk/news/religion /10136888/Scout-Association-amends-vow-to-God-in-bid-to-appease-atheists-and-other -faiths.html.

promise to "do my duty to God" for them. Wouldn't this also be "compassionate, caring and kind"—as Wayne Brock, the chief executive of the Boy Scouts, characterized the decision on homosexual Scouts—to do here as well? No, in fact, it would not be those warm and fuzzy things; it would be derelict in denying the fundamental principle of the importance of belief in God in forming manly character—just as this decision was derelict in ineluctably accepting the rationalization for homosexuality.

Now, to the newly excluded by newly included. The *New York Times* reported :

> Allison Mackey of Hanover, Pa., has five sons—one an Eagle Scout, three now active in scouting and an eight-year-old who had planned to join. The family has discussed the issue and reached a decision, she said: all the sons were willing to abandon the Boy Scouts if openly gay members are allowed. "The Boy Scouts are something we've really enjoyed because they celebrate manliness and leadership," she said. But she added that she and her husband were "looking to encourage our sons in traditional Christian values. To stand by principles would be difficult," she said. "But we're going to have to say no. The organization is giving up freedom."[14]

What freedom might that be? Well, certainly the freedom not to be used by the homosexual movement to move its agenda through society. The Boy Scout leadership must see that this is what it has allowed to happen. And it is only the beginning. Alas, it was the last significant private institution in the United States standing against the homosexual juggernaut, which had taken down the US military only the year before. What does this policy change mean, if not the abandonment of the prohibition of the open promotion of the homosexual cause? If you accept the promotion, you accept what it teaches. No matter how the Boy Scout leadership tries to camouflage it, that is what was so iniquitous about its cave-in.

Also, this decision was like throwing red meat to the wolves. They will want more. And more was immediately asked for. "Scouts for Equality will continue its efforts until discrimination is no longer a word associated with the BSA", announced Zach Wahls.[15] "Today's vote is a significant victory for gay youth across the nation and a clear indication that the Boy Scouts'

[14]Eckholm, "Boy Scouts End Longtime Ban on Openly Gay Youths".

[15]Cheryl Wetzstein, "Opposition to Boy Scouts' Compromise on Gays Grows on Both Sides of Issue", *Washington Times*, April 24, 2013, http://www.washingtontimes.com/news/2013/apr/24/opposition-boy-scouts-compromise-gays-grows/.

ban on gay adult leaders will also inevitably end", GLAAD spokesman Rich Ferraro declared. "We'll continue urging corporate donors and public officials to withhold their support", until the leadership issue is resolved.[16]

Nor will the compromise stanch the loss of corporate support. According to the Associated Press, on June 13, 2013, "Caterpillar spokeswoman Rachel Potts says Thursday that the Caterpillar Foundation made the decision [to withdraw support] while reviewing the groups it supports. She called the Boy Scouts' policy barring homosexual adults from serving as scout leaders discriminatory. She said that policy doesn't square with the Peoria-based heavy equipment maker's own anti-discrimination policies."[17]

How will the Boy Scouts stand in the winds that blow then? They will have to reap the wild wind, and not much will be left standing. Alas, it was a great group, and it need not have acceded to its own demise. It could have continued fighting, even gone down fighting—according to the very principles of courage and leadership that it was supposed to be instilling in the young.

---

[16] Marice Richter, "Boy Scouts of America Votes to End Century-Old Ban on Gay Scouts", *Reuters*, May 24, 2013, http://www.reuters.com/article/2013/05/24/us-usa-boyscouts -ban-vote-idUSBRE94M1A320130524 and Erik Eckholm,"Boy Scouts End Longtime Ban on Openly Gay Youths, *New York Times*, May 23, 2012, http://www.nytimes.com/2013/05/24 /us/boy-scouts-to-admit-openly-gay-youths-as-members.html?_r=0.

[17] David Mercer, "Caterpillar Drops Boy Scout Support over Gay Ban", *Yahoo News*, June 13, 2013, http://news.yahoo.com/caterpillar-drops-boy-scouts-support-over-gay -ban-213446568.html.

11

Sodomy and the Military

From America's founding until 2011, the armed forces of the United States have prohibited sodomy and sought to exclude homosexuals from military service. In 1778, at Valley Forge, General George Washington approved the sentence of dismissal for an officer "attempting to commit sodomy", with "abhorrence and detestation of such infamous crimes", according to Washington's papers at the Library of Congress.[1] The reasons the policy continued until very recently were given in the Department of Defense Directive 1332.14 (Enlisted Administrative Separations), January 1981, which stated:

> Homosexuality is incompatible with military service. The presence in the military environment of persons who engage in homosexual conduct or who, by their statements, demonstrate a propensity to engage in homosexual conduct, seriously impairs the accomplishment of the military mission. The presence of such members adversely affects the ability of the armed forces to maintain discipline, good order, and morale; to foster mutual trust and confidence among service members; to ensure the integrity of the system of rank and command; to facilitate assignment and worldwide deployment of service members who frequently must live and work in close conditions affording minimal privacy; to recruit and retain members of the armed forces; to maintain the public acceptability of military service; and to prevent breaches of security.

I will speak later from my personal experiences as to why I believe this policy was exactly right.

[1] "George Washington, March 14, 1778, General Orders", The George Washington Papers at the Library of Congress, 1741–1799, in John C. Fitzpatrick, ed., *The Writings of George Washington from the Original Manuscript Sources*, 1745–1799, http://memory.loc.gov/ammem/gwhtml/gwhome.html.

Here is how and why it was abandoned. At the beginning of his presidency, Bill Clinton wanted to eliminate any obstacles to homosexuals' serving in the armed services. Congress resisted but in 1993 reached a compromise with President Clinton and established the Don't Ask, Don't Tell policy, which prohibited asking a person if he is a homosexual, but allowed for the removal of openly declared homosexuals or those discovered committing homosexual acts. Summarized by a Department of the Army brochure, the policy still found homosexual behavior incompatible with military service. It said, "In 1993, Congress made a finding that engaging in, attempting to engage in, or soliciting another to engage in homosexual acts is grounds for discharge from the military. Congress said that military service by those who have demonstrated a propensity to engage in homosexual acts creates an unacceptable risk to morale, good order and discipline, and unit cohesion. Therefore, the long-standing element of military law that prohibits homosexual conduct continues to be necessary in the unique circumstances of military service."

In the intervening decade and a half, however, the willingness to consider the moral arguments against homosexual acts and their deleterious effect on the military eroded further. They were not even offered by the purportedly conservative administration of President George W. Bush. Toward the latter part of the Bush administration, in 2007, Marine General Peter Pace, then chairman of the joint chiefs, caused a political uproar by telling the *Chicago Tribune* that, in respect to the military's Don't Ask, Don't Tell policy, "I believe homosexual acts between two individuals are immoral and that we should not condone immoral acts. I do not believe the United States is well served by a policy that says it is okay to be immoral in any way."[2]

Was this man a homophobe? Hysterical reactions from the left suggested as much, but they did so by ignoring the rest of General Pace's statement. He said that he objected to homosexual acts "Just like I would not want it to be our policy that if we were to find out that so-and-so was sleeping with someone else's wife, that we would just look the other way, which we do not—we prosecute that kind of immoral behavior between members of the armed forces".

A *Washington Post* editorial chastised him for "his public expressions of intolerance on the men and women he commands". He had expressed

---

[2] Aamer Madhani, "Top General Calls Homosexuality 'Immoral'", *Chicago Tribune*, March 12, 2007, http://able2know.org/topic/92869-1.

himself only about the immoral Nature of acts against chastity, however, not persons. The real crime of General Pace was that he was in favor of chastity. Would the *Post* have objected if he had said the military does not allow desertion? Would that have been an expression of intolerance, or of an indispensable principle of the military organization? What would be the alternative view? That these acts are moral? Yes, responded the then Republican Senator John Warner of Virginia, a former secretary of the navy, who said, "I respectfully but strongly disagree with the chairman's view that homosexuality is immoral." (This remark blithely ignored General Pace's judgment on homosexual *acts*, not on homosexuality.)

By favoring chastity, General Pace proved himself a good Aristotelian, and he should have been supported. He clearly understood that chastity is not only a moral virtue but also indispensable to good order in the military. That is why he said that the United Sates is not well served by a policy that approves of sexual immorality in its military.

Several days after his indiscretion, a chastened but still unrepentant General Pace, who was not backed up by anyone in the Bush administration, explained that he was expressing his "personal moral views". In other words, the question of the immorality of adultery and sodomy was demoted to a matter of personal opinion, not of objective moral standards. Defense Secretary Robert Gates accepted that demotion ("I think personal opinion really doesn't have a place here") and then expressed the position of the legal positivist: "What's important is that we have a law, a statute that governs Don't Ask, Don't Tell." But is the law based upon a sound moral principle that is necessary for military discipline, or not? Or need we observe it simply because it is the law?

The White House spokesman at the time, the late Tony Snow, obscured the issue by pretending that it is a matter of judging people, rather than the moral Nature of certain acts: President Bush "has always said that the most important thing is that we ought not to prejudge one another". Then Snow also embraced the legal positivist position: "But when it comes to government policy, it's been in place for a long time and we will continue to execute it according to the letter of the law." This nonsense is the only kind of discourse on sexual morality now allowed in the United States.

The unremitting drumroll for allowing open homosexuality in the US armed forces grew louder with President Obama's support. After Obama hosted a homosexual celebration in the White House on the fortieth anniversary of the Stonewall Inn riots in 2009, Secretary of Defense Robert

Gates and Chairman of the Joint Chiefs Mike Mullen began to prepare the ground for what now seems to have been the inevitable rescission of the Don't Ask, Don't Tell policy. In early 2010 Admiral Mullen began his appearances before Congress in favor of eliminating the policy.

From his multiple testimonies, Admiral Mullen appeared not to have had the slightest idea as to why such laws once existed or why his immediate predecessor, General Pace, would have said what he did. The problem with the overturn of this policy was evident in the testimony of those supporting the change. In his appearance before Congress, poor Admiral Mullen never seemed to know when he was shooting himself in the foot and making the very points he haplessly wished to refute. In regard to the "bunk and shower" issues, he said, "I believe, and history tells us, that most of them [the troops] will put aside personal proclivities for something larger than themselves and for each other." But "put[ting] aside personal proclivities for something larger than themselves" is exactly what the Don't Ask, Don't Tell policy asked of serving homosexuals. They were only dismissed when they could not, or would not, put those personal proclivities aside for something larger. The policy Mullen advocated precisely promoted the personal proclivities of homosexual troops who were not content with serving without having their inclinations openly accommodated. Where exactly is the service to "something larger than themselves" in that? Mullen, without noticing it, installed a set of personal proclivities while he thought he was transcending them.

The admiral testified that he had "been serving with gays and lesbians my whole career.... I knew they were there. They knew I knew it. And what's more, nearly everyone in the crew knew it. We never missed a mission, never failed to deliver ordnance on target." Well, if this was so, why change the policy? It seems to have served us well.

Then Mullen trotted out his often-repeated imperative for repealing the policy, saying, "I cannot escape being troubled by the fact that we have in place a policy which forces young men and women to lie about who they are in order to defend their fellow citizens." This, he said "doesn't make any sense to me" because "it was fundamentally an issue of integrity." This was a puzzling formulation because the policy he helped to overturn did not require or force anyone to lie, as it prohibited asking if one was a homosexual in the first place. The more important point that eluded Mullen, however, is that people with integrity cannot be forced to lie. Refusing to lie, even if it is "required", is exactly what defines integrity. In other words,

Mullen was really promoting a policy designed to accommodate people who would otherwise lie as "required". Is that valuing integrity?

Regardless, the sentiment expressed by Admiral Mullen was in sync with the homosexual martyrology that developed with the spread of AIDS. They are not only dying for a cause but willing to lie for one as well. This is all the more noble because it is in defense of the realm. (This is not to disparage the service of those who honorably abided by the Don't Ask, Don't Tell policy.)

In November 2010 the Pentagon issued a report of more than three hundred pages on the subject of repeal, which concluded that it would not cause any serious disruptions in the military—in spite of more than two centuries of military policy and tradition that asserted the exact opposite. The Pentagon's report contained some interesting items. Apparently, some courageous chaplains declared total opposition to the repeal. "In equally strong terms", however, said the report, "other chaplains, including those who also believe homosexuality is a sin, informed us that 'we are all sinners', and that it is a chaplain's duty to care for all Service members." What did the statement that "we are all sinners" mean in the context of a report whose purpose was to pave the way to allow homosexuals to serve openly?

The whole point of repeal was to acknowledge the moral legitimacy of sodomitical acts. Otherwise, why allow the open declaration of the propensity to perform them? Or, since "we are all sinners", what does it matter? Repealing the policy meant that something of which people should be ashamed may now be publicly proclaimed. The permission for the proclamation—which is what the repeal bestowed—had as its exact purpose the removal of shame, and therefore a repeal of the teaching that the act is immoral.

How is that caring for the sinner? It would rather seem to be a reinforcement of the person's rationalization for his immoral behavior, which would serve only to steep him further in it. This is the opposite of "care". It is collusion. How will the clueless chaplains referred to above react when approached to perform homosexual marriages with service members? Declare again that "we are all sinners" and then sacramentalize the sin?

The general conclusion of the parties favoring repeal seemed to be that the only remaining problem was with the prejudices of the military, not with anything homosexuals do. In the many op-eds in the *Washington Post*, in policy papers, and in congressional testimony, none of them actually talked about or even vaguely referred to homosexual acts or examined why anyone might consider such behavior a problem in a military unit. Yes, there were demure references to certain troops (e.g., the Marines, who objected to bunking or showering with homosexuals). In fact, in August 2010 General James Conway, former Marine Corps commandant, said that "an overwhelming majority [of Marines] would like not to be roomed with a person that is openly homosexual." But no one said *why* they would not like it or whether their objections were based upon any good reason.

So, let us get explicit, if not graphic. We begin by noting that the most prized character in the military is masculinity or manliness. It is in the military and, most especially, in battle that a man is at his most masculine. He must call upon all his warlike resources as a man to succeed. Combat requires discipline, self-sacrifice, trust, strength, and valor. Many men enter the military exactly to test themselves, to become or to discover if they are real men—meaning men who can take the hardship, the pressure, the violence, and the mortal danger. Therefore, they prize masculinity in these terms and especially the camaraderie of their fellow warriors.

What is it about active homosexuals that might offend these men? Are active homosexuals somehow less manly? Consider what takes place in a sodomitical relationship. In it, one man behaves toward another man as if that other man were a woman. The other man willingly pretends that he is a woman. For a man to pretend he is a woman in a sodomitical act is, to say the least, the antithesis of maleness. It is its denial. This is why in the old common parlance such a person was often referred to as a "girlie man". He is pretending that he is a girl. He forsakes his masculinity. By Nature there is something cowardly and shameful in this, and that is why "girlie men" are despised. They are being less than men; they are being traitors to their sex.

When a "manly" man is approached by a homosexual to engage in this sexual charade, his natural reaction is outrage and disgust, which can easily turn to violence—one reason overt homosexuality was heretofore banned from the military. He considers it an assault upon his masculinity and an insult to his manhood. Is this man wrong to be outraged at being "hit on" in this manner? If one expects him to be manly, if masculinity is the quintessence of his profession, the answer is obvious. His response to something abnormal is normal. This is, no doubt, why the Pentagon report (p. 74) stated that nearly 60 percent of respondents in the Marine Corps and Army said they believed rescinding the policy would have a negative impact on their combat unit's effectiveness. Among Marines alone the number was 67 percent.

Therefore, what is to be done with these men? They are the obstacle. They must be retrained; they must be reconditioned; they must be reeducated; and, if nothing else works, they must be ordered either to enter the brave new world or leave it. Military discipline, the chain of command, will be used to undermine the very virtue that underlies that discipline. In an extraordinary demonstration of the Chinese proverb that a fish rots from the head, a lesbian professor at the Marine Corps University, Tammy Schultz, in a *Washington Post* op-ed, declared her hope for the successful implementation of the repeal of the Don't Ask, Don't Tell policy by quoting a Marine who said, "If the law changes, we will comply with the law."[3] Indeed they will; they have to. The law is coercive.

Congress finally passed the repeal of the Don't Ask, Don't Tell policy, which had kept a lid on this issue for seventeen years, and President Obama signed it into law on December 22, 2010. By September 2011 it was fully implemented with Mr. Obama's announcement that "patriotic Americans in uniform will no longer have to lie about who they are in order to serve the country they love." But what about the other patriotic Americans in uniform who never lied?

It might be wise to pause for a moment and think about what others may be forced to do now that the policy of Don't Ask, Don't Tell has been abandoned. I may be able to bring a certain perspective to the issue since I have both served in the military and worked extensively in the world of the arts, which the homosexual subculture often dominates.

I keenly recall my induction at army basic training. It was conducted at a former World War II POW camp for Germans. At Indian Town Gap Military Reservation, we first had our heads shaved and then were told to strip naked as we, for several hours, went from station to station being prodded and poked to ascertain our fitness for the coming physical ardors. In the barracks, there were no stalls between the toilets or showers, in case any of us thought there might be some small refuge of privacy left. This was deliberately done to break us down, so that we could then be reshaped into fighting men.

Now imagine inserting into this scenario some naked females. What would happen? All hell would break loose. And whose fault would it be?

---

[3] Tammy S. Schultz, "The Few. The Proud. The Problem: Can the Corps' Warrior Ethos Accept Openly Gay Marines?", *Washington Post*, November 21, 2010, http://www.washingtonpost.com/wp-dyn/content/article/2010/11/19/AR2010111906892.html.

It would be completely unfair to both the men and the women to inject sexual tension into an already highly demanding, emotionally charged situation. Those who contrived such a state of affairs would be largely responsible for the consequences.

Since homosexuals define themselves as being sexually attracted to other men, why would anyone imagine that it is any less combustible to place openly declared, practicing homosexuals into the same setting? It is curious that the military is the only form of association in which it is suggested that people would have to disrobe in front of, and live intimately with, others who find them sexually attractive, but with whom they do not desire any sexual intimacy. Is there a workplace (outside of strip joints) in which women are required to do this in front of men, or men in front of women? For obvious reasons, there is not. Why, then, create such a place in the US military, where men are now required to do this in front of other men who avowedly find them sexually attractive? The answer is, under the faux guise of civil rights, to enforce the rationalization for homosexual misbehavior on the country as a whole. What better way to achieve this than institutionalizing this rationalization in the armed forces?

The question may well be asked: If homosexuals have been serving in the military under the Don't Ask, Don't Tell policy, why hasn't the mayhem described above already happened? The answer is precisely because that policy required homosexuals to be covert in their behavior and not to display their predilections openly. Overturning this policy means "coming out of the closet" inside the military with the consequences described. Adding to the tensions will be the fact that any heterosexual service member who objects or acts in a way that could be interpreted as "homophobic" will be the one brought up on charges or dismissed. He will be forced not to object to homosexual behavior. If a soldier refuses to shower with another person of the same gender who finds him sexually attractive, will he be violating that other person's human rights?

Unlike many who advocated this change in policy, I have actually worked in an openly homosexual environment. As a professional actor, I appeared in productions in which the majority of the cast members were homosexual, as were the directors. When the "gay" subculture takes over, those who do not participate in it are discriminated against. I was not shocked by this. It is human nature to prefer one's own. I left after a season in one regional theater, being told by the public relations director: "You're a good actor; it's too bad you're not a homosexual." More disturbing were the occasions on which I resorted to or threatened physical force to halt unwelcome advances. Does anyone seriously think that things like this will not happen in the military?

It is already happening. According to *NBC News*, May 16, 2013, "The Pentagon estimates that last year 13,900 of the 1.2 million men on active duty endured sexual assault ... or 38 men per day versus 33 women per day."[4] Rates of sexual assault in the military are climbing dramatically—up 34 percent between 2010 and 2012.

The lesson from this experience is that the endorsement of being openly homosexual in the military will lead to the formation of an approved subculture within the armed forces that will seek its own ends and the advancement of its own (based at least partly on sexual favors)—to the detriment of those who are not part of it. This is why, in our saner moments, homosexuality has been considered "incompatible with military service". Of course, homosexuals are not numerous enough to change the dominant military culture, but will gravitate to places within it where they can change it. For instance, based upon the number who were expelled during the Don't Ask, Don't Tell policy, the navy seems to attract more homosexuals than other services.

Once again, this is not shocking. It has to be expected as part of human behavior. What is shocking is that President Obama, Secretary Gates, and Admiral Mullen were willing to let this happen to a military that was already under maximum duress from two wars. It is precisely this point that led General George Casey, the army chief of staff, to say that any such change should be held off until the troops are back from Iraq—as if there would ever be a good time to do this. In the fine tradition of General Pace, General James Conway, the Marine Corps commandant, said that repeal would harm military readiness. But military readiness was not the objective of those seeking to overturn the policy. Moral vindication of homosexual behavior was the goal—no matter what price US service members had to pay for their use as pawns in the homosexual revolution.

This misuse of the military became abundantly clear from President Obama's subsequent behavior. After forcing the repeal of Don't Ask, Don't Tell on the military, he then used the military as the reason for endorsing homosexual marriage. Those poor Marines in the foxholes of Afghanistan

---

[4] Bill Briggs, "Male Rape Survivors Tackle Military Assault in Tough-Guy Culture", NBCNews.com, May 16, 2013, http://usnews.nbcnews.com/_news/2013/05/16/18301723-male-rape-survivors-tackle-military-assault-in-tough-guy-culture?lite.

were just aching to marry each other, and Obama came to their rescue. He shamelessly proclaimed (as quoted earlier): "When I think about those soldiers or airmen or marines or sailors who are out there fighting on my behalf and yet feel constrained, even now that Don't Ask Don't Tell is gone, because they are not able to commit themselves in a marriage, at a certain point I've just concluded that for me personally it is important for me to go ahead and affirm that I think same-sex couples should be able to get married."[5]

This is risible, but one has to admire the audacity of his transparently sophistical argument. What's more, it worked. Obama pulled everyone along with him. Take, for instance, Secretary of Defense Leon E. Panetta, who hosted the first ever "pride" event at the Pentagon "to personally thank all our gay and lesbian service members, LGBT DoD civilians, and their families for their service to our country", as he said on a Pentagon video. I have no problem acknowledging that homosexual Americans have sacrificed for their country. I am equally certain that alcoholic and adulterous Americans have also done so. It is their sacrifice *as* Americans that should be honored. What is the point of celebrating their behavior *as* homosexuals, or *as* alcoholics, or *as* adulterers if not to promote these behaviors? The first is as absurd as the other two.

Panetta, a Catholic, attended Santa Clara University undergraduate and law schools. On the Santa Clara website, Panetta is quoted as saying, "In politics there has to be a line beyond which you don't go—the line that marks the difference between right and wrong, what your conscience tells you is right. Too often people don't know where the line is. My family, how I was raised, my education at SCU, all reinforced my being able to see that line."[6] Where was the line between the proper use of and abuse of sex? Panetta crossed it without apparently being able to see it. Under the cover of "diversity", he publicly endorsed actions that are contrary to the faith he purportedly holds, to say nothing of its effect on military discipline. He endorsed the rationalization for this misbehavior—making wrong into right. That is what rationalizations demand—acquiescence and then cooperation. Panetta gave his. Now no one can serve as secretary of defense, or indeed of any other government agency, without endorsing Gay Pride Month. If you insist on publicly maintaining moral principles, you are officially part of the problem.

The price of open homosexual service is to drive virtue, including the military virtues, further underground as deviancy is defined upward. This is not an accidental effect or simply collateral damage; it was, as mentioned before, the larger purpose of revoking the Don't Ask, Don't Tell policy. The military was the last public bastion within the government for these virtues; so it became the target. It had to be made to kneel before moral abnormity. Men of honor had to be required to acquiesce publicly. Their fall represents the definitive triumph of the moral dystopia that has been eating its way through America's institutions. The subsequent decline in combat effectiveness, the resignations, the dismissals, and the loss of military vocations are a small price to pay for the brave new world's ultimate vindication of the homosexual rationalization. The failure of many of those in public life, including senior military officers, to rally to the defense of these service members and their institution has a name: *trahison des clercs*. It is not an honorable one, but they have earned it.

12

Sodomy and US Foreign Policy

If we are promoting homosexual "rights" within our military and government, what about promoting them overseas? If sodomy and same-sex
marriage are constitutional rights, what is their relationship to US foreign
policy? Despite the tremendous controversy regarding these issues within
the United States, the Obama administration has gone ahead and placed
them at the center of US diplomacy. Why? Recall Jones' remark that the
rationalization of sexual misbehavior "could only calm the troubled conscience in an effective manner when it was legitimized by the regime in
power ... [which] went on in the name of high moral purpose to make
this vision normative for the *entire world*" (emphasis added). Therefore, the
Obama administration has undertaken the task of universalizing the rationalization for sodomitical behavior and is doing so with high moral rhetoric
—as usual, by appropriating the language of human rights.

The effort began in earnest on International Human Rights Day, December 6, 2011, with a powerful pair of events. President Obama issued a memorandum for the heads of executive departments and agencies, directing
them "to ensure that US diplomacy and foreign assistance promote and protect the human rights of LGBT persons". Mr. Obama said that "the struggle
to end discrimination against lesbian, gay, bisexual, and transgender (LGBT)
persons is a global challenge, and one that is central to the United States
commitment to promoting human rights."[1] The departments and agencies
included the Departments of State, the Treasury, Defense, Justice, Agricul-
ture, Commerce, Health and Human Services, and Homeland Security, the

---

[1] Barack Obama, "International Initiatives to Advance the Human Rights of Lesbian,
Gay, Bisexual, and Transgender Persons", December 6, 2011, http://www.whitehouse.gov
/the-press-office/2011/12/06/presidential-memorandum-international-initiatives-advance
-human-rights-1.

United States Agency for International Development (USAID), the Millennium Challenge Corporation, the Export-Import Bank, the United States Trade Representative, and "such other agencies as the President may designate". All US agencies engaged abroad were directed to prepare a report each year "on their progress toward advancing these initiatives".

Austin Ruse, president of the Catholic Family and Human Rights Institute, explained:

> They have directed their embassies everywhere to monitor and assist domestic homosexual movements whether the host country and their people accept it or not. The United States is very powerful and can force governments to submit to its social-policy views. They are intent on forcing homosexual "marriage" and homosexual adoption on countries that are offended by such things. They are intent on forcing sexual orientation and gender identity as new categories of non-discrimination that will trump the rights of religious believers.... Most people recognize that the homosexual lifestyle is harmful to public health and morals. The effect of the Obama policy is to offend billions of people and force this view on reluctant governments. This is most especially offensive to countries that are predominantly Christian and Muslim. In fact, Christianity and Islam are among the chief obstacles of this agenda and policy.[2]

While President Obama took the action, Hillary Clinton, then US secretary of state, gave the rationale in a speech, in which she proclaimed that "gay rights are human rights, and human rights are gay rights." She also announced that the United States would give more than $3 million to a new Global Equality Fund in order to help civil society organizations promote homosexual advocacy.

Mrs. Clinton came energetically to the defense of those "forced to suppress or deny who they are to protect themselves from harm. I am talking about gay, lesbian, bisexual, and transgender people", whom she described with a strong Rousseauian echo as "human beings born free and given bestowed equality and dignity". But if they were born free, why are they not free now? No doubt, because society oppresses them, just as South Africa once oppressed its black population through apartheid—an example Mrs. Clinton gives. But history overcame that, and since, as Rousseau taught, man is a product of history, history can overcome this,

---

[2] Kevin J. Jones, "State Department vs. Catholic Countries", *National Catholic Register,* June 30, 2011, http://www.ncregister.com/daily-news/state-department-vs.-catholic-countries.

too. Thus, Mrs. Clinton ends with the admonition, "Be on the right side of history."[3]

It is a testimony to the influence of Rousseau that Secretary Clinton should have appealed to history for the vindication of "gay" rights rather than to moral principle. Had it been the latter, she would have had to say rather that, in order "to protect themselves from harm", LGBT persons *should* "suppress" precisely that part of themselves inclined to indulge in disordered sexual acts, just as anyone should resist their inclinations to immoral acts, whatever their kind. Mrs. Clinton averred that "being LGBT does not make you less human." That is certainly so, unless you consistently give in to one of these disordered inclinations. In a parallel case, being an alcoholic also does not make you less human. Practicing alcoholism by living life in an inebriated stupor, however, does make you less human in the Aristotelian sense that it impairs your Nature or incapacitates you from fulfilling it. If it is virtue that enables man to reach his natural end in becoming fully human, then it is vice that prevents him from doing so, thus making him less human.

Fully embracing the rationalization of the same-sex cause, Secretary Clinton espoused LGBT "gender identity" as equivalent to being black or being a woman. It is "who they are". In a moment of humility, she stated that, "my own country's record on human rights for gay people is far from perfect. Until 2003, it was still a crime in parts of our country." *It* was? What was *it*? Being homosexual or lesbian was not a crime in the United States, so what was she referring to? Mrs. Clinton never said, but the *it* to which she alluded is sodomy, the elephant in the room. She repeated the mantra that "it is a violation of human rights when governments declare it illegal to be gay" and "it should never be a crime to be gay." One would have to agree insofar as persecution of and violence against homosexuals is concerned but, as Austin Ruse has pointed out, "Such attacks upon individuals are already recognized as violations of human rights in international law particularly in the 1966 Covenants implementing the *Universal Declaration of Human Rights* and other existing treaties."[4] This, then, is moving beyond that to the moral and legal endorsement of certain *behavior*. Some governments continue to

---

[3] Hillary Rodham Clinton, "Remarks in Recognition of International Human Rights Day", U.S. Department of State website, December 6, 2011, http://www.state.gov/secretary/rm/2011/12/178368.htm.

[4] Personal transcript from the video "Debating the Freedom America Promotes", Common Sense Society, October 18, 2012, at: http://dccommonsense.com/debating-the-freedoms-america-promotes/.

have laws against homosexual *acts*, which is not the same thing as violating their rights as human beings. Was Mrs. Clinton saying that it is a violation of human rights to declare sodomy illegal?

Apparently yes, for that would be consistent with an understanding of Section 1 in the Obama directive, instructing agencies abroad to engage in "Combating Criminalization of LGBT Status or *Conduct* Abroad" (emphasis added).[5] What kind of *conduct* might this be? The only conduct that is or has been consistently criminalized by many countries is sodomy. Morally speaking, sodomy is a fairly unattractive act. Why should it not be criminalized? Perhaps there are prudential reasons for not doing so, but what might be the moral objections to such laws? The somewhat evasive answer in the presidential memorandum is, because "no country should deny people their rights because of who they love." In her speech, Mrs. Clinton echoed this response and set this test: "We need to ask ourselves, 'How would it feel if it were a crime to love the person I love?'"

Well, that depends. What if the person one loves is already married? What if the person one loves is a sibling? How about a teacher in love with a student? Or a pastor in love with a choirboy? Or an uncle with his niece? Acting upon any of these loves in a sexual relationship is, in most places, a crime. It is not so much *whom* one loves, but *how* one loves. (As critic and novelist Allan Massie said, "Only in modern times have people been stupid enough to suppose that intense emotional attachments must find physical expression.")[6] How it would *feel* does not really matter since, in each of these cases, it is morally wrong to sexualize the relationship. Feelings do not change the moral Nature of an act. Why, if all the above cases deserve prohibition, do homosexuals deserve an exemption when it comes to sodomy? Secretary Clinton never said why we should *feel* for them and not for any of those mentioned above, nor did she raise any of the above examples of criminal love as violations of human rights. Why not?

As with all rationalizations for misbehavior, Mrs. Clinton's speech was rife with denials of reality—three of which came in one sentence. She said, "Now, there are some who say and believe that all gay people are pedophiles, that homosexuality is a disease that can become caught or cured, or that gays recruit others to become gay. Well, these notions are simply not true." Well, these notions have to be *seen* as not true for her to promote the

[5] Obama, "International Initiatives to Advance the Human Rights".
[6] Allan Massie, "The Unexpected Monarch", *Wall Street Journal*, November 30, 2013, C7.

"gay" agenda internationally and get away with it. I have never met anyone who believes or has said that all homosexuals are pedophiles, but many of them are certainly pederasts. By setting up the pedophile straw man, Mrs. Clinton avoids this unpleasant reality. Whether homosexuality is a disease or not (it is certainly a disorder), there is ample evidence, as we have seen, that it can be cured. Of course, a fair number of people float into homosexuality in their youth and float out again as they mature—no cure required. (So much for its being an immutable characteristic.) Others who have become immersed in this life and who later wish to leave it, even if only a minority, have successfully done so through a variety of therapies. In 1995 the *New York Times* reported that "Dr. Charles W. Socarides offered the closest thing to hope that many homosexuals had in the 1960's: the prospect of a cure. Rather than brand them as immoral or regard them as criminal, Dr. Socarides, a New York psychoanalyst, told homosexuals that they suffered from an illness whose effects could be reversed."[7] As was mentioned earlier, Dr. Socarides said that his cure rate was about one third. For Secretary Clinton to deny this is an enormous disservice to the very people whose rights she purports to be defending. She offered the antithesis of hope.

Lastly, the bigger the lie, the bolder the assertion—as in Mrs. Clinton's outright denial that "gays recruit others to become gay". In my professional career in the arts, I witnessed such recruitment, saw its occasional success, and was several times the object of it. Anyone with a rudimentary knowledge of the homosexual subculture could not possibly make such a statement as Mrs. Clinton's. Those without such knowledge could consult homosexual literature such as *Lavender Culture*, in which Gerald Hannon described the need for a youth recruitment campaign: "I believe ... we have to behave in a certain way vis-à-vis young people. I believe that means we have to proselytize.... The answer is to proselytize. Aggressively so." He added, "To attract young people to the gay movement in large numbers should be the challenge to the next phase of the movement. It is a challenge we have set ourselves."[8] This is not to say that all homosexuals recruit, but to assert that none do is a complete denial of reality—which, after all, is the point of the rationalization.

[7] David W. Dunlap, "An Analyst, a Father, Battles Homosexuality", *New York Times*, December 24, 1995, http://www.nytimes.com/1995/12/24/us/an-analyst-a-father-battles-homosexuality.htmlscp7&sqcharles%20socarides&stcse.

[8] Gerald Hannon, "Gay Youth and the Question of Consent", in Karla Jay and Allen Young, eds., *Lavender Culture* (New York: NYU Press, 1994), 362–64.

What this is all about was very clear from the 2006 *Yogyakarta Principles on the Application of International Human Rights Law in Relation to Sexual Orientation and Gender Identity*, adopted by the International Commission of Jurists, the International Service for Human Rights, and homosexual activists. The purpose of the document was to influence the interpretation of the articles of the *Universal Declaration of Human Rights*, all UN human rights treaties, and international law as a whole. One requirement of the *Principles* is to "repeal criminal and other legal provisions that prohibit or are, in effect, employed to prohibit consensual sexual activity among people of the same sex who are over the age of consent."[9] This is the nub of the issue. It is not the status of homosexuals that is so much the matter as it is the status of their conduct.

In 2008 the sixtieth anniversary of the *Universal Declaration of Human Rights,* at the UN General Assembly, France introduced a *Joint Statement on Sexual Orientation, Gender Identity and Human Rights.* It proclaimed, "We urge States to take all the necessary measures, in particular legislative or administrative, to ensure that sexual orientation or gender identity may under no circumstances be the basis for criminal penalties, in particular executions, arrests or detention."[10] The statement was signed by sixty-six nations. Under the George W. Bush administration, the United States declined, but in 2009 the Barack Obama administration signed the statement. While the statement did not go as far as the *Yogyakarta Principles*, it was clearly headed in that direction. The majority of the criminal penalties it was decrying were not, as the statement disingenuously suggests, aimed at orientation, but at activity. It is the activity that must be vindicated and blessed as a universal human right.

One of the most immediate results of the priority given to the homosexual cause by President Obama and Secretary Clinton has been the profusion of "gay pride" commemorations and celebrations in US embassies abroad. June is the month singled out for this because, in 2000, President Bill Clinton declared June "Gay and Lesbian Pride Month", with the last

[9] International Commission of Jurists (ICJ), *Yogyakarta Principles—Principles on the Application of International Human Rights Law in Relation to Sexual Orientation and Gender Identity*, March 2007, http://www.refworld.org/docid/48244e602.

[10] *Joint statement on Sexual Orientation, Gender Identity and Human Rights at United Nations, 2008*, ILGA Europe website, accessed August 2, 2013, http://www.ilga-europe.org/home /issues/ilga_europe_s_global_work/united_nations/ilga_europe_and_joint_statements /joint_statement_on_sexual_orientation_gender_identity_and_human_rights_at_united _nations_2008.

Sunday reserved as Gay Pride Day. June was chosen to commemorate the anniversary of the Stonewall Inn riots as the beginning of "gay liberation". Ever since, every government agency has observed it. As of 2011, it moved overseas as part of US foreign policy.

Therefore, the US embassy in Islamabad celebrated its first-ever lesbian, gay, bisexual, and transgender "pride celebration" with an event on June 26, 2011. The embassy said the purpose of meeting was to demonstrate "support for human rights, including LGBT rights, in Pakistan at a time when those rights are increasingly under attack from extremist elements throughout Pakistani society". Richard Hoagland, the US deputy chief of mission, was quoted on the embassy website as saying, "I want to be clear that the US Embassy is here to support you and stand by your side every step of the way."[11] It is Pakistan's penal code, however, not extremist elements, that, in Section 377 (introduced at the time of British colonialism), states, "Whoever voluntarily has carnal intercourse against the order of nature with any man, woman or animal, shall be punished ... with imprisonment of either description for a term which shall not be less than two years nor more than ten years, and shall also be liable to fine."

If the Pakistani embassy in Washington, DC, held a public event in which it encouraged the United States to change its domestic laws in order to recriminalize sodomy, we might be somewhat surprised and irritated. Why should the Pakistani people be less annoyed by the US embassy telling them to change its laws in order to decriminalize sodomy? Why exactly is that our business? All Islamic groups in Pakistan condemned the "pride" event as a form of "cultural terrorism" against democratic Pakistan. Students protested against what they called "the attempts of the United States to promote vulgarity in Islamic societies under the pretext of human rights". One speaker at a demonstration said, "Now the United States wants to project and promote objectionable, unnatural, abnormal behaviors under the pretext of equality and human rights, which is not at all acceptable.... If you destroy the morality of the society, you have destroyed it completely."[12]

---

[11] U.S. embassy in Islamabad, "Embassy Islamabad Hosts GLBT Pride Celebration", press release, website of U.S. embassy in Islamabad, June 26, 2011, http://islamabad.usembassy .gov/pr_062611.html.

[12] Patrick Goodenough, "Pakistani Islamists Protest U.S. Embassy's 'Gay Pride' Event", CNSNews.com, July 5, 2011, http://cnsnews.com/news/article/pakistani-islamists-protest -us-embassy-s-gay-pride-event.

In Nairobi, Kenya, in June 2012, the US embassy hosted what is thought to be the first "gay pride" event in that country. John Haynes, a public affairs officer at the US embassy, introduced the event: "The US government for its part has made it clear that the advancement of human rights for LGBT people is central to our human rights policies around the world and to the realization of our foreign policy goals."[13] Homosexual acts are illegal in Kenya, just as they were in parts of the United States until 2003. Now, as part of our foreign policy, we tell Kenya to change its laws in this respect.

The US embassy in Laos, proudly displays web-page news from its 2012 "first-ever Lesbian, Gay, Bisexual, and Transgender (LGBT) Pride event on June 25 in Vientiane. The event, called 'Proud to be Us!', was produced by a group of young Lao LGBT activists and featured music, dance, skits, and dramas exploring issues faced by LGBT people in Laos today, such as discrimination, gender roles, and sexual health."

On the web page of the US embassy in Prague, Czech Republic, a joint statement was issued that the US ambassador, Norman Eisen, had signed. It declared:

> On the occasion of the 2nd annual Prague Pride Festival (2012), we express our solidarity with the lesbian, gay, bisexual and transgender communities of the Czech Republic in their celebration. . . . The Prague Pride Festival reminds us that ensuring LGBT rights is an important aspect of fulfilling our broader international human rights commitments since the full recognition of those rights is still one of the world's remaining human rights challenges. Safeguarding human rights and guarding against intolerance requires constant vigilance in the Czech Republic, as in all our countries. Therefore today, we align ourselves with the Prague Pride participants.[14]

This type of thing at US embassies has become standard. As Secretary of State Clinton proclaimed in June 2012:

> United States Embassies and Missions throughout the world are working to defend the rights of LGBT people of all races, religions, and

---

[13] Roopa Gogineni, "US Embassy in Nairobi Hosts Gay Pride Event", VOANews.com, June 26, 2012, http://www.voanews.com/content/us-embassy-in-nairobi-hosts-gay-pride-event/1252825.html.

[14] U.S. embassy in Prague, "Joint Statement Expressing Support for the 2012 Prague Pride Festival", website of U.S. embassy in Prague, August 13, 2012, http://prague.usembassy.gov/prague-pride-support-2012.html.

nationalities as part of our comprehensive human rights policy and as a priority of our foreign policy. From Riga, where two US Ambassadors and a Deputy Assistant Secretary marched in solidarity with Baltic Pride; to Nassau, where the Embassy joined together with civil society to screen a film about LGBT issues in Caribbean societies; to Albania, where our Embassy is coordinating the first-ever regional Pride conference for diplomats and activists to discuss human rights and shared experiences.[15]

As in Pakistan, there has been some blowback from the effort to legitimize sodomy and promote same-sex marriage. When the acting ambassador in El Salvador, Mari Carmen Aponte, wrote an op-ed in a major Salvadoran newspaper, *La Prensa Grafica*, implying that the disapproval of homosexual behavior is animated by "brutal hostility" and "aggression" by "those who promote hatred", a group of pro-family associations fought back.[16] On July 6, 2011, they wrote:

> Ms. Aponte, in clear violation of the rules of diplomacy and international rights laws, you intend to impose to [*sic*] Salvadorans, disregarding our profound Christian values, rooted in natural law, a new vision of foreign and bizarre values, completely alien to our moral fiber, intending to disguise this as "human rights".... The only thing we agree with from your article, is to repudiate violence against homosexuals, bisexuals, transsexuals, etc.; against these, just the same as against skinny, fat, tall or short.... This of course does not mean accepting the legal union between same sex individuals or to add new types of families like bisexual, tri-sexual, multi-sexual and the full range of sexual preferences. Not accepting the legitimacy of "sexual diversity" does not mean we are violating any human right. There can be no talk of progress if this is how "modern" is defined. We prefer to feel proudly "old fashioned", keep our moral values, preserve our families and possess the clarity of what defines good and evil.[17]

In the spring of 2013, the US Agency for International Development announced a public-private partnership designed to promote LGBT rights around the world. "This partnership leverages the financial resources and skills of each partner to further inclusive development and increase respect for the human rights of LGBT people around the world", said Claire Lucas, senior

[15] Hillary Rodham Clinton, "Video Remarks for 'Pride Month'", U.S. Department of State website, June 8, 2012, http://www.state.gov/secretary/rm/2012/06/192136.htm.
[16] "Obama's Foreign LGBT Agenda Experiment in El Salvador", *Obama's Corrupting Foreign Policies* (blog), accessed August 2, 2013, http://valoressalvadorenos.blogspot.com/.
[17] Ibid.

advisor of the USAID Office of Innovation and Development Alliances. "It can be a real game-changer in the advancement of LGBT human rights."[18] The project will contribute $11 million over the next four years to advocacy groups in Ecuador, Honduras, Guatemala, and other developing countries.

Secretary of State John Kerry has continued in this vein. On November 20, 2013, he delivered remarks, which were then posted on the State Department's website, memorializing the Transgender Day of Remembrance. While he celebrated progress "in advancing the rights of LGBT persons", he deplored that "people continue to be harassed, arrested and even killed simply because of who they are and who they love." Yes, we all deplore murder, but as usual with such pronouncements, there was no mention of what LGBT persons *do,* or whether there might be anything wrong with it. Failure to protect what they do apparently "threatens our common humanity".[19] But are their actions in accord with our "common humanity"?

As mentioned earlier, Secretary Clinton said, and it is clear that her successor, Mr. Kerry agrees, that "gay rights are human rights, and human rights are gay rights." The problem with this should be self-evident. The promotion of "gay rights" must come at the expense of the promotion of human rights because the two are immiscible. One is founded on the "Laws of Nature and of Nature's God" and the other on moral relativism, which eviscerates the very idea of natural rights and the natural law on which they are based. If you have one, you cannot have the other. You have your rights by virtue of being a human being and not by anything else—not ethnicity, not religion, not race, not tribe, not sexual orientation.

I deplore, for instance, the persecution of Baha'is in Iran and the persecution of Ahmadis in Pakistan. Being a Baha'i or being an Ahmadi no doubt constitutes the identity of these people who are being persecuted. Nonetheless, there is no such thing as Ahmadi rights or Baha'i rights; there are only human rights. And our defense of them comes precisely at the level of principle in the inalienable right to freedom of conscience, freedom of religion, and freedom of expression. Were we to construct such a thing as Ahmadi rights or Baha'i rights or gay rights, we would be eviscerating the foundations of human rights, which have to be *universal* by definition in order

---

[18] Michael K. Lavers, "USAID Launches Partnership to Promote LGBT Rights", *Washington Blade*, April 9, 2013, http://www.washingtonblade.com/2013/04/09/usaid-launches-partnership-to-promote-lgbt-rights/.

[19] John Kerry, "Transgender Day of Remembrance Remarks", http://www.state.gov/secretary/remarks/2013/11/217776.htm, accessed December 1, 2013.

to exist. If one has rights as a Baha'i, what happens to those rights if one converts to, say, Christianity? Does one then lose one's Baha'i rights and obtain new Christian rights? What happens to one's gay rights if one goes straight? One does not possess or attain rights in this way. They are inalienable because one possesses them by virtue of one's human Nature—not due to any other specificity. Either they exist at that level, or they do not exist at all. If someone tries to appropriate human rights for something that applies to less than everyone, then you may be sure that they are undermining the very notion of human rights. If there are abuses, and this includes abuses against homosexuals, then they should be opposed from the perspective of human rights, not manufactured rights that obtain to a specific group.

If the United States wishes to promote democratic principles and constitutional rule in other countries, but insists on inserting a manufactured right as integral to that program, it will be rejected overall by religious people and by those who, through the examination of moral philosophy, have arrived at the existence of human rights from natural law. If we wish to make ourselves not only irrelevant, but an object of derision in the Muslim world and in other parts of the globe, all we have to do is openly promote the rationalization of homosexual behavior, which is explicitly taught as inherently immoral by Islam and, in fact, by every minority religion in those Muslim-majority countries, including Christianity and Judaism. If we wish to make this part of American public diplomacy, as we have been doing, we can surrender the idea that the United States is promoting democracy in those countries, because they are already responding, "If this is democracy, we don't want it, thank you; we would rather keep our faith and morals."

But, of course, democracy is not the goal; the goal is the universalization of the rationalization for sodomy. This is now one of the depraved purposes of US foreign policy. How successful has it been? Formerly active homosexual Ronald G. Lee reported, "When I lived in the United Kingdom, I was struck by the extent to which gay culture in London replicated gay culture in the United States. The same was true in Paris, Amsterdam, and Berlin. Homosexuality is one of America's most successful cultural exports. And the focus on gay social spaces in Europe is identical to their focus in America: sex."[20] The United States government has officially embraced this culture in its foreign policy. The light from the City on the Hill is casting a very dark shadow.

[20] Lee, "The Truth about the Homosexual Rights Movement".

Conclusion

This brings us to the conclusion of this sad story and its lessons. In his debates with Stephen Douglas on slavery, Abraham Lincoln said that one "cannot logically say that anybody has a right to do wrong".[1] The insistence of certain homosexuals to foist their personal moral confusion—as a "right" mandated by the courts or state legislatures—upon the general populace so that it becomes public moral confusion is not some harmless caprice. They claim the right to do wrong, or more accurately, that the wrong they do is their right. I have tried to demonstrate that this is dangerous for more than them.

To paraphrase Roger Scruton's remark about the phony in modern art, activist homosexuals and others campaigning for same-sex marriage are asking us to conspire in their own self-deception, to help them create a fantasy world, to join in their flight from reality.[2] Their goal is to make the flight enforceable, in fact mandatory, to have society reorganized around it so that nothing can interrupt the flight. I have endeavored to show how the homosexual rationalization has eaten its way through America's civic and political institutions with dire results. Since the moral acceptance of sodomy requires the denial of a teleologically ordered Nature, it, in turn, necessarily affects everything—including the ultimate ends of life, as perceived by Socrates and Aristotle. They are part of the loss.

Nevertheless, same-sex proponents insist that their unreality will not affect the reality of others. Same-sex marriage, they say, will leave real marriage untouched, but the denial of reality never remains partial. The unreal part is in tension with the real part, even if the two are not directly in contention on a specific issue. The ultimate vulnerability of the rationalization is reality, which remains despite the rationalization's denial of it. To support itself, unreality must advance, or be advanced upon. Assertions of unreality

[1] Abraham Lincoln, *Political Debates between Lincoln and Douglas* (Cleveland: Burrows Brothers, 1897), Bartleby.com, 2001. www.bartleby.com/251/.

[2] Roger Scruton, "The Great Swindle: From Pickled Sharks to Compositions in Silence, Fake Ideas and Fake Emotions Have Elbowed Out Truth and Beauty", *Aeon*, December 17, 2012, http://www.aeonmagazine.com/world-views/roger-scruton-fake-culture/.

are always aggressive—not only because they are a negation of something, but because, like Napoleon, they must conquer to survive.

A perfect example of this is the spread of heterosexual sodomy subsequent to its moral approval in homosexual relationships. Dr. Mark Regnerus reports that "there's been a wide and comparatively recent uptake of anal sex in heterosexual relationships, boosted by the normalization of gay men's sexual behavior in the American [male] imagination."[3] And the purveyors of sex education and contraception are keeping up with, or perhaps even promoting, the trend. Recently at a public high school in San Francisco, a heterosexual female student was provided with a flyer that included instructions on how to use female condoms, including in anal intercourse. The information is the same as that on the Planned Parenthood website, which says that women can use such condoms "for vaginal and anal intercourse." (Interestingly, the Mayo Clinic website instructs women *not* to use a female condom for anal sex.) It is worth repeating Mary Eberstadt's line, quoted earlier, but now in reverse order: "Once homosexuals start claiming the rights of heterosexuals, it would not be long before heterosexuals started claiming the right to act as homosexuals."

The denial of reality imperils even prohibitions that some homosexuals may wish to keep. But on what grounds can they now be retained? As formerly active homosexual Ronald G. Lee observed, "If you support what is now described in euphemistic terms as 'the blessing of same-sex unions,' in practice you are supporting the abolition of the entire Christian sexual ethic, and its substitution with an unrestricted, laissez faire, free sexual market. The reason that the homosexual rights movement has managed to pick up such a large contingent of heterosexual fellow-travelers is simple: Because once that taboo is abrogated, no taboos are left."[4] Exactly. All rationalizations for sexual misbehavior, no matter of what sort, are allied to and reinforce each other. The rationalization being complete, anything goes, including "bug chasing"—the new craze in which homosexuals actively seek HIV infection because of the added sexual thrill. They call the men who infect them "gift givers". One bug chaser said, "It's about freedom."[5] Freedom is slavery. Others claim that the virus and its treatment

---

[3] Mark Regnerus, "Yes, Marriage Will Change—and Here's How", Witherspoon Institute, June 7, 2012, http://www.thepublicdiscourse.com/2013/06/10325/.

[4] Lee, "The Truth about the Homosexual Rights Movement".

[5] Gregory A. Freeman, "Bug Chasers: The Men Who Long to Be HIV+", *Rolling Stone*, February 6, 2003, http://www.solargeneral.com/library/bug-chasers.pdf.

impart a better quality of life.⁶ Indeed, sickness is health, just as death is life—remember Dr. Brandt?

Lee needed only add that, in addition to Christian morality, the "Laws of Nature and of Nature's God" are also abolished—with some rather grave political consequences. The price for this has not yet been paid in full. The nineteenth-century French political philosopher Frédéric Bastiat warned: "When misguided public opinion honors what is despicable and despises what is honorable, punishes virtue and rewards vice, encourages what is harmful and discourages what is useful, applauds falsehood and smothers truth under indifference or insult, a nation turns its back on progress and can be restored only by the terrible lessons of catastrophe."⁷

The celebration of the "rich diversity" to which we are all being invited or coerced is not diverse enough to include those who have not shared in the unreality or who have refused to join in the flight—that would include the observant followers of every major religion. Those religions, including Christianity, Judaism, and Islam, hold that homosexual acts are morally repugnant. Therefore, their teachings must be privatized, while homosexuality is publicized and celebrated. Fr. James Schall remarked that "we are seeing more and more not just the legally enforced living of disordered lives but the official effort to repress any speaking or information that suggests anything is wrong with it. This is really what is behind the establishment of 'diversity' as the only criterion of truth. It is a form of relativism that seeks to silence any possibility that 'the goodness and humanity of God' are the true keys to human living and its ultimate destiny in eternal, not political, life."⁸ This is no longer permitted speech.

The problem with our civilization is that the moral convictions underlying its public order have been undermined to the point of near collapse. No doubt there are many fine families and individuals continuing to live very good lives in the United States and the Western world, and this is a cause for hope. But those are now "private" lives, based upon "personal" choices, and all choices are therefore equal. What has been lost from public discourse

---

⁶ Gemma Aldrige, "Bug Chasing: Men Deliberately Trying to Catch HIV for Sexual Thrill in Astonishing Craze", *Mirror*, July 7, 2013, http://www.mirror.co.uk/news/uk-news/bug-chasing-men-deliberately-trying-2033433.

⁷ Frédéric Bastiat, *Economic Harmonies*, trans. George B. de Huszar, ed. W. Hayden Boyers, (Irving-on-Hudson, NY: Foundation for Economic Education, 1996), 21, 35, http://www.econlib.org/library/Bastiat/basHar21.html.

⁸ Schall, "The Goodness and Humanity of God".

is the rhetoric with which to address what distinguishes the very goodness of their lives as essential to our survival as a republic from the public immorality that is bringing about its demise.

Evidence of legal enforcement is present wherever the homosexual ethos has been publicly embraced. After all, what is the good of a rationalization if it cannot be made compulsory? A woman in Washington State was sued for refusing to arrange wedding flowers for a homosexual couple.[9] An inn owner in Vermont paid a large fine in a dispute over hosting a lesbian wedding reception.[10] A photography studio in New Mexico that refused to shoot a same-sex wedding was found guilty of "sexual orientation discrimination" and given a fine.[11] A Hawaii judge found against a woman who refused to rent a room to a lesbian couple at her in-home bed and breakfast.[12] An African-American woman lost her job at Toledo University because of her op-ed in the local newspaper disputing that the "gay rights" movement had anything to do with the civil rights struggles of African-Americans.[13]

A friend from Great Britain reports that a police chaplain was removed from his post because he voiced his support for traditional marriage on his personal Internet blog. "Strathclyde Police say Rev. Brian Ross can believe in marriage in private if he so wishes, but he can't express his opinions in public—not even when he's 'off duty'. It's a breach of their equality and diversity policies, say the police."[14] This happened even before the law on same-sex marriage was changed by Parliament. Since then, a wealthy

---

[9] Sue Ellen Browder, "Washington State Sues Florist for Declining to Beautify Same-Sex 'Wedding'", *National Catholic Register*, April 16, 2013, http://www.ncregister.com /daily-news/washington-state-sues-florist-for-declining-to-beautify-same-sex-wedding/.

[10] Ben Johnson, "Vermont Catholic Couple Pays $30,000 in Dispute over Hosting Lesbian 'Wedding' Reception", LifeSiteNews, August 24, 2012, http://www.lifesitenews.com /news/vermont-catholic-couple-pays-30000-for-not-hosting-lesbian-wedding-receptio/.

[11] Matthew Cullinan Hoffman, "Photographers Guilty of 'Discrimination' for Refusing to Shoot Same-Sex 'Wedding': New Mexico Court", LifeSiteNews, June 7, 2012, http:// www.lifesitenews.com/news/photographers-guilty-of-discrimination-for-refusing-to-shoot -same-sex-weddi/.

[12] Kirsten Andersen, "Judge Rules Against Christian Innkeeper Who Refused to Rent Bedroom to Lesbian Couple", LifeSiteNews, April 16, 2013, http://www.lifesitenews.com /news/judge-rules-against-christian-innkeeper-who-refused-to-rent-bedroom-to-lesb.

[13] http://www.americanfreedomlawcenter.org/press/59/full-court-rehearing-requested -before-sixth-circuit-in-case-of-christian-woman-fired-by-university-for-speaking-out -against-homosexuality.html.

[14] Colin Hart, campaign director of the Coalition for Marriage, letter to "Marriage supporter", "Most Eastleigh Voters Backed Pro-Marriage Candidates", Patria, March 2, 2013, http://www.patria-uk.org/cameron-queers-the-pitch-at-eastleigh/.

homosexual couple in Great Britain has already threatened to sue the Church of England to force it to perform same-sex weddings. Logically enough, Barrie Drewitt-Barlow said: "The only way forward for us now is to make a challenge in the courts against the church. It is a shame that we are forced to take Christians into a court to get them to recognise us. It upsets me because I want it so much—a big lavish ceremony, the whole works.... As much as people are saying this is a good thing I am still not getting what I want."[15] There are many such stories. There will be many more.

Ultimately, of course, none of this is going to work because reality will always, if only eventually, win over unreality. Those involved in this effort, both homosexuals and their allies, are simply contributing to what Italian law professor Francisco D'Agostino calls the "illusion that a more pervasive legalization of their existence can give homosexuals that interior balance whose lack they so clearly suffer".[16] Unfortunately for them, as former lesbian Linda Jernigan said, "There is not a law that can bring you peace." To repeat the quote at the beginning of this book from former lesbian Melinda Selmys, "A man may lie to himself very prettily, but he can never really escape from the knowledge that it is a lie." Illusion will finally lead to disillusion, perhaps at the cost of the catastrophe that Bastiat predicted.

Of course, we cannot blame homosexuals for all of this. As mentioned before, first came contraception and the embrace of no-fault divorce. Once sex was detached from diapers, the rest became more or less inevitable. If serial polygamy is okay, and contraceptive sex is okay, and abortion is okay, what could be wrong with a little sodomy? First, short-circuit the generative power of sex through contraception; then kill its accidental offspring; and finally celebrate its use in ways unfit for generation. Contraception used to be proscribed, then it was prescribed, and now has become almost obligatory in the contraceptive mandate in the Affordable Care Act, which proposes to penalize employers who do not provide it, along with abortifacients and sterilization procedures, to their employees with fines of $100 per worker per day. I only wish there were survivors from the 1930 Lambeth Conference—which first endorsed a limited use of contraceptives—who

---

[15] Christian Institute, "Gay Couple to Sue Church Over Gay Marriage Opt-Out", Christian Institute website, August 1, 2013, http://www.christian.org.uk/news/gay-couple-to-sue-church-over-gay-marriage-opt-out/.

[16] Francesco D'Agostino, "Christian Anthropology and Homosexuality—10: Should the Law Recognize Homosexual Unions?", *L'Osservatore Romano*, English edition, May 21, 1997, 9; available at http://www.ewtn.com/library/humanity/homo10.htm.

might be forced to attend the Gay Pride events and officiate at same-sex "marriages", so they could dwell upon what they hath wrought. Just as there is no such thing as being a little bit pregnant, there is no such thing as a little compromise on moral principle, as the Boy Scouts will soon discover. If the ideology behind the *Casey* decision is correct, then the homosexual position is the right one. It substitutes the primacy of will for the primacy of reason. If we can make it all up as we go along, then there are no moral standards in Nature to distinguish between the use and the abuse of sex, only personal taste. The broad embrace of this view has opened the floodgates to a sexual dystopia. The problem with this inundation is that it threatens the very democracy that allows it.

Evil is particularly contagious when it is institutionalized. The institutionalization of immorality leads to more moral disorder, not to its attenuation, and then to political disorder and eventual collapse. There is a kind of Gresham's law of morals: just as bad currency drives out good currency, so bad morals drive out good morals. The *Spectator* provided a compelling example of this regarding legalized prostitution in the Netherlands: "Legalization has not been emancipation. It has instead resulted in the appalling, inhuman, or degrading treatment of women, because it declares the buying and selling of human flesh acceptable."[17] The institutionalization of homosexual marriage likewise declares sodomy acceptable, even sanctified. Similarly, it will make things worse, not better.

If life is sacred, then the means of generating it must also be sacred. If generation is intrinsic to the Nature of sex, then sex possesses immense significance. It is not a toy, or simply an amusement, or an item for sale. It is profoundly oriented to creation—creation emanating from union. It has a telos. Dr. Jennifer Roback Morse said: "The human person is meant for love, and the human body cries out to be fruitful."[18] As stated earlier, the fruit is the incarnation of the love. If generation is artificially separated from it, sex lapses into insignificance and triviality. This denial leads to its desecration and is contemptuous of what human beings are meant to be.

For everyone's sake, it is essential to recover the sensibility underlying the prohibition against the desecration of sex. That it must be recovered is not simply the agenda of the religious right, but a deeply political concern for

---

[17]Julie Bindel, "Why Even Amsterdam Doesn't Want Legal Brothels", *Spectator*, February 2, 2013, http://www.spectator.co.uk/features/8835071/flesh-for-sale/.

[18]Jennifer Roback Morse, "What to Expect When No One's Expecting", *MercatorNet*, March 19, 2013, http://www.mercatornet.com/articles/view/what_to_expect_when_no _ones_expecting.

the future of freedom. That freedom is already imperiled by the effects of the sexual revolution: widespread divorce, single parenthood, cohabitation, child abuse, rampant pornography, and the promotion of homosexual acts and homosexual marriage. Sex is so important that its misuse has become the principal means for dismantling our culture and political order.

We have blinded ourselves to the connection between the abuse of sex and the dissolution of the American family, which can be seen in these results: as of 2010 those with children now represent only 20 percent of American households, according to the US Census Bureau;[19] 35 percent of children are in single-parent families; sexual crime is up more than 200 percent in public schools since 1994; there has been a precipitous rise in illegitimate births (now 40 percent of all births); 60 percent of African-American children are born out of wedlock; some 50 percent of marriages end in divorce;[20] there are some one million abortions per year on average, or 55 million since 1973; and our culture has coarsened in brutal ways. Yet the misuse of sex has so corrupted our society that no one dares mention it as a principal cause of our debasement. As Justice Kennedy teaches, unassailable "private conduct between consenting adults" made under the inviolable "autonomy of self" is at the heart of liberty. But this cannot be right, particularly if it leads to self-destruction.

The reason is that the key to democracy is not free choice. As we know from the Weimar Republic, people can freely choose anything, even Hitler. The key, as our Founding Fathers knew, is virtue. Only a virtuous person is capable of rational consent because only a virtuous person's reason is unclouded by the habitual rationalizations of vice. Vice inevitably infects the faculty of judgment. No matter how democratic their institutions, a morally enervated people cannot be free. And people who are enslaved to their passions inevitably become slaves to tyrants. Thus, our Founders predicated the success of democracy in America upon the virtue of the American people.

Our culture no longer corners us into virtue, however, but impels us into vice. Almost every contemporary cultural signal militates against chastity, which is why the fabric of society is falling apart. The effort to construct a political order on Eros, of which homosexual marriage is simply the capstone, will end in the same way as Pentheus' Thebes—in slavery, subjection, and destruction. A society that is no longer willing to guarantee the

---

[19] Sabrina Tavernise, "Married Couples Are No Longer a Majority, Census Finds", *New York Times*, May 26, 2011, http://www.nytimes.com/2011/05/26/us/26marry.html.

[20] Centers for Disease Control and Prevention, Data for the United States on unmarried childbearing, last updated January 18, 2013, http://www.cdc.gov/nchs/fastats/unmarry.htm.

institution that is fundamental to its survival—marriage, the family—and that so loses a proper sense of the Founding principle of equality that it uses it to undermine the family will not long endure. Will we lament with Euripides' Agave, "Dionysus has undone us. Too late I see it"?

Fr. Schall's diagnosis is that

> we would like to "free" ourselves from nature in order that we become what we "want" to be. And what we "want" to be must, logically, eliminate any sign that something in us is better made than what we ourselves could conjure up. This result is why so much of our contemporary life is taken up with ways of life that deny marriage, children, and seek to glorify ways of life that are intrinsically opposed to them. To achieve this latter goal of complete independence from God, we must lie to ourselves about what we are.... No one, Plato said, wants a "lie in his soul about the most important things." But if we do want to replace God with our own definition of ourselves, we must lie to ourselves, deceive ourselves, about what we are. We must seek ourselves independently of what we ought to be. If we succeed in this endeavor, we will make ourselves into monsters and oddities.[21]

These remarks are flares in the night, distress signals, calls for moral rescue before a tsunami engulfs all memory of moral order. Signals have been sent. They still hang in the night sky, the last illumination before bearings are lost. In the darkness that descends, who will answer the cries for help? Will it be those who have been told to be less than men and women in marriage?

Controversies about life, generation, and death are decisive for the fate of any civilization. Each distinction we erase makes it harder for us to see or make other distinctions. The ability to discriminate is, of course, essential to the ability to choose correctly. If we lose it, the change in our own moral character cannot help but profoundly change the character of our government. This is because, as Fr. Schall has written, "Where truth cannot be spoken, no one can reform his life."[22] With the loss of the possibility of virtue goes everything that depends upon it. A society can withstand any number of persons who try to advance their own moral disorders as public policy. But it cannot survive once it adopts and enforces the justification for those moral disorders as its own. This is what is at stake in the culture war. This is why everything is changing.

---

[21] Schall, "The Goodness and Humanity of God".

[22] James V. Schall, S.J., "On Philosophical Eros", *The Catholic Thing*, December 11, 2012, http://www.thecatholicthing.org/columns/2012/on-philosophical-eros.html.

Acknowledgments

I would especially like to thank Angelo Codevilla for looking over some early chapters of this book and suggesting improvements, and Katie Gorka and Richard Bastien for reading its first draft. I am very grateful to Vivian Dudro for her patient and superb editing and to others at Ignatius Press who have helped bring this book to fruition. Lively conversations with Fr. Joseph Fessio, S.J., were the instigation for this work, though he should not be blamed for its outcome. When I would emerge from my study enveloped in gloom from having looked at some of the extremely distressing research material for this book, my daughter Teresa would restore my spirits by accompanying me on long walks in the woods. I am very grateful to her and to my wife, Blanca, for her help in proofreading and improving the manuscript.

Appendix

Disease and Mortality

The US Department of Health and Human Services provides the following statistics on its AIDS.gov website, reflecting the most current data available from the Centers for Disease Control as of March 2012 ("MSM" means men who have sex with men):

- MSM accounted for 61 percent of all new HIV infections in the United Sates in 2009, as well as nearly half (49 percent) of people living with HIV in 2008 (the most recent year national prevalence data is available).

- CDC estimates that MSM account for just 2 percent of the US male population aged 13 and older, but accounted for more than 50 percent of all new HIV infections annually from 2006 to 2009. In 2010, MSM accounted for 61 percent of HIV diagnoses.

- In 2009, white MSM accounted for the largest number of annual new HIV infections of any group in the United States (11,400), followed closely by black MSM (10,800).[1]

Dr. Richard Fitzgibbons:

The sexually compulsive, highly reckless, and life-threatening behavior in a large percentage of homosexuals would indicate the presence of an addictive disorder in these individuals. These addictions resemble substance abuse disorders in that individuals engage in compulsive behaviors that are medically hazardous. This clinical view of much homosexual

[1] U.S. Department of Health and Human Services, "HIV in the United States", AIDS.gov, http://aids.gov/hiv-aids-basics/hiv-aids-101/statistics/.

behavior as being addictive in nature is supported by numerous studies of the sexual practices of homosexuals and by the recent best estimates that one half of all homosexual males in New York City are HIV positive (C. Horowitz. *New York* February, 1993: 30). The National Institutes of Health estimated that at current rates of infection, a majority of twenty-year-old gay or bisexual men nationwide will eventually have the AIDS virus (*Newsweek*, September 19, 1994: 50–51). The addictive nature of much homosexual behavior explains why HIV infections have quadrupled in San Francisco since 1987. These studies support the clinical view that homosexuality is a disorder with extremely compulsive, highly reckless, and self-destructive features.[2]

The Gay and Lesbian Medical Association warns that lesbians have the richest concentration of risk factors for breast cancer than any subset of women in the world. They have higher risks for cervical cancers. They are more likely to be obese. They use more tobacco, alcohol, and illicit drugs. A study of over 1,400 lesbians found the following:

- Lesbians experience higher rates of bacterial vaginosis and hepatitis C.

- They have more than twice the number of male partners than heterosexual women (only 7 percent of those who identify themselves as lesbians never have sex with men).

- They are 4.5 times more likely to have 50 or more male sexual partners in a lifetime.

- They are 3 to 4 times more likely to have sex with men who are at high risk for HIV—homosexuals, bisexuals, and IV drug users.

- They are 6 times more likely to abuse drugs intravenously.[3]

According to Paul Cameron and Kirk Cameron of the Family Research Institute:

In general, wherever a comparison could be drawn between homosexual and nonhomosexual groups, life expectancy at birth was significantly less for homosexuals (p < .0001; p < .01 for Norwegian females), typically

---

[2] "Origin and Healing of Homosexual Attractions and Behaviors", Second Pan-American Conference on Family and Education, Toronto, Ontario, May 1996.

[3] Katherine Fethers et al., "Sexually Transmitted Infections and Risk Behaviors in Women Who Have Sex with Women", *Sexually Transmitted Infections* 76, no. 5 (2000): 345–49, http://sti.bmj.com/content/76/5/345.full.

on the order of 20+ years. This was true for men and women in the United States, Denmark, and Norway, whether partnered or unpartnered at time of death, and also whether or not AIDS was judged the cause of death. In the United States, MSM who died of AIDS had estimated life expectancies at least 30 years less than either official US figures for males-in-general or estimates from Washington Post obituaries for all males or ever-married males.[4]

In 2009 the *Journal of Human Sexuality* offered the following set of risk figures for homosexuals and lesbians as compared with heterosexuals.

Compared with heterosexuals, homosexual men demonstrated the following:

- 2.58 times increased risk of lifetime prevalence of depression

- 4.28 times increased risk of lifetime prevalence of suicidal attempts

- 2.30 times increased risk of lifetime prevalence of deliberate self-harm

- 1.88 times increased risk of 12-month prevalence of anxiety disorders

- 2.41 times increased risk of 12-month prevalence of drug dependence

Compared with heterosexuals, homosexual women demonstrated the following:

- 2.05 times increased risk of lifetime prevalence of depression

- 1.82 times increased risk of lifetime prevalence of suicidal attempts compared

- 4.00 times increased risk of 12-month prevalence of alcohol dependence

- 3.50 times increased risk of 12-month prevalence of drug dependence

- 3.42 times increased risk of 12-month prevalence of any substance use disorder[5]

[4] Paul Cameron, PhD, and Kirk Cameron, PhD, "Federal Distortion of Homosexual Footprint (Ignoring Early Gay Death?)", Eastern Psychological Association Convention, City Center Sheraton, Philadelphia, March 23, 2007, http://www.lifesitenews.com/ldn/2007 _docs/CameronHomosexualFootprint.pdf.

[5] James E. Phelan, Philip M. Sutton, and Neil Whitehead, "What Research Shows: NARTH's Response to the APA Claims on Homosexuality", *Journal of Human Sexuality* 1 (2009), 74–81.

The results of this meta-analytic study by King et al. (2008)—as well as those reported above from Herrell et al. (1999), Fergusson et al. (1999), Gilman et al. (2001), Jorm et al. (2002), Sandfort et al. (2003), and Conron et al. (2008)—offer clear evidence that people who are homosexually oriented are at significantly greater risk for serious medical and mental health problems than are heterosexually oriented persons.

Index of Proper Names

Index of Subjects

Sin, 188
  original sin, 30, 48
Society, 29, 214
  family as foundation, 16, 26, 30–31,
    33–34, 49, 64–66, 69, 86, 95, 109,
    128–29
  marriage as foundation, 69–70, 106,
    112
  shaping behavior to benefit, 95
  soul of, 65
  See also Civilization
Sodomy, 51, 207–8, 211–12
  in America, history of moral/legal
    status, 68–71
  and Aristotle's laws of Nature, 22,
    24
  biology and, 52, 57, 64–65
  Blackstone on, 68–71
  and the Boy Scouts, 173–83
  criminal sodomy laws, 71
  the culture wars, 4, 7, 9–10, 13–14
  and education, 154–72
  essence of, 60
  and the military, 184–94
  morality, inventing, 73, 82–85,
    87–88, 91–92, 94–96, 99–102,
    108, 112–13
  Rousseau and, 36–41, 43–44, 47
  and science, 117–42
  and US foreign policy, 195–205
  See also Homosexual acts
Soul, 19, 23–25, 150
  beauty and, 23
  corruption of, 150
  disordered, 71
  Eros and, 25
  evil in, 24–25
  good, as ordered toward, 19, 21, 48,
    104
  happiness and, 21
  right order of, 24–25
  of society, 65
  and the worst thing, 106, 142, 214
Spousal love, 38, 42, 59, 62, 64–65

State,
  power of, 88
  See also under Family: Rousseauian
    ideal; Society

Ta onta, 18
Telos, 18–19, 28, 31, 34, 36, 212
Therapy. See Conversion therapy
Thought, 17–18
Trahison des clercs, 194
Transgender people. See LGBT (lesbian,
    gay, bisexual, and transgender)
Transvaluation of values, 42–45
Truth, 10, 43, 88, 118, 122, 126, 179, 214
  diversity and, 209
  language and, 47–48
  source of, 21
Tyranny, 47–49

Union, marital/sexual, 13, 26, 36, 38,
    41, 53, 70, 86, 93, 109
  creation emanating from, 212
  and fertility/infertility, 101–2
  See also under Marriage: "one flesh"
    union in
Unions, same-sex, 5–6, 62–63, 101–2,
    108, 208
  See also Same-sex marriage
Universal law, 19
Universe,
  intelligible, 17–18
  meaning of, 48, 80, 89–90
  order in, 15–27
  teleological, 19
Unreality, 179, 207, 209, 211

Values, 158, 182, 203
  transvaluation of, 42–45
Vice, 7–9, 23, 27, 29, 157, 179, 197,
    209, 213
Virtue, 32, 179, 213–14
  beauty and, 24
  happiness and, 21
  life of, 27, 72